Violent Modernity

HARVARD MIDDLE EASTERN MONOGRAPHS
XLII

Violent Modernity

France in Algeria

Abdelmajid Hannoum

DISTRIBUTED FOR THE
CENTER FOR MIDDLE EASTERN STUDIES
OF HARVARD UNIVERSITY BY
HARVARD UNIVERSITY PRESS
CAMBRIDGE, MASSACHUSETTS
LONDON, ENGLAND

ISBN-13: 978-0-674-05328-1
Printed in the United States of America

Library of Congress Cataloging-in-Publication Data

Hannoum, Abdelmajid, 1960–
Violent modernity : France in Algeria / by Abdelmajid Hannoum.
p. cm. — (Harvard Middle Eastern monographs)
ISBN 978-0-674-05328-1
1. French—Algeria—History. 2. French—Algeria—Politics and government.
3. Algeria—Colonization. 4. Algeria—Politics and government. 5. Algeria—
Foreign relations—France. 6. France—Colonies—Africa—Administration.
7. France—Foreign relations—Algeria. 8. France—Politics and government.
I. Title. II. Series.

DT283.6F7H36 2010
965'.03—dc22

2009042529

In memory of Tamou, Salem, and Houda

Contents

Acknowledgments

This book was supposed to be finished several years ago, but a number of unfortunate events interrupted its writing more than once. This was rather fortunate for the book; the delay made it richer and, to me at least, more meaningful. In the process of its writing and in moments of its interruption, numerous friends, colleagues, helped me in a variety of ways. I would like to acknowledge Gabriel Asfar for his loyal friendship and his comments on earlier drafts of several chapters. Thomas Glick, Laura Bunt, and Sahar Bazzaz graciously commented on the first chapter. Joshua Cole, Bill Lawrence, Brent Metz, Bartholomew Dean, Daniella Gandolfo, Heather Meiers, Marwa Ghazali, and Naima Boussofara kindly read parts of it and provided insightful comments and constructive criticism. Bob Antonio generously read drafts of parts of the book and provided very useful comments. Laura Veal, Aidan Peters, and Stephen Rea witnessed and even participated in the elaboration of its main arguments in oral forms while I was teaching courses on colonialism, nationalism, and violence. Martin Bernal offered much encouragement upon reading chapter 1 and chapter 2. Deborah Kapchan, then an anonymous reader, along with a still anonymous reader, offered many comments and suggestions without which the book would not be what it is now.

The idea of the book was born while I was at the Institute for

Advanced Study in Princeton. I was fortunate to discuss the project with the late Clifford Geertz and benefited from his insights and directions. The late Daniel Reig discussed issues of Orientalism, for which he was one of the important specialists in France; also his support was very critical in times of its interruptions. Jean-Paul Dumont commented on a draft of the project and on a first draft of a chapter. As a postdoctoral fellow at the Harvard Center for Middle Eastern Studies, in 1999–2000, I benefited then from the encouragement, support and friendship of Ahmed Jebari and Susan Miller. The Moroccan forum, a postdoctoral seminar devoted exclusively to the study of the Maghreb, organized by Susan Miller, was a stimulating source of inspiration. The Department of Anthropology at Columbia University allowed me to devote much time to writing during Spring 2004. Nicholas Dirks graciously made such a wonderful stay possible. It is there that the first draft of this book was accomplished. The Department of Anthropology and the Department of African and African American Studies at the University of Kansas generously released me from one semester teaching during which I rewrote the final drafts of several chapters. I would also like to extend my acknowledgments to my colleagues Garth Myers, Don Stull, John Janzen, Allan Hanson, and Mohamed El Hodiri for their encouragement and support. Pam LeRow spent hours and hours proofreading a version of the entire manuscript.

Working in Algeria, especially on a topic such as violence, was not easy, to say the least, especially for someone from a neighboring country. Several of my friends and colleagues in Algiers and in Constantine made this research possible through unusual acts of generous hospitality.

I also would like to thank Steve Caton for his enthusiasm for and interest in the project. It was he who early on drew my attention to the relation between culture and event, which constitutes an important dimension of this book. I am grateful to Rosemary Winfield for her meticulous editing of the manuscript.

Dick Tonachel's impeccable assistance and his patience have been decisive.

I would also like to express my deep gratitude to Gananath Obyesekere, James Boon, and Larry Rosen for their continued support ever since I was a student. Their exemplary scholarship has continued to inspire me in every scholarly project I undertake.

My heartfelt thanks to Joseph Shovelin, Diane Sorrel, the late Anne Clark, and MaryAnn Pixely for their loyal friendship, care, and affection. Without each one of them, the book would have been delayed even further.

The book is dedicated to the memories of my mother, my brother, and my niece.

Copyright Acknowledgments

The author gratefully acknowledged permission to reproduce the following material:

An earlier version of chapter 1 appeared as: "Colonialism and Knowledge in Algeria: The Archives of the Arab Bureau" in *History and Anthropology,* vol 12, no. 4, pp. 343–379. A slightly different version of chapter 4 also appeared in *History and Anthropology.* "The Historiographic State: How Algeria Once Became French," *History and Anthropology,* vol. 19, No. 2, June, pp. 91–114. Both reprinted by permission.

An earlier version of chapter 2 appeared in *History and Theory,* "Translation and the Colonial Imaginary: Ibn Khaldûn Orientalist," *History and Theory,* vol. 42, no. 1, pp. 61–81. Reprinted by permission.

Introduction

During one of my interviews for this book, a Moroccan academic told me that his father was shot at and killed by French soldiers during an anticolonial protest in Fez in the 1930s. He did not seem angry, bitter, or accusatory. I did not sense from his tone of voice or his bodily gestures that he felt that he was a victim. Yet I was aware that being the son of a martyr, a *shahîd* (anyone killed by the French during the struggle for independence), is a source of pride for many people. In Morocco and even more so in Algeria, to be a son of a *shahîd* constitutes impressive social capital that can lead to tremendous economic privileges. In my interviewee's speech, however, there was no sense of sorrow or pride. His talk about the French colonial presence in Morocco was a bit different. It had an unmistakable tone of deference. He said: "For us, colonialism is the equivalent of Europe's industrial revolution. It brought us modernity." As a Moroccan, I felt I was included in his "us." Later, I thought about how he juxtaposed the tragic death of his father with a modernity imported from France, a modernity that he cherished. One concludes from talking to him that modernity was worth the price of the conquest and its violent tragedies, including the death of his father, the violence of modernity.

My interviewee's discourse about colonial casualties and modernity is not unfamiliar to me, for this is a discourse that is

1

found in literature and even national historiography. While I was growing up in a country that the French ruled and "left" only a few years before I was born, colonialism *(ist'mar)* was a bad name for a bad thing, but was somehow balanced by the "progress" that it brought to the country. Progress *(taqaddum)* and modernity *(hadatha, tajdid)* were undoubtedly associated with France, despite narratives about colonial occupation and its ugly deeds. In this discourse, modernity redeems violence. Kateb Yacine, the celebrated 1950s novelist and poet of anticolonialism, expressed this, echoing a general sentiment about colonialism for people of his generation and later of mine: "the conquest was a necessary evil, a painful graft promising growth for the nation's tree slashed by the foreign axe."[1] Sociologists and historians of modernity rarely consider that colonialism is a tragic effect of modernity, or that colonialism is modernity imported somewhere else. For instance, when sociologist Anthony Giddens cites the sombre sides of modernity, he mentions the horrors of the two world wars, the holocaust, and totalitarian regimes, but not colonial expansion in 85% of the world.[2] The reason may lie in the common belief that colonialism was redeemed because it brought modernity to the rest of the world.

This book looks into the adventure of modernity in Algeria during and after the colonial age. In 1998, when I undertook this project (initially and ambitiously about both Morocco and Algeria),[3] "the nation's tree" had continued to grow and its fruits were many and varied. Independence had long since been granted, the French had "left" and the nation-state of Algeria was founded as Arab and socialist, and was for decades the model for revolutionaries in the Third World. Visited as a Mecca by those dedicated to universal freedom, justice, and equality, Algeria constituted a model for revolutionary success and the hope of "the wretched of the earth" as Fanon calls them.[4] In addition to these euphoric results of independence, aftershocks of colonialism loomed. Francophony has introduced a part of the cultural landscape that Kateb Yacine himself suffered from—

alienation. Perhaps the darkest aftershocks were the seeds that sprouted in Algeria (beginning at the funeral of Kateb Yacine, when his supporters clashed with Islamists) but whose severity could not yet be understood. This most recent and dreadful aspect of modernity was fully revealed in 1992 when Algeria plunged into one of the bloodiest conflicts of the second half of the twentieth century, resulting in the deaths of over 150,000 people and the disappearance of several thousand others.[5]

Even then, the brutal war ravaging the country was not seen as the effect of modernity but rather as the age-old pitting of Islam against modernity. This was viewed as just another case of Muslims who were carrying out the orders of God to build an Islamic society by fire and iron. The insurgents were seen as opposing modernity, and their actions were seen as taking Algeria to a premodern stage, one of barbarism. What had previously taken place in Iran was seen as happening in Algeria but this time in Europe's backyard. The danger seemed real and imminent, at least for French modernity—"the modernity of modernity," as Henri Meschonnic calls it.[6] Islam versus modernity became once again the dominant discourse and the easy way to understand the emergence of fundamentalism, their adherents' pursuit of power, and their slaughtering of civilians, without distinction of armed and unarmed people, men and women, and old and young, and unborn.[7]

By 1990, it was common to use academic discourse on Islam to explain what was happening in Muslim countries and also in European countries where there was a strong Muslim presence. Algeria seemed to confirm the thesis of the return of the religious and, more specifically, the return of Islam. In this discourse, there is modernity on the one hand and Islam on the other. The former is marked by democracy, freedom for the individual, and separation between church and state. In the latter there is no individuality and no freedom, but only the rule of *shari'a*—the government application of God's commandments. The first is based on persuasion and debate in the public sphere; the second recognizes no sphere but God's. Modernity's view of religion holds that because it is based on sacred texts and their interpretations, it lacks reason, which entails critiquing and questioning, which lead to change and progress. Further, in religion, the world is God-ordained, whereas in modernity, the world entails "a very strong emphasis on the autonomous participation of members of society in the constitution of the social and political order, on the autonomous accesses of all members of the society to these orders and to their centres."[8] Religion appears thus as diametrically opposed to modernity in the discourse of modernity and its critics. Alain Touraine, in his book *Critique of Modernity,* asserts: "It is impossible to call modern a society that seeks first of all to organize itself and act according to a divine revelation or to a national essence."[9]

But most nations are founded on the idea of "a national essence." The phrase "national essence" is a modern term that would not have made sense in Europe in its premodern era. Moreover, some societies have organized themselves on human interpretations of what are believed to be divine revelations, and these interpretations may include the fact that although "In God we trust," God left the business of ordering society to be decided according to our own human principles. Thus because "In God we trust," "He blesses us" even when our interpretations exclude these words from the realm of politics. Touraine's statement reveals a strong Enlightenment belief in the separation of religion and state, which was initially an ideological separation. Nicolas Sarkozy, president of the French republic, was more coherent and in some sense more critical when he asserted that the reason Turkey will not be part of the European Union is because "Europe is fundamentally Christian."[10]

The interweaving between the religious and the secular has always been noticed. For some authors, the secular cannot be understood without what precedes it, and some of the main ideas of Western secular societies were derived from Christianity.[11] Hans Blumenberg, for instance, argues that modernity is the product of the secularization of Christianity and that the secular has a theological background. Thus, for instance, he shows that the idea of progress itself is a secular transformation of the idea of salvation.[12] But for Blumenberg, this seems to be a passing phase of the secular; because it had just come out of the religious, the religious needed to be understood. But this passing phase has refused to pass, and all the signs indicate that the religious is part and parcel of the secular. The religious seems to be more assertive in politics and academia than it has ever been since the triumph of the secular. This phenomenon has been noted by Etienne Balibar in the debates and the ideological confusions over the Islamic headscarf for women. He writes about the political considered "fundamentally secular" and the religious considered "religious" and outside of politics:

> The two terms have never been, and are now less than ever, "exterior" to one another. In the current period, for reasons involving the circulation of populations and mixing of cultures connected to "globalization" and the crisis of the symbolic bases of the nation-state ("sovereignty"), leading at once to the mobilization of institutional "authorities" and the interventions and claims of "citizens," and consequently making politics more than ever a site in which religious beliefs are invested, and the place of religion in the public space a political matter.[13]

If the two terms, *secular* and *religious,* have never been "exterior," how then did we fail to see them all this time?

A few months before he passed away—at the end of a long career devoted to the study of religion, and more specifically to the study of Islam—Clifford Geertz maintained that social science, because of the conditions of its emergence, developed a myopia to the religious phenomenon and that the "return of the religious" is not a return after all but a blindness to a phenomenon that has always existed.[14] Although there might never have been a return as Geertz affirms, there is surely a surfeit of the religious not witnessed a few decades ago, and it problematizes both categories. One would argue that what is called religious has been so transformed that the traditional features of the religious seem unrecognizable. Social science and its founding figures established the limits of the religious by focusing on the secular in an age when the former was in crisis. The crisis of the religious means mainly that religious beliefs, practices, signs, symbols, and subjects were all confined to a space created for them that was far from the public space, which is the space of the secular. The question becomes: "How does one rethink the new individual who does not recognize himself in a public space and the terrible void left when the religious departed?" How can one account for this alienation (Karl Marx), disenchantment (Max Weber), anomie (Emile Durkheim)? These founding fathers of social science offered to remedy the crisis created by the assumed waning of religion by elaborating systems of thought that promise salvation.[15]

Not only has the religious been secularized, but the opposite is also true. Some secular societies were so blinded by the religious that they lost many of the recognizable features of secularism. The most obvious examples of this are communism and nationalism. A less obvious example is the discourse of democracy which has been promoted with a zeal that seems to approach the religious zeal of the "age of religion." Not only is social science unable and ill equipped to tackle the religious, but the religious and the secular are indeed intertwined and thus no longer present themselves in recognizable ways. Talal Asad argues that the religious cannot be thought about without the secular and vice versa because both are modern categories that were born together in the age of Enlightenment and inherited today as part of the ideology of modernity.[16] However, seeking the religious in the secular and the secular in the religion might reveal that the old distinctions inherited from the Enlightenment no longer hold. Hence, there is a need to rethink categories and invent more appropriate ones that reflect a social reality that is different than the one that predominated in the Enlightenment and its aftermath.

There are debates about whether nationalism is a religion or whether religious movements are nationalisms, and the arguments for and against each stem from the idea that although the secular models itself on previous religious systems, religious systems of the modern world (including the Islamic one) have also been transformed and transfigured by the secular. The challenge for the scholar of either religion or modernity lies in pinpointing what is and is not religious in a modern social reality. Both the secular and the religious affect each other or rather work within one another. One can speak about the religious of the secular and the secular of the religious, if one has no alternative but to use these old categories.

None of the violence of which Islam has been part can be distinguished as merely religious. Although its leaders declared the Iranian Revolution to be Islamic, they guided it from a Parisian suburb through cassettes and videotapes, and the revolution has been viewed by many observers, including Muslim Arabs, as a nationalist revolution, whose aim was to reassert Persian domination in the region. The 2003 invasion of Iraq was defended by millions of Christians in churches and on radio stations, its success was prayed for by the president and his administration, but it has been seen by many inside and outside of the United States as a war against Islam, even another crusade.

The point here is that the religious is modern and also that the dividing line between secular and religious is blurred. Algeria's culture is modern, and its modernity was brought to it by conquest and implemented through violent colonial machinery that combined modern technologies and the instrumentalization of knowledge by disciplines of the human sciences *(les sciences de l'homme)*. Modernity came with implements of violence and contained within itself a structural violence that had already been experienced by people in Europe.[17] It is this founding violence of modernity that constituted an important theoretical tradition in social science that stretches from Karl Marx, Max Weber, and Vilfredo Pareto to Antonio Gramsci, Hannah Arendt, and Michel Foucault. For these critics, modernity triumphed through violence by using bureaucracy—new institutions that are either openly violent such as the army, the police, or appear nonviolent (the universities and hospitals, for example). Modernity was therefore a project of restructuring of society by regulating space, politics, and subjectivity of the individual—language, education, body, sexuality, values and ideas, family, health, feelings, taste, judgements, and so forth.[18] This in addition to the unprecedented level of violence, especially throughout the nineteenth and twentieth centuries, the bloodiest ever by any standard.

In Algeria, the transformation brutally destroyed lives, local forms of knowledge, religious practices, traditions, and languages. Modernity was created from within Europe's preexisting philosophical, religious, economic, and social structures, and it was imported by French forces as part of a conquest into a land with its own different historicity. In Algeria, the French found Islam, against which France had long defined itself. Algeria became France's civilizing mission. The question was not "How can one modernize that which is by definition antithetical to modernity?" This is a postcolonial question that France debates through the discourse of migration, the veil, and mosques. Initially, modernity and religion were perceived to be polar opposites. The question was "What mechanisms, strategies, and implements can be used to defeat Islam and make civilization (a widely accepted synonym for modernity) triumph?"

Establishing modernity was a violent process through which the landscape of the country was transformed and became unquestionably French modern. Modern violence had multiple faces and included the violence of modern armaments (inscribed in modern technology) and the violence of modern texts (with their power to create and transform). The two are intertwined. The violence of armaments (large-scale expeditions, famine, destruction of lands and lives, and imprisonment of women and children) is often preceded or conditioned by modern knowledge (texts that create and transform by representing the local population as others, a racial monstrosity whose very existence threatens "us").

Alexis de Tocqueville is one of the most eloquent theorists of political modernity because of his uncompromising belief and defense of its core values, including its commitment to the use of physical violence to assert itself:

> In France, I often heard men I respect but do not agree with not like the burning of harvests, the emptying of granaries, and the seizing of unarmed men, women, and children. For me, those are unfortunate necessities that any people wanting to wage war against Arabs must accept. . . . I believe the laws of war entitle us to ravage the country and that we should do this either by destroying crops at harvest time or frequently by making rapid incursions we call *razzias* [raids], the objective of which is to seize men or flocks.[19]

According to this statement, violence is inscribed in the very processes of modernity. Without violence, progress is impossible, and the violence of and for modernity is a core value that must be upheld and defended—whatever the cost. Because modernity takes precedence over all costs, violence is necessary for modernity (again in the discourse of modernity). Both progress and freedom require violence. And the discourse of violence expresses modernity, via speaking, hearing, arguing, agreeing, disagreeing, and dialoguing. Making violence a requirement for progress (and thus for modernity) makes the discourse on violence a violent discourse because the discourse of modernity itself inflicts and creates the conditions of violence. As a discourse of race, for instance, modernity is violence that stripped the colonized people of their humanity and relegated them to a space of noncivilization, and of no right and no freedom. While they are there, they become good candidates for colonial genocide in times of conquest and in times of land reform. The discourse of progress makes the natives into children who must be spanked when they misbehave—when they resist or reject colonialism and its violent practices (even then called modernity or civilization). There is no massacre or genocide—small or large, organized or spontaneous—that was not preceded by a discourse in which the Other is created as a dangerous enemy and a threat to "our" own existence.

This book is about the violent processes of political modernity in Algeria and the violent practices—physical, textual, and symbolic—that have been inflicted on Algeria and its people. The book shows how modernity, in its colonial turn, was envisioned and set in place by various modes of modern forms of knowledge—ethnography, anthropology, archeology, history, and translation. The book also explores the different and constantly changing facets of modernity. For reasons I clarify below, it privileges political modernity and looks at the dynamics of the colonial state through its ethnographic and historiographic discursive practices and examines their unique power of transformation. Violence, which this book associates with the project of modernity, lies initially in this work of transformation, which presupposes the destruction of what is there—not only what is not modern or what is premodern but also what is seen to be unethical and thus to threaten modernity, which is the antimodern. Examples of the not modern include those forms of life that were considered premodern: the primitive, the backward, and even the savage.[20] In political terms, those are tribalism, revolts, anarchy, native criminality, and religion, which has always been seen as the archenemy of modernity. Historically, modernity triumphed against religion in Europe, and religion ferociously opposed, resisted, and often fought modernity (colonialism). In all Algerian wars—from those of Abd el-Qader to the ones of FLN—religion was the motor and the battle cry against colonial domination and its ideology of modernity. When Ben Badis claims: "Islam is my religion, Arabic is my language, Algeria is my nation,"[21] he is asserting precisely what France negated: Islam as a religion, Arabic as a language, and Algeria as a nation. The irony is that this seemingly religious and antimodern statement of Ben Badis is a modern statement. It would not have been said in 1830 at the time of the conquest. Political modernity, as I discuss in this book through the analysis of forms of modern knowledge and political institutions, set out to destroy these forms, whether premodern or antimodern, and implement itself instead. This was done in Europe, and the French Revolution epitomizes its triumph there.[22] Once triumphant in Europe, modernity was exported to the rest of the world mainly or rather exclusively via conquests.

It is no coincidence the architects of colonial knowledge were military men. When Charles Richard wrote one of the earliest colonial books about Algeria, he noted in his introduction that "the pages of this book are tainted with blood."[23] The point is not that there is violence on the one hand and a harmless knowledge on the other but rather that institutions such as the army and the university may produce forms of knowledge that are themselves forms of textual violence. These texts conditioned violent events such as those that happened in 1864, 1871, 1945—and also created the conditions of postcolonial violence in both Algeria and France.

Through an analysis of the formations of modern knowledge, the book traces the genesis of the political present in Algeria. It explores how modern colonial culture has conditioned the emergence of a number of postcolonial events (the most important of which is the killings that tore apart Algerian society throughout the 1990s).

Ever since Edward Said and Bernard Cohn, scholars of colonialism and of postcolonial societies have discovered new venues in the study of colonial societies. Knowledge has become the focal point of their analyses because of the crucial role it plays in the dynamics of rule and governance. The power that knowledge deploys has become a defining characteristic of modern power.[24] However, power has always been exerted by physical force and by powerful symbolic forces, and such phenomena are not typically modern. That societies can be ruled by systems of symbols has been observed and noted in antiquity and in medieval times. Tacitus speaks about the cultural policy of the Romans in Britain immediately after its conquest:

The following winter passed without disturbance and was employed in salutary measures. For, to accustom to rest and repose through the charms of luxury a population scattered and barbarous and therefore inclined to war, Agricola gave private encouragement and public aid to the building of temples, courts of justice, and dwelling-houses, praising the energetic and reproving the indolent. Thus an honorable rivalry took the place of compulsion. He likewise provided a liberal education for the sons of the chiefs and showed such a preference for the natural powers of the Britons over the industry of the Gauls that they who lately disdained the tongue of Rome now coveted its eloquence. Hence, too, a liking sprang up for our style of dress, and the toga became fashionable. Step by step they were led to things which dispose to vice, the lounge, the bath, the elegant banquet. All this in their ignorance, they called civilization, when it was but a part of their servitude.[25]

Even in antiquity, force was not the only means by which to establish domination. Education—organized knowledge—was an instrument by which to subdue a population, and education was first aimed at the native elite. Other means, such as the imposition of the symbols of the dominant (dress, architecture, and ceremonies) were also expression and instruments of domination.

In medieval Mediterranean Islam, Ibn Khaldûn noted the same phenomenon:

The dominated [*maghlūb*] is enamoured of imitating the dominant [*al-ghālib*]. It is because humans always see perfection in those who subjugate and dominate them. Inspired by a fearful reverence toward them, they see them wrapped in all the perfections, or they attribute them to him so they cannot admit that their subjugation is achieved by ordinary means. If such an illusion is perpetuated, it becomes certitude. They then adopt the usage of the master, and they seek to imitate him in all aspects. It is by a spirit of imitation that they act in this way, or it is because they imagine that the dominant owes his superiority not to his strength and ethnic solidarity [*'asabiya*] but to his usage and practices by which he is distinguished.[26]

Ibn Khaldûn also states that the imitation of the dominant by the dominated is "a sign of servitude" (*'alâmat al-istîlâ*).[27]

Colonialism in modern times is not the only enterprise of domination that operated by both force and knowledge. Conquests and domination were always the work of force and ideas conjointly. Perhaps this is because the former is not possible without the latter. In essence, modern Europe did not invent the politics of culture in the strategy of domination. It only applied its own cultural modern forms to suit its objectives. The specificity of European colonialism, especially that of French colonialism in Algeria, may be founded on the fact that this knowledge expressed modernity and was diffused and therefore implemented by modern institutions—what Weber calls *bureaucracy*, itself a manifestation of modernity. Although modernity was undoubtedly violent in Europe, colonialism expanded modernity elsewhere, and this modernity has had a power of transformation that we still witness today. To understand the present in a country such as Algeria, one must consider it as the work of a modern and even brutal transformation in which everything was modified, changed, and transfigured.

The purpose of this book is to show that the advent of modernity was a violent process and that the modernity that now constitutes the present—referred to by Appadurai as "modernity at large,"[28] and by others as "coloniality at large"[29]—has in turn generated violent events. When analyzed historically, these events are themselves manifestations of a culture that contains within itself what is traditional, modern, religious, even though it is difficult to say which is what.

Several chapters in this book are devoted to various techniques that have been used to implement modernity. They focus on the processes by which a country was evaluated and then transformed according to the political wishes of the colonial administration. These chapters show that this process was first possible after a violent endeavour, called *conquest* or *pacification* that was based on a system of representation that itself was regulated by violence. This system of representation had the power to depict, name, and create the other in ways that were negative, but these systems of representation created an ontological separation between "us" and "them" and entailed rights or lack thereof.

This book is not a history of colonialism in Algeria, a history of modern Algeria, or a history of the violence of modernity in Algeria. It examines a violent modernity that Algeria endured and continues to endure in its postindependence era. The major thesis of the book—the violence of modernity—is highlighted through examples that show how the processes of producing knowledge, undertaken by the army in the midst of conquests, were violent. Violence was both physical and textual at the same time. The book also argues that local responses to the violence of modernity were violent from beginning to end. I focus on the Algerian uprising of 1871 because it illustrates how violence has a dialectics of its own by generating a similar response from the local population. I also focus on the example of the war waged in Algeria during the 1990s, which is interpreted as an attempt by Islamists to seize power. Although I maintain that violence was dominant, the crisis of the 1990s was only a spectacular manifestation of what has operated in Algerian society since before independence in 1962. The goal is to show through this example from the present that postcolonial violence is a continuation and transformation of the culture of colonial modernity and its powerful ability to generate violence. I argue that what happened through 1992 was a continuation of this violent restructuring of Algerian life, including Islam itself. The point here is not that Islam has returned but rather that Islam has been transformed by colonial modernity and that the ways it expresses itself through political parties, campaigns, fund raising, political speeches, elections, and so forth are all modern. Modernity transformed the "religious" and was transformed by it as well.

Lastly, I would like to say few words about the transcription of names in this book. I have kept names as they appear in colonial literature, except for the name of Ibn Khaldûn. I use quotes sometimes when terms are colonial and thus are a manifestation of colonial power. Because of our postcolonial condition, it is difficult and sometimes even impossible to say things differently.

NOTES

1. Kateb Yacine, *Nedjma* (Paris: Seuil, 1956), 135.
2. Anthony Giddens, *The Consequences of Modernity* (Stanford: Stanford University Press, 1990), 8–9.
3. The study of modernity in Morocco is still in progress.
4. Frantz Fanon, *Les damnés de la terre*. Paris: Maspero,1961. English translation, *The Wretched of the Earth*. New York: Grove Press, 1963.
5. The Algerian state claims that the number is 100,000.
6. Henri Meschonnic, *Modernité, modernité* (LaGrasse: Verdier, 1988), 17. Meschonnic also asks the rhetorical question: "Who is more modern than us?" (ibid).
7. There were several accounts of destruction of fetuses of killed pregnant women.
8. S. N. Eisenstadt, "Multiple Modernities," *Daedalus* 129, 2000: 1.
9. Alain Touraine, *Critique de la modernité* (Paris: Fayard, 1992), p. 23.
10. Nicolas Sarkozy makes frequent references to "the Christian roots of Europe," and during an official meeting with the Pope in Latran on January 20, 2007, he argued for a *laïcité positive,* which meant being tolerant of and in dialogue with other religions. But the *laïcité positive* in the discourse of Sarkozy privileges Catholicism. Consider this statement, which sounds more missonary than secular: "France has always shined in the world by its generosity and intelligence. This is why it needs Catholics who are fully Christians and Christians who are fully active." See his speech at Catholique.org (accessed September 9, 2009). Some media intellectuals, such as Max Gallo, a self-declared defender of *laïcité,* endorsed Sarkozy's statements and noted that *laïcité positive* was initiated by Lionel Jospin, the minister of interior affairs. He adds that "the old definition of *laïcité* is outdated. . . . One needs to recognize the Christian origin of France. . . . Reason is the base for our society, but it has its limits. It needs to engage faith." Gallo

here means the Catholic faith. See www.liberation.fr/evenement/
010189216-l-ancienne-conception-de-la-laicite-est-depassee   (accessed September 19, 2009). But Gallo asks his Muslim compatri-
ots to have "a personal relationship with their faith." See
his column in *Figaro,* www.lefigaro.fr/debats/20060208.FIG0209
.html?073334 (accessed September 19, 2009). The same *laïcité* is
dubbed by philosopher Paul Ricoeur, a self-declared Christian, a
"*laïcité* of exclusion" in the context of the ban of the veil. But
Ricoeur is not fully Catholic. See Paul Ricoeur and Monique
Canto-Sperber, "Laïcité d'exclusion," *Le Monde,* December 11,
2003), 000.

11. Hans Blumenberg, *The Legitimacy of the Modern Age* (Cam-
    bridge: MIT Press, 1983), 13–26.
12. Ibid., 27–36
13. Etienne Balibar, "Dissonances within *Laïcité,*" *Constellations* 11,
    no. 3 (2004): 353–367.
14. Clifford Geertz, "La religion, sujet d'avenir," *Le Monde,* May 6,
    2006, 000.
15. This intent is more obvious with Marx and Durkheim and less so
    with Weber. See the commentary of Raymond Aron, *Les étapes de
    la pensée sociologique* (Paris: Gallimad, 1967).
16. See Talal Asad, *Genealogies of Religion* (Baltimore: Johns Hop-
    kins University Press, 1996); Talal Asad, *The Formation of the
    Secular* (Stanford: Stanford University Press, 2001). For this spe-
    cific point, see also Asad, "Religion, Nation State, Secularism," in
    Nation and Religion, edited by Peter van der Veer and Hartmut
    Lehmann (Princeton: Princeton University Press, 1999), 187–203.
17. See for the case of France, Eugen Weber, *Peasants into Frenchmen.*
    (Stanford: Stanford University Press, 1976).
18. This is what Charles Taylor calls "modern social imaginary." His
    conception of the social imaginary is very similar to the one sug-
    gested by Cornolius Castoriadis; for Taylor "the social imaginary
    is that common understanding which makes possible common
    practices, and a widely shared sense of legitimacy. It incorporates a
    sense of the normal expectations that we have of each other; the
    kind of common understanding which enables us to carry out the
    collective practices which make up or social life." See Charles Tay-
    lor, "Modern social imaginaries," *A Secular Age* (Cambridge:
    Harvard University Press, 2007), 171–172. For the concept of the

imaginary as developed by Castoriadis, see discussion in chapter 2 of this book.

19. Alexis de Tocqueville, *Oeuvres complètes,* vol. 3 (Paris: Gallimard, 1962), 227–228.

20. Here there is the exception of a modern discourse that romanticized the so called "savage" and "primitive," a discourse that goes from Rousseau to Claude Lévi-Strauss. But such discourse in addition to the fact that it has never been transformed to a state ideology, the way several race theories have, still casts a segment of humanity as "others" with little or no civilization. The question, especially for Rousseau, was whether civilization was good for Europe, not whether the "savage" people were capable of reaching it.

21. Ben Badis, cited in Roger Le Tourneau, *L'évolution politique de l'Afrique du Nord musulmane* (Paris: Colin, 1962), 314.

22. François Furet, *Interpreting the French Revolution* (Cambridge: Cambridge University Press, 1981).

23. Charles Richard, *Etudes sur l'insurrection du Dhara (1845–1846)* (Algiers: Besancenez, 1846), 194.

24. Bernard Cohn, *An Anthropologist amongst Historians* (Oxford: Oxford University Press) and *Colonialism and Its Forms of Knowledge* (Princeton: Princeton University Press, 1996); Edward Said, *Orientalism* (New York: Vintage, 1978).

25. Tacitus, *Agricola* (Cambridge: Harvard University Press, 1970), 62.

26. Abderrahmane Ibn Khaldûn, *Muqaddima* (Beirut: Dâr al Kutub al 'Ilmiya, n.d.), 155–156

27. Ibid., 156.

28. Arjun Appadurai, *Modernity at Large* (Minneapolis: University of Minnesota Press, 1996).

29. Mabel Marona, Enrique Dussel, and Carlos Jauregui, *Coloniality at Large* (Durham: Duke University Press, 2008).

ONE

Conquests and Archives

Large-scale expeditions are more and more necessary—first, to show the Arabs and our soldiers that there are no obstacles in the country that can stop us, second to destroy anything that looks like a permanent aggregation of population or in other terms a town.
—Alexis de Tocqueville

On August 22, 1837, Alexis de Tocqueville published a letter addressing the state of colonial politics in Algeria.[1] Imagine, he suggested, that France is suddenly occupied by the emperor of China and that once the emperor landed, he immediately gathered the governing elite and sent them to a remote country. Will the Emperor—ignorant of the country, its language, its peoples, and its culture and without any local elite to inform him—be able to sustain order? The country will be plunged into anarchy. This is exactly the situation of Algeria, Tocqueville concluded. He drew attention to the importance of knowledge for the colonial enterprise. Conquering a country, according to him, depends on courage and force, but colonizing requires knowledge.

A year later, in 1838, General Thomas Robert Bugeaud recommended that the French government should first establish military settlements in Algeria, principally because a fundamental condition of colonization is security, and this is not possible without force.[2] Yet neither was this possible without knowledge. Whether through politicians or military officers, the conquest of Algeria was in fact a "conquest of knowledge" to borrow an expression from Bernard Cohn.[3] At this time, France was still debating whether Algeria should be completely colonized, or whether only the shores should be colonized for French use.

The year 1841 was significant in the history of French colonialism in Algeria. In this year the French government finally decided to annex Algeria and make it a French territory. This same year saw also another important decision—the appointment of Bugeaud as governor of Algeria. His mission was to establish French rule and put an end to the movement of the Algerian leader Abd el-Qader, who had led the resistance against the French since their arrival. In 1837, Abd el-Qader's resistance had forced France to sign a peace treaty and recognize his sovereignty over Rachgoun, Tlemcen, and larger parts of western Algeria.[4] In addition, the mountainous region of Kabylia remained out of French control.

Bugeaud immediately reestablished the Arab Bureau [*le Bureau arabe*] as a military institution in August 16, 1841.[5] Bugeaud gave the Arab Bureau a new mission and reorganized it so that it became the strongest instrument for administering the still uncertain colonial enterprise. Charles Richard, an officer of the Arab Bureau, wrote that "the Arab Bureau will now be the instrument of our actions, the force behind our ideas."[6] *Bureaux arabes* were created throughout Algeria. In 1847, there were forty-three officers in the Arab Bureau of Algeria, and forty to forty-five subsidiary circles or annexes were created by 1856. This number grew to a hundred thirty-six officers by 1859, a hundred ninety by 1868, and a hundred ninety-five by 1870.[7] From the year of its reinstatement by Bugeaud in 1841,[8] this institution played a major role in the colonial enterprise. It also determined the colonial objects of French scholarship and set in place the foundations of French colonial knowledge about North Africa and not only Algeria.

An officer of the Arab Bureau was almost always a graduate

of an elite school with a strong background in the humanities. At the beginning of his career in the bureau, he would have had little or no knowledge of either Arabic or Berber.[9] But there were interpreters at his command, usually Jewish or Armenian native speakers of Arabic. A number of French interpreters who were trained at the Ecole des Langues Orientales, the greatest European Orientalist institution, were also available to the Bureau.[10] After the conquest of Algiers, Silvestre De Sacy recommended many of his students for service as interpreters in the army during the time of the conquest.[11] The Arab Bureau had principally an informative function—to ensure the intellectual conquest of Algeria—but it also served as a military instrument for maintaining order. Thus, the Arab Bureau was an institution that, from its inception, operated by both force and knowledge. By its French opponents, the Arab Bureau was considered an "Arab government" and "a state within the state." This is because the Arab Bureau had a larger and more extended task than simply gathering information about Algerian society. As Captain Ferdinand Hugonnet, a former officer of the Bureau, recalled:

> The Arab Bureau has at times been compared to the authority of the Pashas of the Orient. The Arab Bureau had a more extended power over Muslims, for, in addition to all that a Pasha could do, in Algeria it controlled anything that concerned Muslim religion with much more independence than that of a successor of the satraps. The Arab Bureau also had, as a role, the task of fulfilling all the needs, all the demands, as well as all the initial endeavors of the conquering race in the conquered territory. This is, by itself, a quite large and often a quite thankless task.[12]

In 1844, Bugeaud published a brochure for the use of military men in Algeria. After a brief description of the "races that inhabit Algeria," he gave a detailed description about the local form of governance. This, Bugeaud added, should be kept intact, but the recently created Arab Bureau should play a major role among the natives. He then clearly states the mission of the Arab Bureau, its goals, and its methods for achieving them:

The officer in charge of Arab affairs should be concerned with gradually collecting information for a good statistical survey, in the larger meaning of the word. He should confine himself as much as possible to all facts relating to religious customs, public morality, local and general laws. He will write down everything that relates to the soil, the culture, the delimitation of the tribes, tribal fractions, etc., etc. He will describe with particular attention everything concerning relations of tribes with each other, public markets, rights, and weights and measures in use. But the most essential part of his statistical work is the one related to the history of the tribe, to which should be added, little by little, information about all its families and its political leaders. The collection of these documents, however incomplete they may be at the outset, will end up constituting, in each division, archives, so that accumulated knowledge will not be lost or forgotten. This will prevent personnel changes from becoming a source of confusion. . . . As for the content of these archives, we will not hesitate to write down even contradictory information; for it is only by comparing different data about the same question that we can discover the truth.[13]

At the time of the reestablishment of the Arab Bureau by Bugeaud, there was a growing literature about Algeria. Most of it was created by individuals for whom writing was a hobby and their statements about the country struck a rather exotic chord.[14] The numerous texts produced by the Arab Bureau, however, show a serious scholarly effort to extract the truth about Algeria to determine exactly what it was and how it should be governed. In 1848, only four years after the publication of Bugeaud's brochure, the archives of the Arab Bureau were impressive. The officers of the Arab Bureau and their interpreters turned out to be prolific ethnographers and historians. As I describe these archives, I examine both the dominant, popular, and conventional representations, and also the marginal ones that constituted intellectual heresies. I also explore how some representations were imposed as valid and even true, whereas others were eliminated or disregarded as false, mediocre or irrelevant. My intent is to show how the foundations of

French knowledge of Algeria (and by extension North Africa) were set in place, under what circumstances this occurred, and what politics were involved in representing the population in the early phase French colonialism.

THE POLITICS OF REPRESENTATION

In 1847, Colonel Eugène Daumas and Captain Paul-Dieudonné Fabar, officers of the Arab Bureau, published their first book, *La Grande Kabylie*.[15] The book was different from anything that was available at that time regarding the population of Algeria. First, it focused principally on a population of native Algerians in an area not yet accessible to the French—the still autonomous area of the Great Kabylia. Second, by representing the inhabitants of this specific region, it orders the colonial situation differently than previous writers had done. At this juncture in the history of French colonialism, various studies depicted Algeria as inhabited by various groups, but the most common view was that Algeria was an Arab land taken away from the Turks.[16]

Daumas and Fabar constructed their object geographically and in tandem with history. The Great Kabylia is a mountainous area that extends from Dellys, Aumale to Setif and Bougie. The region had always been independent, although it was once occupied by the Romans and later the Vandals. According to the authors, one could still find Roman ruins and see Germanic phenotypes in most of the region. In a few areas these European traits are absent, which suggested that the region had never been totally occupied. Thus, the authors construct their objects as seemingly heterogeneous: it is indigenous in some parts and yet Roman and Vandal in the rest of its parts. One would then conclude that the region, as a whole, was therefore European, and this European characterization does not disappear when the authors describe episodes of warfare. For instance, the authors speak of Kabyles who fought Rome in the name of Christianity, and after Rome adopted Christianity, they fought it again in the name of another Christian sect, Donatism. Before they became

Roman, the Kabyles were Christian and coveted their own independence. The Kabyle was both Christian and nationalist.

Daumas and Fabar introduce the Arabs in a significant way that later caught on. The Arab invasion is seen as a natural disaster. The Arabs invaded like "resplendent lightning."[17] This is a persistent theme in colonial representation of the Arab conquest of North Africa.[18] It is an invasion whose very act is completely disastrous. It "swept away the plains with its successive waves."[19] The inhabitants were either massacred or forced to convert to Islam. The Arab is destructive and invades to kill and subjugate people by force of arms. By contrast, Europeans—whether Roman, Greek, or Vandal—build, civilize, and enhance lands and peoples wherever they journey. There it is the Orient, here it is the Occident, and what makes them mutually exclusive is the difference between barbarism and civilization. For the authors, the Orient is not only Arab but also Turkish. In the sixteenth century, the authors continue, "new factors took part in the religious struggle between the Orient and the Occident."[20] Thus, having constructed the Great Kabylia as an Occident composed of a population of Christian natives, of German descent, and long-time Romans, the authors opposed it to the Orient (Arabs and Turks). Europe in North Africa—the occidental North Africa—had been assaulted twice by both Arabs and Turks. Thus, this particular colonial discourse creates and enlists its own logic.

At this time, in the 1840s, Bugeaud was waging a systematic war against the inhabitants of Algeria, Kabyles and Arabs—destroying their villages, burning their fields, and taking away their wives and children. The natives were perceived as the aggressors in this situation because the area is represented as a previous point of contention with Arabs and then with Turks. Therefore, the same struggle continued into modern times and was marked by the taking of Algeria from the Turks, and that same land still had to be snatched from the hands of the Arabs. In other words, the present French actions are a continuation of a response to past aggression.

Daumas and Fabar construct Kabyles as historical European figures as well as contemporaneously Europeans. After describing a territory, the two authors examine Algeria's current inhabitants. What are they like? How similar or different are they from the rest of its inhabitants, particularly in contrast to the Arabs? How can one determine their relationship with the French? Daumas and Fabar develop these issues throughout the rest of their narrative, as their tone shifts from a historical narrative to an ethnographic work based on their observations of the inhabitants of the Great Kabylia.[21]

Daumas and Fabar describe the inhabitants as opposed to the Arabs in origins, culture, social organization, and even skin color. For example, the Kabyles are white, whereas the Arabs are dark. The Kabyle wives are free, whereas Arab wives are repressed. Kabyles are monogamous, while Arabs are polygamous. Kabyles are studious and busy themselves with primitive industry and agriculture, and Arabs are lazy and embody a nomadic lifestyle. Kabyles, although Muslim, do not concern themselves with religion. They are liberal and their lives are regulated by local laws that have nothing to do with Islam. Daumas and Fabar conclude that these laws are derived from Roman law because of their name—the *Qanoun* (Canon). By contrast, Islam constitutes the bedrock of the political and social life of Arabs. Whereas Arabs live in an oligarchy, Kabyles, the authors continue, live in a primitive democracy, a "sort of savage Swiss."[22] They elect the members of their ruling group which they call *djemaa*. Their region is made up of a number of independent tribes, each with its own government and each is allied, by interest, with a number of other tribes that together constitute a political entity called *soff*. Only the *marabout* (the holy man) stands outside and above these political alliances. His authority remains uncontested.

Thus, one might well conclude that the Great Kabylia has always been European, despite a Turkish and Arab presence. Kabyle land still shows traces of its European heritage and its the inhabitants are living artifacts of this heritage close to the

French. They are white and secular, live in a democracy and still adhere to Roman law. They do not obey the rules of the Qu'ran and therefore do not recognize it as legitimate. Historically Christian, they are only superficially Muslim. The authors see the proof for this in Kabyle women, who have at the center of their forehead a tattoo in the shape of a cross.

Daumas published his description of the Kabyles several times, often with a different title. He discussed Arabs in a number of other books in which he consolidated the same categories.[23] In sum, Daumas fashioned a new way of conceptualizing the Kabyles as an ethnic and cultural group. His discourse became authoritative. Not only was it the most credible, but it generated a number of other historiographic and ethnographic texts. By the 1850s, works openly acknowledged Daumas as an authority on Algeria and some placed him among the most competent scholars.[24]

Another text was published a year earlier than *La Grande Kabylie*. In 1846, Edward Lapène, another officer of the Arab Bureau who did extensive fieldwork in the Kabyle area,[25] published his results a year before Daumas and Fabar published theirs. Lapène describes the origin of the Kabyles, their culture, and their social organization. He maintains that the Kabyles were not homogeneous, but were the result of various emigrations from Europe and around the Mediterranean as well as of a mixed indigenous population. Lapène defines *indigenous culture* by framing it directly against French culture. The Kabyles hate the French, but the Kabyle are what the French are not—liars, polygamous, violent, vain, arrogant, and fanatic. The Kabyles live in tribes *(harch)*, but each tribe is made of factions *(karouba)*; and villages *(taddarts)*. Lapène notices that the Kabyles have a *djemaa* (a council that elects the sheik or *amghar* of the tribe) and that the *amghar*'s rule is not absolute. Instead, he obeys the orders of the *djemaa*. Lapène describes this social organization as a republic. Nevertheless, the Kabyles, whether *amghar* or commoner, have a blind faith in another character that has the upper hand over both of them—the *marabout* (saint).

He is the holy man who serves as a mediator for peace, but he is also an organizer of war.

The conclusion is that although the Kabyles have a different social organization than the Arabs, they are more similar to the Arabs than to the French. In a few instances, Lapène himself uses the word *Arab* interchangeably while talking about the Kabyles. In doing so, he extends the already existing opposition between Arabs and French, between Christians and Muslims, to the Kabyles. Despite differences, the Kabyle is essentially no different from the Arab. Both oppose the French, and their hatred toward the French is religiously based.

Making the Kabyle (and by extension, the Berber) an Arab is an interpretation that was reformulated in 1848 by another colonial author and officer of the Arab Bureau, Charles Richard. However, unlike Lapène, Richard wrote about the Arabness of Algeria. Richard does not make a distinction between Arab and Kabyle. For him, there is only the Arab. From the outset, he asserts that "Arabs live in a milieu that is not ours. His tradition, his religious beliefs, his culture are in flagrant opposition to our moral order."[26] Richard reformulates all the descriptions that Daumas attributed to Arabs without making an opposition between Arabs and Kabyles. But Richard takes the formulations of Daumas further. For instance, while Daumas asserts that Arabs are liars, Richard adds that they tell the truth only by accident.[27] Here is a quote from Richard's summary of the Algerians:

> Here is what the Arab people are: almost three million souls who live in the confusion of all the imaginable abominations, an orgy of all known immoralities, from the one of Sodom to the one of the Mandarins. A man plunders and robs his neighbor. The latter pays him back. He marries four women and runs after others. When he is strong, he eats the weak. When he is weak, he stabs from behind. The woman is condemned to the virtue of seclusion, sold like a pig in the market, appraising herself for being appraised, signifying nothing, giving herself to prostitution with the first man that comes along.[28]

Knowledge is a means by which and through which an institution justifies its practices and rules others. Thus, it is a weapon and a disputed realm of conflict and struggle. Knowledge is supposed to be at the service of the institution that made it possible, but it may be appropriated by others and used against that institution. The Arab Bureau was officially a secular institution, producing a discourse that overtly proceeded by a secular binary opposition. The French were opposed to the Arabs in terms of religion, language, history, culture, and social organization. The Kabyles, on the other hand, were either in apposition or in opposition to the Arabs, by the same description. Although colonial discourse is secular, it operated with religious categories. Daumas himself once quipped: "Take a Frenchman and an Arab and put them in a pot and let them boil on high together. After 24 hours, you will still recognize the Christian from the Muslim."[29]

Captain Daumas does not express something new in this statement. Opposing Christianity to Islam is an idea that had long been shared by his countrymen. It was inherited from the theological scholarship of the Middle Ages. The statement reveals the colonial ideology. Captain Daumas intends to oppose Arab and French, two categories based on the European idea of nation and civilization, but instead opposes two religions. Thus, the Arab Bureau appropriated the ideology of the church. Yet if Kabyles were already Christian and Islam was forced on them, why not help them to become Christian again? If the Berbers were originally European and still have traces of Christianity, was it not a moral obligation to help them find their original way?

The church in Algeria, under the leadership of Cardinal Charles Martial Allemand Lavigerie, adopted this discourse and constituted a third political force in Algeria that was reinforced by another locus of emerging civil discontent, that of French settlers against the politics of the French Arab Bureau.[30] However, both church and settlers opposed each other, despite the fact that they formed a common front against the military. The church sought to Christianize Algeria, and the settlers wanted to Frenchify it. The church wanted the people; the settlers wanted land. The members of the Arab Bureau, aware that their discourse could be usurped, fought to prevent it from being adopted by the church and by the settlers.

Richard offered a religious solution with secular coloring. Because he was a pantheist, he believed that Arab resentment of the French was religiously based. Arabs were not protesting the taking of their lands and lives. Arab resentment was based on the "invincible repulsion" that Islam has for Christianity.[31] Richard is not against conversion, and suggests that conversion could be achieved through the implementation of French institutions that embody Christian values and ideals. Arabs and French (Muslims and Christians) are too different to work together or to hope for a reconciliation. What should be done? To kill them all, Richard says, is a solution, but realistically it is a "deplorable impossibility."[32] Therefore, there is only one way to remedy the problem of the natives: make them disappear like "a drop of poison in a glass of water."[33] In fact, the native should be absorbed by a massive European immigration. In Algeria, the Tell, the area most hostile to the French, was inhabited by 2500, so importing 15,000 Europeans would doubtlessly swallow the Arabs in a way that would make them harmless. Richard suggested a scheme in which a book that was highly favorable to the French would be distributed among the natives to convince them that it was written by the Prophet Mohammed and recently found under his grave.[34]

The entire archives of the Arab Bureau were linked to the politics of colonization. For instance, most of its members claimed the Tell was too large for the inhabitants and that an appropriation of Arab land was required by political exigency and the need for security. Furthermore, this could also be justified legally from an Islamic point of view. Such a justification was available in 1844 and had been formulated by a physician known as Doctor Worms.[35] This man was interested in lending colonization the force of the law. However, the law is "a manner of imagining the real," as Geertz puts it, and is not "a bounded set of norms."[36] Worms does not so much imagine the real as he presents a representation of the real by interpreting a law differently. For Worms, Algeria (like the rest of the Islamic countries, including India and Persia) was conquered by the Arabs by force of arms. Thus, most of its territory is a land of *kharadj* (it belongs to the Turkish state that France inherited by virtue of conquest). The tribes are allowed to use it in exchange for annual tribute. Only a small portion of the territory is considered personal property, and it is subject to another type of taxation, *zekkat* (in Islamic law, the tithe; *le dime* in French; in Arabic, *ùshur*). How can the French government distinguish between the two?

Worms believes that the "Turkish state" distinguished between the two by the manner in which the land is used: anything that could be ploughed with more than two cows is a land of *kharaj*. In other words, it is principally the larger fields of agriculture that are domains of the state. The logical conclusion, which nicely coincided with the Arab Bureau's position on land, is that the Arabs live in vast territories that necessarily belong to the French government by virtue of its conquest of the Turks. Because the Kabylia area is ploughed on a smaller scale, as fields of subsistence and not of agriculture, it does not constitute a state-owned property. It is personal and subject to sale. In other words, both kinds of land are subject to colonization, but Arab land could be taken (that is, expropriated) legally because it technically belonged to the state, and Kabyle land could be bought and sold legally. Colonial discourse—whether ethnographic, historical, or legal—is systematic in its divisive view of the natives.

Representation of the natives was usually overtly intended to shed light on the best way possible to govern them. To govern, one needed to know, and knowing is nothing more than representing. In this context, understanding what the natives were

like also meant understanding the proper way to manage, neu-
tralize, and govern them in the most efficient way for the success
of the colonial enterprise. This meant lowering the cost of governing the natives, and taxes were also drawn from native labor
which colonial officers were to maximize. Making the natives
inferior was linked to a policy of *containment*. If the natives are
half-savage, "plunged in a state of barbarism," and respects
only force, how should they be managed?

The conquest was a means to colonialism, and colonialism
was a means to civilization, or as a colonial author put it, "colonization is not the means of action to the conquest, it is a means
of civilization after the conquest."[37] Civilizing the natives meant
colonizing them. In the political language of the Arab Bureau,
the natives had to cede parts of their lands to the Europeans in a
way that allowed the two communities to live harmoniously side
by side. By this time, the officers of the Arab Bureau were mostly
in favor of these politics, known as containment. Richard
pushed it to its limits. For him, the natives were all the same fanatic Arabs. So, any part of their land was available for colonial
expansion. Daumas, who was often described as someone "who
likes the natives," had a more ambivalent position. He represented the Arabs in a way that opposed them to the French,
making them an enemy whose excesses could be justified by that
same representation, but his description of the Kabyles makes
them familiar which inspires compassion for these "primitive
ancestors of" Europe. In this way, the politics of containment,
so central in the discourse of the Arab Bureau, found its legitimacy in the very representations provided by the Arab Bureau,
despite its cleavages.[38]

Although representations of Algeria differed in the 1840s and
1850s, officers of the Arab Bureau seemed to agree that the
Arabs had too much land and that therefore expropriation of
the tribal land was the way to implement European settlement.[39]
By the 1860s, some officers opposed and denounced the policy
of expropriation.[40] The political position of some of the coloniz-

ers had changed, but their representations of Algerians that inspired and justified the policy of containment remained, which served to generate other projects. For those who later changed their political positions, it was too late, for they had established a discourse that they no longer controlled. In fact, the discourse fabricated by the Arab Bureau was soon appropriated by its opponents—the church and the settlers. The first sought to justify an agenda of religious conversion, and the second sought to defend the policy of containment that had once been defended by members of the Arab Bureau. The settlers believed that Algeria had been conquered by force of arms and so they had the right to occupy any part of it. This is what was meant by "making Algeria French." The natives, especially the Arabs, should be contained, removed, and separated from the European community and if necessary remitted to the desert.[41] Representing the natives and policing them were so tightly linked that, as Charles-André Julien has put it, for a settler to show that he is republican, he has to show his hostility and disdain for the Muslims.[42]

Nevertheless, in this colonial period, a discursive formation emerged within the colonial enterprise. There were not scholars on one hand and the colonial enterprise on the other. Colonialism produced its own intellectual institutions, its own authorities, and its own knowledge. Colonial institutions, such as the Arab Bureau produced knowledge that was to a certain extent, heterogeneous. There was no consensus about the Arabs and the Berbers. For Lapène and Richard, the Kabyles were not Europeans but were either Arabs or close to Arabs. Envisioning the Kabyle as European and different from the Arab was not a common discourse at this point, although it soon became dominant. In fact, Daumas and Fabar articulated a discourse that came to constitute the norm and succeeded in gaining the adherence of major politicians and decision makers. During the rise of this discursive formation, one also finds representations that were considered untrue and others that were ignored or dismissed. It is this type of representation that I now examine.

COLONIAL HERESIES

Paying attention to conflicting interpretations can help us address some important questions. Was French colonial knowledge homogeneous and entirely antinative? Does it reflect conflicting ideologies and contradicting statements? If so, how does one account for the differences or contradictions that occurred within the archives of the same institution? Among the scholars I discuss in the nineteenth century is Thomas Urbain. He is often considered an anticolonialist who rebelled against his own colonial society,[43] and he produced a discourse that questioned most of the colonial interpretations of the population of Algeria.

Thomas Urbain wrote his first article about the Kabyles in 1857, a decade following Daumas, and he too offers a new interpretation.[44] Urbain notes that the Kabyles do not constitute a separate, opposing entity among the inhabitants of Algeria. For him, the Kabyles are "an agglomeration of tribes."[45] They are Berbers, no different from the Berbers of the plains or the plateaus. But who are the Berbers?

For Urbain, the Berbers at the time of the Arab conquest were themselves of diverse origin that included the Senahdja, Ketama, and Zenata. The Kabylia area from Dellys to Bone (Hippo) was inhabited by these groups and totally absorbed the natives of that area. At the time of the colonial conquest, Berber divisions disappeared, and two denominations appeared, Kbail and Chouai. The name Kbail, which Urbain contends was invented by the French, designates the Berbers who resided in the mountains and in Senhadja and Ketama territories. The Chouai indicates the Berbers of the plain, descendants of the Zenata and Houara. Drawing from a number of authors that include Ibn Khaldûn, Ernest Carette, and even Daumas,[46] Urbain dissolves the Berbers into a heterogeneous population whose origins are quite murky. He then concludes: "From the point of view of the French conquest, we should consider them as mountaineers, Algerians and Muslims, in the same way as all other Berbers that still inhabit our possessions of North Africa."[47]

Having constituted the Kabyles as Berber and the Berbers as Algerian, Urbain examines and refutes each of the characteristics that the dominant discourse attributed to them, one by one. In other words, he seeks to blur the opposition made by Daumas. For instance, the Kabyles do not only busy themselves exclusively with industry and gardening, but they are involved, along with Arabs, in agriculture. They do not possess a special law called *qanoun*, a term brought to them by the Arabs. They have rules regarding the affairs of their tribes, but they possess no written law. Being independent tribes and without a central government, the strict application of the Quranic law is not easy.

Urbain is attacking, through the use of a historical narrative, the predominantly ethnographic representation articulated by Daumas. Although Urbain lacks ethnographic authority, he gives his discourse the effect of self-evident truths by narrating the history of the various groups in North Africa from the seventh-century Arab invasions to the nineteenth-century French occupation of Algeria.

For Urbain, the Kabyles are the same as all of the inhabitants of Algeria: they are Algerian and Muslim. Here again, unlike Daumas, Urbain defines Islam differently. In an article significantly and defiantly called "The Tolerance of Islam,"[48] Urbain maintains that Islam has historically shown a high level of tolerance for other religions. He concludes that the "fanaticism" of the Muslims in the Algerian context is caused by the occupation of their land. Urbain suggests that only a just policy that assures equality between the natives and the European immigrants would permanently eradicate fanaticism. For Urbain, the Algerians can progress, emulate, and even become French.

This was the mission of the Arab Bureau, according to Urbain, and the mission that would serve both natives and French. He suggested a policy that focused on the "politics of the *kaids*" (the notables of the tribes), but he also advocated the merciless use of force for the "fanatics" or the "recalcitrant." A civilizing mission, for him, should go through three phases: the native administration is exclusively Arab but under French control; after French influence takes root, the Arab Bureau governs; and finally, the Arab tribes either live side by side with the French community or are absorbed by it.[49]

Urbain was not expressing an isolated position.[50] In colonial Algeria, one finds similar representations. Pellissier de Reynaud—another officer of the Arab Bureau and known as an authority in the colonial period for his exhaustive three-volume history of the French conquest of Algeria, *Annales algériennes*—expressed a similar position.[51] Reynaud, who was a more potent historian and ethnographer than either Urbain or Daumas, begins with philosophical remarks:

> Humanity is one: the differences that one notices between diverse societies that constitute humanity are more of a façade than a reality. The forms change, but the content is always the same. Submitted to the same essential needs, man has everywhere the same passions. He is endowed with a natural sentiment of kindness towards his fellow men, without which society could not exist for one moment. But born progressive, man has also a sentiment of individualism which is much more developed than in animals whose organization is fixed.[52]

Reynaud believed that the differences between societies are caused by differences in their soil and climate. The Arabs had a different "public spirit" that was the result of their soil and climate. Among Arabs, the tribes were independent from and often at war with the state. Arab tribes were always ready to use any means to preserve their freedom from the central power and this state of rebellion created anarchy and led to "barbarism" among them. They are in contrast to Europeans, whose desire for liberty forced them to settle down and create civilization. Thus, Reynaud echoes Ibn Khaldûn and his views on dynastic power and on the effects of soil and climate,[53] although it is precisely this "state of things" that makes colonization legitimate.

That is, due to their social organization, the population was in a state of "anarchy" that only the French mission could curtail. Colonial discourse, even among the heretics, had to maintain a crucial device—"a situation of lack." There had to always be a lack of progress, a lack of order, a lack of civilization, or lack of security. Even in the heretical colonial discourse, there was a line that it would not transgress.

The postulate shared by all the members of the Arab Bureau was that the population lacked civilization. Divergences occurred in the ways the natives as objects were constructed but seldom in the political solution offered. The differences that Reynaud highlighted among the inhabitants of North Africa does not oppose them to each other. For instance, he did not discern any opposition between Arabs and Kablyes. There was much more conflict among Kabyles themselves than there was between Kabyles and Arabs. Neither was bad. On the contrary, Reynaud constructs an Arab that contradicts, on almost every point, the common image: he is as intelligent as the European, has higher morals, and enjoys a superior family organization. Arab women hold a better position than European women because although they have their share of difficulties in life, they are not exposed to the abuses that European peasant women endure due to the effects of alcoholism. Moreover, in the city aristocratic native women enjoy tremendous freedom, and common women seem to have the upper hand in the home. Reynaud constructs his object, the native of North Africa, differently than the majority of the members of the Arab Bureau do. He initially wants to show the inaccuracy of the dominant discourse, misconceptions that justify the worst forms of colonial practice. Indeed, as he wrote:

> By accepting without examination, these old expressions of *the perfidious Arab, the ferocious Arab, the Arab that can be ruled only by force,* we expose ourselves to ignoring the voice of humanity that should always be heard from a people that have in their hands the noble cause of civilization. It would be very fortunate, one would agree, that by exaggerating the fierceness of these

peoples, we will come to believe that we are allowed to use against them procedures worse than those we blame them for.[54]

The natives, according to him, were unjustly judged in a situation of war capable of transforming the kindest of people into the most ferocious ones. The erroneousness of the descriptions of his contemporaries, according to him, is based on the fact that they focused on limited areas, thus providing "fodder for the heinous prejudice of some Europeans."[55] But his study is based on extensive fieldwork over an area that extended from Libya to Morocco:

> For me, without hiding the fact that I have always had as a goal to weaken these pretensions, I declare that I have always told the truth as I saw it. It is thus with full conviction, the most complete good faith, that I establish the following conclusions: Arabs are neither better nor worse than the French. Good and evil are distributed unequally among the second than among the first. This makes our civilization present types that are clearer-cut in virtue and in vice than theirs. It is the same in the domain of intelligence: the masses have more among them, but they have no great foyer. As for happiness, I am convinced, as much as one can be, that the majority suffers less in Africa than in Europe.[56]

The heretical colonial discourse, as articulated by both Urbain and Reynaud, has a number of characteristics. It tends to eliminate the opposition between the French and the natives and between Christianity and Islam, but not to obliterate the differences. In this discourse, the differences are carefully noted but not in terms of bad and good. For Urbain, Islam is tolerant, a Muslim can be French, and Islam historically has shown a high level of tolerance. Sociologically, the "fanaticism" that some of the Muslims showed in the colonial period was a consequence of an unjust colonial policy rather than an effect of Islam. For Reynaud, Islam as a system was not against progress and did not obstruct French colonization.[57]

The heretical discourse also investigates national characteristics—what Reynaud calls "the spirit of a people" *(volks-*

geist), a famous Hegelian concept common in the nineteenth century. Europeans and the natives of North Africa were both intelligent but because of their social organization, the natives were hindered from progressing. Humanly, so to speak, the population was as good as the Europeans and often better, for they had not experienced the negative side-effects of civilization, such as alcoholism, individualism, and materialism. The heretical discourse also tends to be less essentialist. In Urbain and Reynaud, the population were "an agglomeration" of "Algerians," made up of a number of different ethnic groups that are not reduced to only two categories, Arabs and Berbers. One could consider them all Algerian Muslims, but their Islam was malleable. It changed and could change in a way that would not be an obstacle for integrating them into the French nation.

The heretical discourse was not anticolonial in the twentieth-century meaning of the term.[58] It supported the civilizing mission, cast the population as inferior, and recommended their subjugation. Its description of the native as "good" tended to sustain the possibility of civilizing him. Its description of "retardation" tended to legitimate the colonial enterprise. Nevertheless (and this is why this discourse is heretical), it did not make the population an enemy, a negation of Western civilization, or an opposition to the very being of Europe. Rather, it made them perfectible. Their social organization caused them to be "plunged into a state of barbarism" not some "inherent nature." In other words, the heretical discourse contained the dichotomy of "us" versus "them," an anthropological one that presupposes the unity of humanity. The others were once a part of us, but they have not progressed as we did. Historically, we were all once the same.[59] This dichotomy is not an Orientalist one that totally opposed West versus East, two entities that mutually exclude each other.[60] How can one account for this contradiction within the archives of the Arab Bureau?

Contradiction is not an error by which truth is defined and thus recognized, but it creates the possibility of another discourse.[61] It is a discursive alternative that reflects a diversity of

opinions and ideologies and that is an option to be considered
when a discourse exhausts its possibilities. Both orthodox representations, and their contradiction, constitute the archives of the
Arab Bureau. Each is potentially true or false, and each participates in defining the other.[62] Let us now see how discourse and
place can intertwine to produce truth.

CANONIZING KNOWLEDGE

Why would scholars who belonged to the same institution and
wrote at the same time produce highly conflicting representations of the same population? In most theories of representation,
knowledge is the product of an operation that involves an observer (a subject) who examines an observed (an object). However, following Maurice Merleau-Ponty, I suggest that representation is the product of both observer and observed and that
each is simultaneously an object and a subject: what the observer perceives is also what the observed offers for perception.[63]
The contradicting representations created for the Arab Bureau
may be explained by the fact that its officers had not observed
the same aspects of the population. Reynaud seems to be aware
of this. He points to some of the causes of the differences between himself and his contemporaries. They saw the population
in a "state of excitement," he says, during the war against for-
eigners, whereas his inquiry was made in a larger area, from
Libya to Morocco, that was not subject to the same aggression
as Algeria. Richard, on the other hand, notes that he saw the
population who confirmed his idea of the hostility of the inhabitants. He made an ethnographic argument based on eyewitness
accounts: "This book was written in the midst of the upheaval,
in the stormiest of circumstances and it is with the most serious
preoccupations that many of these pages have been written, at
the sound of the musketry of our front posts, and some of these
pages are tinged with blood."[64]

   "Being there" is a device that regulates ethnographic discourse and makes it more powerful.[65] Colonial authors such as

Richard, Reynaud, and Urbain were there in a variety of ways. Reynaud was there extensively—from Libya to Morocco—and he has seen all of the population. Richard was there extensively as well—during peace and war—and he saw the Arabs in all their states (he also risked his life to bring forth this knowledge). Urbain was there but not in large area or for an extensive period of time. Because of this, he uses an additional device that is common to the historical narrative. He has read history, where nothing is invented, and all events speak for themselves.[66] Colonial discourse makes use of devices that are all valid. Why is one accepted as true and the other as untrue? The status of the veracity (or falsity) of a discourse should be sought in the discourse itself and the things that may affect it and make it either persuasive or unconvincing. For this purpose, I examine the case of Daumas, whose writings acquired an unparalleled legitimacy and in the process compare him with Urbain and Reynaud.

Soon after his arrival in Algeria in 1835, Captain Daumas participated in Marshal Clauzel's expeditions to Mascara and Tlemcen against Abd el-Qader. Daumas perceived his object of investigation from the battlefield. For him, the Arabs were mostly Arabic-speaking and nomadic. Most were involved in the struggle against the French, and most were motivated by a religious ideology. Urbain's experience was quite different. As a Muslim convert,[67] Urbain's descriptions were made far from the battlefield, among the passive and peaceful population of the city. As suggested earlier, the observer is also a part of the observation. What conditions the perception of each observer may also explain why one discourse becomes more palpable and dominant and why another discourse becomes baseless and marginalized.

Daumas was both an officer and a director of the Arab Bureau. At the time of his appointment, he gained tremendous prestige. He was one of the few officers who spoke fluent Arabic and Algerian dialect,[68] he had the most extensive field experience among the population, and he was the French ambassador to Abd el-Qader from November 15, 1837, to October 15, 1839.[69]

Daumas used a common academic strategy. By multipliying his publications, if necessary by repetition, he appeared to be the most knowledgeable expert of the day in Algerian affairs. Indeed, by 1857, Daumas had expressed more or less the same ideas in dozens of books.[70] Some of them were a mere reproduction of Daumas and Fabar's *La Grande Kabylie* (1847), which was published again under different titles, in the process of which the name of his coauthor Fabar was dropped and forgotten. By 1857, because of his service to the Arab Bureau, Daumas was promoted from captain to the rank of general, which meant this his writings were now coming from a general of the Arab Bureau, a dominant institution with impressive scholarly credentials. Daumas was also close to General Bugeaud, whose ideas he shared and expressed.[71] From 1841 to 1848, they worked together. *The Brochure of 1844,* which covered the organization of the Arab Bureau, was a product of that collaboration. "When Daumas wrote," one of his biographers said, "he did so as if Marshal Bugeaud was holding the pen."[72] The colonial careers of both men were so intertwined that they ended at the same time. When Bugeaud left Algeria, Daumas immediately followed, even though the Arab Bureau had begun to lose some of its authority before the time of the departure of Bugeaud.

During his tenure, Daumas continued to exert tremendous influence over the Ministry of War as director of indigenous affairs. In fact, war minister Saint-Artaud depended almost completely on Daumas, and as time passed, Daumas accumulated more and more "symbolic capital," to use Bourdieu's expression,[73] and the more firmly his discourse was established as authoritative, which meant true knowledge, this discourse gained strength as its author continued to solidify it from the most powerful sites of French colonial administration.

By contrast, Reynaud, although an officer of the Arab Bureau, was critical of his superiors, including Bugeaud. He was known to be a difficult person who had many enemies.[74] He made himself known not as an ethnographer but as an historian of the French conquest of Algeria. His ethnographic work was published as an appendix of his *Annales algériennes* (1854) giving it a secondary status. Although he was the author of the most exhaustive chronicles of French colonial adventures from 1830 to 1853, he was not considered an authority on Algerian affairs. Moreover, as time passed in the colonial enterprise, the less complete and therefore the less authoritative his contemporary history of colonization became. In addition, the colonial enterprise was more interested in knowledge about the local population than in knowledge of its own history. Reynaud witnessed a different war than Daumas saw. Reynaud saw the same brutal war that Bugeaud waged against the population, ruthlessly killing them, imprisoning children and women and destroying villages and crops. In 1839, early in his career, Reynaud resigned from the Arab Bureau to protest the policies of his superiors.[75] Furthermore, he expressed a position that corresponded to neither the Arab Bureau nor the Saint-Simonians. Instead, he echoed the sentiments of Jean-Jacques Rousseau in his reference to the population (good half-savages not yet corrupted by civilization),[76] and Ibn Khaldûn (who insisted on the influence of the soil and the climate on human cultures).[77]

Urbain, on the other hand, was not an officer of the Arab Bureau but only an interpreter. His ideas reflected less the ideology of the Arab Bureau than that of the Saint-Simonians, who insisted on the idea of unifying Orient and Occident. They also put forward a program of colonization that stressed work, industry, and progress to improve human well-being.[78] Unlike Daumas, Urbain did not develop a strategy: most of his publications were short articles. His two later books were political treatises: one was published anonymously, and the second one under a pseudonym, George Voisin.[79] Urbain was aware that his discourse expressed a heresy in French Algeria of that time— that the populations are all Muslims, that because they are Muslims, they are good, and that they therefore should be assimilated into the French nation. In addition, Urbain had against him a number of factors that initially impeded the wide circulation of his discourse: he was a Muslim convert, he was an illegitimate son, he was black, and last but not least, he was married to an Algerian woman.[80]

Nevertheless, his interpretation was adopted by Napoleon III in the early years of 1860s. By this time, the Arab Bureau had undergone a drastic transformation. By 1860, all of Algeria was conquered, and Napoleon himself no longer believed in its mission, especially after the conquest of the Great Kabylia in 1857. The policy of containment to which most of the members of the Arab Bureau adhered was itself revealed as colonial malpractice. It had alienated the Arab tribes and empowered the civilian settlers whose ultimate aim was to replace the military regime. In 1856, the Arab Bureau, already under attack, offered to its opponents a golden opportunity when one of its officers killed an *agha* and was sentenced to death.[81] Napoleon had a different policy: he was more concerned with a liberal economy that would make Algeria a source of income instead of an economic burden for the French government. His position coincided with the Saint-Simonian doctrine. It was no accident that he took Urbain as his adviser, as an expert on native affairs with a position that called for the reconciliation between the two communities for the benefit of colonization. For Napoleon, there was only a nation that he often referred to as an Arab kingdom, proclaiming that "this country is at once an Arab kingdom, a European colony, and a French camp."[82] Moreover, Napoleon did not categorize the population but referred to them as Arabs, "a warrior and intelligent nation"[83] that could effectively participate in the success of colonization.

Napoleon was influenced by the work of those inspired by the Saint-Simonians, especially Urbain and Lapasset. But his policy alienated both the army and the French settlers, who dismissed him as the emperor of the Arabs.[84] Even top army officers (such as General Pellissier) did not dare to attack the emperor. Rather, he attacked his adviser Urbain, calling him: "a renegade," "the circumcised one, a fox with a trimmed tail."[85] This underscores the notion that even when it became official, the heretical discourse remained unpopular.

The archives of the Arab Bureau were, therefore made of heterogeneous and even conflicting representations about the natives of Algeria. But for sociological and ideological reasons, only one emerged as the most valuable, the most authoritative, and therefore the most truthful. Indeed, the discourse articulated by Daumas became the most dominant because it expressed the official ideology of Arab Bureau. This gained tremendous strength due to its multiplication in a magnitude of other texts, initially by the author himself and then by his colleagues, hence Jacques Berque's description of the scholarship of the Arab Bureau as in a state of "precocity" and "stagnation."[86] *Precocity* exemplifies the fact that the members of the Arab Bureau were the first to construct a number of objects in French knowledge of North Africa. *Stagnation* describes the way in which the discourse of the Arab Bureau proliferated by repetition without constructing new objects, at least until 1870, when France's war with Prussia led to the fall of the French empire, a defeat that was blamed on the officers. In Algeria, things were no better. The population of the Kabylia area organized a massive revolt that threatened the entire colonial enterprise. That, too, was blamed on the officers (who plotted and orchestrated the revolt to save the Arab Bureau) by the settlers.[87]

By 1871, the Arab Bureau was practically dismantled, yet its ethnographic work remained the source of French knowledge of North Africa. The knowledge constructed by the Arab Bureau was indispensable to the civil regime, which now was dominant. This knowledge ordered the colony and even its politics of representation admirably fit the civil regime. Is not Algeria divided between Arabs and Berbers? Is not the Berber, specifically the Kabyle, of European origins? Is not the Arab the dreadful enemy with too much land? In short, the knowledge constructed by the Arab Bureau carried meanings that were common to that whole era. But 1871 opened up a new one. The whole of Algeria, including the region of Kabylia, was then "conquered and pacified," to use a colonial expression.

In the 1860s, the colonial enterprise became certain, at least for many, and seemed well established. Yet more knowledge was needed, but not mere indications of who lived there, how different or similar were they from the French, and how they could be managed so they would not become a nuisance for colonization. Instead, colonial administration needed more details about those objects, more statistics about the tribes, and their relations to each other, and more details about their agricultural and industrial production. In short, what was needed was knowledge that would make the area as familiar as a canton to a Frenchman. This knowledge was provided at the right time, precisely when the Arab Bureau had fallen down.

This new knowledge came from two of its former officers, Adolphe Hanouteau and Aristide Letourneau, who built on the scholarship of the Arab Bureau in a three-volume book called *La Kabylie et les coutumes kabyles*.[88] They reproduced all the objects constructed by the officers of the Arab Bureau, expanding on most of them, sometimes correcting them, and sometimes refuting them. For the authors, the Kabyles are Berbers. They have been mixed with other peoples, such as the Greeks, the Romans, and the Vandals, throughout history. The conclusion is that "today a good number of Kabyle families have had ancestors of European race."[89] There is no evidence that they were Christians, even though this may be possible. The crosses that women tattooed in the center of their forehead do not constitute an argument, the authors contend. It is a mere motif that artists had developed, though it is not common. The authors believe that the Kabyles could be closer to the French, not by religion but rather by material interests alien to religion. The Kabyles were "greedy and poor," so France could use these qualities to initiate them to industry, develop trade routes, and tie them to itself by a set of common interests.[90]

Hanouteau and Letourneau also created new objects and investigated the details of Kabyle life. They re-presented the Kabyles in many of their aspects and fully described their agriculture (its methods, means, varieties, and results), diseases, medicine, industry, and penal code *(qanoun)* with texts that the authors collected for the first time. In sum, no other text was as comprehensive about Great Kabylia as the text by Hanouteau and Letourneau. The book synthesized the Arab Bureau's archives and ultimately replaced it, even though it owed its existence to the old archives. From that time onward, Hanouteau and Letourneau's book became the foremost reference on the Kabyles and it eclipsed all previous works.[91] In a review of the book in 1873, Ernest Renan wrote:

> The Berber race has now not only been unquestionably established in the field of anthropology; but it is also the object of a science. An ensemble of studies have been created about this indigenous race of North Africa similar to the worlds of Semitic and Indo-European [studies], which have given it its materials.[92]

What had been created was a body of knowledge about North Africa, with the Berber as its focal point, that is significantly different from Orientalism; the latter which focuses on the Orient, with Islam as its privileged discursive site. In his review, Renan had to place this new knowledge in the Orientalist framework. Thus, for Renan, the Berbers are distinguished from the people of the Orient by their social and political structures. Whereas the Orient was despotic and governed by an intolerant religion, the Berbers had a democracy. Whereas the Orient was organized on a feudal system, the Berbers lived in a republic. Were the Berbers European or equal to Europeans? In fact, the Berber republic did not extend beyond the tribe, and there was no notion of a nation. Berber democracy was based on a penal code that did not distinguish acts that affect society and acts that affect only individuals, and it enforced laws that unduly restricted individual liberty. Renan concludes:

> The great service that Rome did for the world was dissolving these old local customs and creating the notion of a liberal law that fixes penalties to the crimes that society cannot withstand without destroying itself. It protects each, in their person and in their possessions, and abandons the rest to the morality of the individual.[93]

In the Orientalist taxonomy established by Renan, the Berbers
are opposed to the Orient by their social organizations and depend on Europe to make laws that distinguish between social order and individual liberties. As Rome had imposed its laws in
the past in other societies, France, its heir, must do to the
Kabyles. In any case, Berbers needed to be colonized by the logic
of colonial representation, whose genealogy can be traced to the
Arab Bureau and on which civil institutions would continue to
build even after 1871.[94]

NOTES

1. Tocqueville, *Oeuvres complètes,* 3: 139–153.
2. Thomas Bugeaud, *De l'établissement de légions des colons militaires dans les possessions française du nord de l'Afrique* (Paris:
   Firmin Didot, 1838), 5, 26.
3. Cohn, *Colonialism and Its Forms of Knowledge,* 16.
4. The treaty was signed by Bugeaud, who was then a commander of
   the division of Oran. For more details, see Charles-André Julien,
   Histoire de l'Algérie contemporaine (Paris: Presses Universitaires
   de France, 1964), 128–140.
5. In 1830, immediately after the conquest of Algiers, the French created an *agha* through which they intended to communicate with
   local tribes. In November 18, 1834, the *agha* post went to a French
   officer, Captain Marey-Monge. In April 1833, an Arab Bureau
   was created in Algiers and was headed by Captain Lamoricière. In
   1835, the Arab Bureau was abolished. In 1837, after the treaty of
   Tifna with Abd el-Kader, the Algerian Arab Bureau was reestablished under the direction of Captain Pellissier de Reynaud. But its
   function had drastically diminished to watching the borders that
   separate the Algerian occupied territory from the area under Abd
   el-Kader's rule. Ferdinand Hugonnet, *Français et Arabes en
   Algérie* (Paris: Sartorus & Challamel, 1860), 173–198.
6. Charles Richard, *Du gouvernement arabe et de l'institution qui
   doit l'exercer* (Algiers: Bastide, 1848), 20.
7. These numbers are from Vincent Monteil, "Les Bureaux arabes au
   Maghreb (1833–1961" in *Esprit,* 1962; 575.
8. Another officer of the Arab Bureau, Hurbert Lyautey, later reestab-

lished it under a different name—*Service des affaires indigènes et des renseignements*—and made it his instrument for colonizing Morocco. See Daniel Rivet, *Lyautey et l'institution du protéctorat au Maroc, 1912–1925* (Paris: L'Harmattan, 1988), especially vol. 2, 35–55. For a general view on the production of the Arab Bureau in Morocco, see Abdelmajid Hannoum, "L'auteur comme autoritéen ethnographie coloniale," in François Pouillon and Daniel Rivet, eds., *La sociologie de Robert Montagne* (Paris: Maisonneuve & Larose, 2000), 251–266.

9. Jacques Frémeaux, *Les Bureaux arabes dans l'Algérie de la conquête* (Paris: Donël, 1993). This work about the Arab Bureau is quite apologetic. More balanced views are expressed by both Monteil, *Les Bureaux arabes,* and Julien, *Histoire de l'Algérie.* The richest book about the Arab Bureau remains Xavier Yacono, *Les Bureaux arabes* (Paris: Larose, 1953).

10. For details about this institution and its role in the formation of Orientalists, see Daniel Reig, *Homo orientaliste* (Paris: Maisonneuve & Larose, 1988).

11. Charles Feraud, *Les interprètes de l'armée d'Afrique* (Alger: Jourdan, 1876), 49.

12. Ferdinand Hugonnet, *Souvenirs d'un chef du Bureau arabe* (Paris: Michel Levy, 1858), 5.

13. Thomas Bugeaud and Eugène Daumas, *Exposé de l'état de la société arabe, du gouvernement et de la législation qui la régit* (Algiers: Imprimerie du gouvernement, 1844), 79.

14. The Mission Scientifique de l'Algérie was launched by the Ministry of War in 1839. Its unfinished work was published in the 1840s but was excluded from the archives of the Arab Bureau for ideological reasons. This is because the Mission Scientifique was dominated by Saint-Simonians. For a discussion of the conflict between the Saint-Simonians and Bugeaud, see Marcel Emerit, *Les Saint-Simonians en Algérie* (Paris: Société d'édition, 1941), 131–134, 142–143. For example, the historian Ernest Curette, one of the most important members of the Mission, once commented that the regime of Bugeaud was full of "flat sycophants, false and hateful hearts, degraded intelligence, this that swarms in Algiers. . . . No, in truth, this must change, and the only cure is to break this court" (Ibid., 44).

15. Eugène Daumas and Paul-Dieudonné Fabar, *La Grande Kabylie* (Paris: Hachette, 1847).
16. See for instance the early work of Adrian Berbrugger. For a discussion of this book, see Abdelmajid Hannoum, "Notes on the (Post)Colonial in the Maghreb" in *Critique of Anthropology,* vol. 29, number 3, 2009: 324–344.
17. Ibid., 12.
18. For more details about the myth of Roman North Africa, see Abdelmajid Hannoum, *Colonial Histories, Postcolonial Memories* (Portsmouth: Greenwood, 2001), 29–69.
19. Daumas and Fabar, *La Grande Kabylie.*
20. Ibid., 14.
21. The term *ethnography* was not in use yet although the practice was. Daumas and Fabar describe their work as "a contemporary chronicle" (see v). Nevertheless, the case of the Arab Bureau shows that within the French tradition, ethnography was initially a military practice.
22. Daumas and Fabar, *La Grande Kabylie,* 43.
23. Eugène Daumas, *Moeurs et coutumes de l'Algérie* (Paris: Hachette, 1953) (originally published 1855); Eugène Daumas, *La vie arabe et la société musulmane* (Paris: Lévy, 1869).
24. See, among many, Henri Aucapitaine, *Le pays et la societé kabyle* (Paris: Bertrand, 1857); Charles Devaux, *Les Kebailes du Djerdjera* (Marseille: Camoin, 1859); Eugène Monglave, *La Kabylie* (n.p., 1857?).
25. Edward Lapène, *Tableau historique, moral et politique sur les Kabyles* (Metz: Academie Royale, 1846).
26. Richard, *Du gouvernement arabe,* 5.
27. Richard, *Etudes sur l'insurrection du Dhara.*
28. Charles Richard, *De la civilisation du peuple arabe* (Algiers: Dubos, 1850), 5.
29. Quoted by Ernest Waterbled, "L'insurrection Kabyle," *Revue des Deux Mondes,* 108 (1873), 625.
30. Marcel Emerit, "Le problème de la conversion des musulmans de l'Algérie," *Revue Historique* 223 (1960): 63–84; Marcel Emerit, "La lutte entre les généraux et les prêtres au début de l'Algérie française," *Revue Africaine* (1949): 65–125.
31. Richard, *Etudes sur l'insurrection du Dhara,* 122.
32. Richard, *De la civilisation du peuple arabe,* 5.

33. Richard, *Du gouvernement arabe*, 9.

34. Richard, *Etudes sur l'insurrection du Dhara*, 192–193.

35. Indeed in 1844, Worms wrote a text that became crucial for any discussion of the containment issue. M. Worms, "Recherches sur la constitution de la propriété territoriale dans les pays musulmans et subsidiarement en Algérie," *Journal Asiatique* (1844): 000–000.

36. Clifford Geertz, *Local Knowledge: Fact and Law in Comparative Perspective* (New York: Basic Books, 1983), 173.

37. M. Walsin-Esterharz, *De la domination turque dans l'ancienne regence d'Alger* (Paris: Gosselin, 1840), 37.

38. One finds a similar representation in an earlier work by a settler who preached a total occupation of Algeria and the possibility of taking away Arab land. Anonymous, *La Kabylie: recherches et observations sur cette riche contrée de l'Algérie par un colon* (Paris: Maistrasse et Wiart, 1846).

39. The expression "The Arabs have too much land" was uttered by Lapasset in the 1840s. He became an opponent of expropriation after he witnessed the colonial practices of the settlers and even the Arab Bureau.

40. Such as Lapasset, who describes the containment as "theft and spoliation." See Yacono, *Les Bureaux arabes*, 167–171.

41. See Charles-Robert Ageron, *Les algériens musulmans et la France, 1871–1919* (Paris: Presses Universitaires de France, 1968), 37–54.

42. Julien, *Histoire de l'Algérie contemporaine*, 344.

43. Edmund Burke compares him with Franz Fanon. See Edmund Burke, "Two Critics of French Rule in Algeria: Ismael Urbain and Frantz Fanon," in Carl Brown and Mathew Gordon, editors. *Franco-Arab Encounters* (Beirut: American University of Beirut, 1996), 329–344.

44. Ismael Urbain, "Les Kabyles du Djurdjura," *Revue de Paris*, 36 (1857): 36, 91–110.

45. Ibid., 94.

46. Ernest Carette provided Ismael Urbain with information about the history of Algeria that he himself took from Ibn Khaldûn. Daumas provided data about the Kabyles, which Urbain reinterprets. Carette was also a major ethnographer and a historian, although he was not a member of the Arab Bureau. He participated in the Exploration Scientifique de l'Algérie between 1840 and 1842. His work was published in 1848. It gained more importance with the

triumph of the civil regime and the fall of the military regime. He was a Saint-Simonian, a fierce opponent of Bugeaud, whom he openly criticized with the acerbity. His works include, especially, Ernest Carette, *Etudes sur la Kabylie proprement dite* (Paris: Imprimerie Nationale, 1848), and also *Recherches sur l'origine et les migrations des principales tribus de l'Afrique septentrionale et partculièrement de l'Algérie* (Paris: Imprimerie Nationale, 1853).

47. Urbain, "Les Kabyles du Djurdjura," 98.

48. Urbain, "La tolérance de l'Islamisme," *Revue de Paris* (XXXI) (April 1856): 61–83.

49. Ismael Urbain, "Du gouvernement des tribus de l'Algérie," *Revue de l'Orient et de l'Algérie* 2 (1847): 241–259.

50. A Few others expressed the same position, such as Walsin-Esterharz, *De la domination turque;* M. Walsin-Esterharz, *Notices sur le maghzen d'Oran* (Oran: Perrier, 1849); also Ferdinand Lapasset, *Aperçu sur l'organisation des indigènes* (Paris: Dubos, 1850).

51. In the appendix, "Mémoire sur les moeurs et les institutions sociale des populations indigènes du Nord Afrique," of the third volume of his *Annales,* he describes both the inhabitants of Algeria and their religion. Pellissier de Reynaud, *Annales algériennes* (Paris: J. Dumain, 1854), 3: 426–457.

52. Ibid., 426.

53. Reynaud must have known Ibn Khaldûn through the work of Ernest Carette, who was a member of the Expedition Scientifique de l'Algérie along with Reynaud. Ibn Khaldûn was made known to the public between 1847 and 1851 by de Slane's translation of a portion of his work. William de Slane, *Histoire des Berbères d'Ibn Khaldûn* (Algiers: Imprimerie du Government, 1852–1856). His theoretical work that appears in Reynaud's ethnography was translated a decade later. William de Slane, *Prolegomènes historique d'Ibn Khaldun* (Algiers: Imprimerie du Gouvernement, 1863).

54. De Reynaud, *Annales algériennes,* 449.

55. Ibid., 456.

56. Ibid.

57. Pellessier de Reynaud, "De l'Islamisme considéré principalement dans l'Afrique du Nord et dans son action sur les moeurs des peuples qui le professent," in *Annales algériennes,* 457–503.

58. Raoul Giradet, *L'idée coloniale en France* (Paris: La Table Ronde, 1972).

59. Claude Lévi-Strauss, "Race and History," *Structural Anthropology* II, trans. M. Lyton (Chicago: University of Chicago Press, 1983), 323–362.

60. Said, *Orientalism*.

61. Michel Foucault, *L'archéologie du savoir* (Paris: Gallimard, 1969), 195–204.

62. My definitions of *true* and *false* are ultimately semiotic. Following Greimas, I believe that a statement is true when it is adequate within the cognitive universe of the receiver; it is false when there is an inadequacy. See Algirdas-Julien Greimas, *Du sens II: essais sémiotiques* (Paris: Seuil, 1983), 103–113, 115–133. However, unlike orthodox semioticians, I maintain that both the adequacy and inadequacy of a statement are the mechanisms by which a statement or an ensemble of statements is constituted as true. The sociological sites that impose a statement as true forcefully affect even the internal mechanisms of a statement.

63. Maurice Merleau-Ponty, "Le corps comme expression et la parole," *Phénoménologie de la perception* (Paris: Gallimard, 1945), 203–232.

64. Richard, *Du gouvernment,* 194.

65. Clifford Geertz, "Ethnography and The Scene of Writing," *Works and Lives: The Anthropologist as Author* (Stanford: Stanford University, 1984), 1–24.

66. Roland Barthes, "Le discours de l'histoire," *Social Science Information* 6 (1967): 56–75. See also Michel de Certeau, "L'histoire et le réel," *Dialectiques* 14 (1976): 42–62.

67. Thomas Urbain converted to Islam in Egypt. He took the name of Ismael to make a parallel between him and Ismael, the son of Abraham from a slave. To Enfantin, Urbain justified his conversion to Islam as an attempt to bring Orient and Occident into union within himself. For more details about his conversion, see Philip Régnier, *Ismayl Urbain: voyage d'Orient* (Paris: L'Harmattan, 1993). After his first wife died, Urbain converted again to Christianity so he could marry a French woman who agreed to marry him on that condition.

68. During his stay with Abd el-Qader, Daumas served as a spy for Bugeaud and communicated to him the smallest details about the

emir, his army, the European deserters at his service, and his diplomatic relations with Morocco. He was not a friend of Abd el-Qader, and he did not like Arabs, as many historians later asserted, such as Feraud, *Les interprètes de l'armée d'Afrique;* Hugonnet, *Francaiset Arabes en Algérie;* and Julien, *Histoire de l'Algérie contemporaine.* For more details about Daumas during this period, see Georges Yver, *Correspondance du Capitaine Daumas (1837–1839)* (Algiers: Soubiron, 1912), (reprinted Algiers: Editions el Maarifa, 2008).

69. Thomas Bugeaud, *Par l'epée et par la charrue* (Paris: Presse Universitaire de France, 1948).

70. Daumas, *Moeurs et coutumes de l'Algérie;* see also Daumas, *La vie arabe et la sociéte musulmane.*

71. Bugeaud, *De l'établissement de legions de colons militaires.*

72. Raymond Peyronnet, *Livre d'or des officiers et des affaires indigenes* (Algiers: Imprimerie Algérienne, 1930), 124.

73. Pierre Bourdieu, *The Logic of Practice,* trans. Richard Nice (London: Polity Press, 1990), 112–121.

74. Peyronnet, *Livre d'or,* 48.

75. Hugonnet, *Français et Arabes en Algérie,* 180.

76. For Rousseau, see Claude Lévi-Strauss, "Jean-Jacques Rousseau, Founder of the Sciences of Man," *Structural Anthropology,* 33–48.

77. This idea was also common in nineteenth-century Europe—for instance, as a key concept in the work of Hyppolite Taine. See his *Histoire de la littérature anglaise* (Paris: Hachette, 1863), especially the introduction to volume 1.

78. See Prosper Enfatin, *Colonisation de l'Algérie* (Paris: Bertrand, 1843).

79. George Voisin, *L'Algérie pour les Algériens* (Paris: Michel Levy Frères, 1861); Anonymous, *Indigènes et immigrants* (Paris: Challamel, 1862).

80. Emerit, *Les Saints-Simonians,* 67–83; see also Charles-Robert Ageron, *L'Algérie algérienne de Napoléon III à de Gaule* (Paris: Sindbad, 1980), 17–36.

81. This incident is known as the Doineau affair. The trial revealed many cases of abuses by and corruption of officers. Julien, *Histoire de l'Algérie contemporaine,* 339–341.

82. Napoleon III, *Lettre sur la politique de la France en Algérie*

addressée par l'Empereur au Marechal de Mac Mahon (Paris: Imprimerie Nationale, 1865), 9.

83. Ibid.
84. See Ageron, *L'Algérie algérienne.*
85. Emerit, *Les Saint-Simonians,* 144.
86. Jacques Berque, "Vingt ans de sociologie maghrebine," *Annales: Economie, Société, Civilisation* 11 (1956): 302.
87. The Arab Bureau was accused by the settlers of instigating revolts and insurrections. For the major revolt of 1871, see especially Julien, *Historie de l'Algérie contemporaine,* 453–500); see also Ageron, *Les Algériens musulmans et la France,* 3–36.
88. Adolphe Hanouteau and Aristide Letourneau, *La Kabylie et les coutumes kabyles* (Paris: Imprimerie Nationale, 1872).
89. Ibid, 302.
90. Ibid., 311.
91. Emile Durkheim used this in his discussion of solidarity. Emile Durkheim, *The Division of Labor in Society,* trans. G. Simpson (London: Free Press, 1933), ch. 6.
92. Ernest Renan, "La société berbère," *Revue des Deux Mondes* (September 1873): 138–157.
93. Ibid., 156.
94. For a general survey about the production of the Faculty of Algiers until 1930, see Stéphane Gsell et al., *Histoire et historiens de l'Algérie* (Paris: Alcan, 1931). From 1931 to 1956, see Louis Balout et al., *Ving-cinq ans d'histoire algérienne: Recherches et publications* (Algiers: Latypo-Litho et Carbonel, 1956).

TWO

Translation and the Colonial Imaginary

*No translation would be possible if its ultimate essence
strove for likeness to the original.*
—Walter Benjamin

Imagining is first and foremost restructuring semantic fields.
—Paul Ricoeur

Translation was part of the enterprise that the early French colonial administration in Algeria set in place to make knowledge indispensable. To know the local population, one had to observe them, study them, understand their culture and their society, and know their past—for the past made their present. Although the present was believed to be "out there" and able to be apprehended by observation, the past was assumed to be recorded in documents. It could be grasped only in translation, either direct or indirect.

The French officers of the Arab Bureau—the military institution that established order in Algeria and produced knowledge about the country and its people—were mainly ethnographers who had relatively little concern for history. The later interest in history among the scholars of the civilian regime was an attempt to go beyond the stagnate research of the Arab Bureau and beyond the Bureau's politics, which were seen as being too sympathetic to the Arabs. After an opposition between Arabs and Berbers had been established and gained the self-evidence of truth, it needed to be explained. This meant seeking its origin and development and establishing what was Arab and what was Berber in colonial Algeria. Only historical research could respond to the challenge. Whereas the ethnographers of the Arab Bureau conducted their research in the field among the inhabitants, observing them and translating their cultures into words, the scholars of the civilian regime were faced first with the search for documents. Usable documents already existed. The Exploration Scientifique de l'Algérie (the Scientific Exploration of Algeria) translated Arab historiography on a small scale in the first decade after the conquest of Algiers. Of the thirty-nine published volumes dedicated to the study of Algeria, three volumes were translations of Arabic works.[1] Especially important was the translation of the *Histoire de l'Afrique* by Qayrawani. Ibn Khaldûn, the fourteenth-century Maghrebi historian, was not translated by the members of the Exploration Scientifique, but he was extensively used by one of its scholars, Ernest Carette, who was the first to trace the history of the tribes and to reveal the locations of Arabs and Berbers in colonial Algeria. Ibn Khaldûn was already a subject of indirect translation in the context of the Exploration Scientifique.[2]

William de Slane's translation of a fragment of Ibn Khaldûn related to the history of the Berbers might well be considered the greatest textual event in the history of French Orientalism.[3] The translation of Ibn Khaldûn, with the title *Histoire des Berbères,* made the work of Qayrawani less significant because of its richness and also because Ibn Khaldûn built on previous historians, including Qayrawani himself. The main aim of this chapter is not to write a history of Ibn Khaldûn in European scholarship,[4] however, but to examine how the translation of native historical knowledge formed the foundation of French historical knowledge of North Africa. It shows the mechanisms and the politics by which an Arab text, a fragment of the *Ibar* of Ibn Khaldûn, was discovered by French Orientalists and converted into a co-

lonial text with colonial categories. This text became central in
the French colonial historiography of North Africa, and all colonial historians built their work on it. This same colonial historiography became, from 1930 onward, the foundation of national
historiography in North Africa.

TRANSLATION AND THE IMAGINARY

This chapter also has a theoretical dimension for it attempts to
show both how knowledge is regulated by power and also how
colonialism introduced and established a specific imaginary by
transforming local knowledge and converting it into colonial
knowledge.

Translation is not the reproduction of a foreign text in one's
own text, not a transmission (faithful or not) of a message from
one language to another, and not even a betrayal of the initial
message. Translation is a domestication of a foreign text. Lawrence Venuti's remark about literary translation are also valid in
the case of historiography: "Not only does a translation constitute an interpretation of the foreign text, varying with different
cultural situations at different historical moments, but canons of
accuracy are articulated and applied in the domestic culture and
therefore are basically ethnocentric, no matter how seemingly
faithful, no matter how linguistically correct."[5] I argue that a
translated text is not only an interpretation but also the production of a new text. Translation is also creation, imagination—"a
restructuring of semantic fields."[6] The foreign text serves as the
raw material, almost an excuse, for the production of another
text that emerges within a specific discursive formation, with its
own rules and constraints. Just as the foreign text is the expression of an imaginary structure, which is the product of a historical moment, the translated text is the expression of an imaginary
structure, that is the product of a historical moment. Maybe this
is why Antoine Berman notes that "a translator without a historical consciousness remains a prisoner of his representation of

translating and to those representations that convey the 'social discourses' of the moment."[7]

I use the concept of the imaginary in the rich sense given to it by Cornelius Castoriadis. "The imaginary about which I talk," he says, "is not an image of [something]. It is an incessant and essentially determined creation (sociohistorical and psychic) of figures, forms/images, from which it must be only a question of 'something.' What we call 'reality' and 'rationality' are its products."[8] Imaginary refers both to the product of imagination (our worlds made up of systems of meanings) and activity (the ability by which we create the world—this system of meaning that we identify as our world). Anthropologists have already explored the domain of the imaginary in a certain way. They consider knowledge as a part of that "complex whole" that Walter Tylor calls culture, and culture is a system of meaning, the product of the function that Clifford Geertz calls a "program." Geertz writes:

> Culture is best seen not as complexes of concrete behavior patterns—customs, usages, traditions, habits clusters—as has, by and large, been the case up to now, but as a set of control mechanisms—plans, recipes, rules, instructions (what computer engineers call "programs")—for the governing behavior.[9]

The imaginary is a function of producing meanings, and it is the product of this function. However, unlike Castoriadis, I maintain that the imaginary does not create *ex nihilo* but operates within systems of meanings and transforms them to create new meanings out of old ones. Knowledge, in all its forms, is in fact a product of imagination, and it was the means by and through which colonialism governed. Knowledge is also regulated by the power of the mental structure that produces it. Its function went beyond providing an understanding of the population so that they could be governed. It assured colonial domination even long after the collapse of the colonial enterprise. Colonial knowledge shaped postcolonial identities by introducing colonial categories and institutions that outlived colonialism. Indeed, colonialism produced knowledge by and through which it governed and transformed the product of imagination and the function of imagination. The local culture has been transformed. The native people have been caught in webs of significance that they have not spun, but their native function (program) has been transformed to continue producing similar webs of significance in the absence of colonial scholars or with their collaboration. In short, colonialism produced a body of knowledge, implemented the colonial function of the production of knowledge, and transformed native culture to produce colonial webs of significance. This function was implemented by the existence of a powerful discursive formation and by colonial institutions, which were themselves the product of the imaginary. In fact, society as a whole is the product of the imaginary insofar as it is a system of interpretation. As Castoriadis writes:

> It would be superficial and insufficient to say society "contains" a system of interpretation of the world. Each society *is* a system of interpretation of the world, and again, the term "interpretation" is flat and inappropriate here. Each society is a construction, a creation of a world, of its own world. Its own identity is nothing but this "system of interpretation," this world it creates. And that is why (like every individual) it perceives any attack as a mortal threat, as an attack upon its identity, upon itself.[10]

Society is a system of meaning; it constitutes "who we are today." To answer the Kantian question of "Who are we today?," we should first attempt to answer the implicit question of "Who were we yesterday?" To be more precise, one has to find out "How we have become who we are today." The present is made up of the past, and the past itself is our present—hence the fundamental importance of historical knowledge in human societies. Thus, a system of meaning is always historical; it always draws from the past, or as Ernest Cassirer put it: "Historical knowledge is the answer to definite questions, an answer which must be given by the past; but the questions themselves are put and dictated by the present—by our present intellectual interests and our present moral and social needs.[11]

However, the past is available to us mainly through documents—narratives that, however close to the event they may be, are themselves representations of the real and not the real itself. Therefore, the historian does not find answers in the past but makes them from documents of the past—from answers given by others. The past does not provide answers to questions of the present, but the historian does, using other representations of the past.[12] Further, the historian is the official producer of meaning in a society. His knowledge not only is informative about things past but constitutes and shapes identities and determines relations. Identities, whether collective or individual, are by definition historical. "History," Merleau-Ponty says, "is a strange object, an object which is ourselves."[13] However, the historian is not a solitary man busy looking at documents of the past and making meaning out of them. His function takes various forms in different social institutions—schools, the family, the media, the press, the church. The social is historical, and the historical is everywhere; it is not only a realm but also the "whole of reality."[14] To say with Croce that all history is contemporary history is to say that "above and beyond the realm of history there is no other realm of being."[15]

This chapter, through its investigation of translation and the imaginary, also explores the relation of a colonial present to another past, by asking, what questions the colonial present produced and how it answered them using the past of another culture. In fact, the colonial questions and answers were regulated by a European epistemology (a way of knowing made up of certain categories that were specific to the nineteenth century), and the past as written by the natives contained another epistemology (another way of knowing relative to a specific time and culture, the Arabic Islamic culture of the fourteenth century). Examining the Arabic text, its translation, and its subsequent interpretations sheds light on what Michel Foucault would call "the conditions of emergence" of the colonial discourse in the form of a translation.

DISCOVERING IBN KHALDÛN

Ibn Khaldûn was part of a larger Orientalist project that was linked to the discovery of Islamic manuscripts that Silvestre de Sacy undertook with an uncanny vitality and vigor. One of de Sacy's achievements was that he "put before the profession [Orientalism] an entire systematic body of texts, a pedagogic practice, a scholarly tradition, and an important link between Oriental scholarship and public policy."[16] Ibn Khaldûn was an important part of that "body of texts" that de Sacy put at the disposal of both Orientalism and public policy. He discovered Ibn Khaldûn for Orientalism by making fragments of his work known in 1808.[17] In 1818, de Sacy wrote about the *ʿIbar* that "among the historical books written in Arabic there is none that deserves more the honor of publication than this one."[18] Soon afterward, de Sacy's students began to write about to make Ibn Khaldûn. In 1822, Joseph de Hammer published in the *Journal Asiatique* a summary of the same book and insisted on the importance of translating Ibn Khaldûn.[19] Two years later, Garcin de Tassy presented another review.[20] F. E. Schulz gave a review of the whole book the following year in the same journal.[21] The following general view on the organization of the book also discusses the circumstances of its composition.[22]

Ibn Khaldûn undertook his project about the history of the Maghreb in the fourteenth century, soon after he became dissatisfied with politics. He then retreated to the castle of Salama (in what is today Algeria), a place that has since vanished. There he wrote the first part of his project (known as the *Muqaddima*), and most of the second part (related to the history of the Berbers). Because he needed to verify some materials to complete his manuscript, Ibn Khaldûn moved to Tunis, where he ultimately offered the first copy to the Hafsid Sultan, Abu al-

'Abbâs. In the initial project, Ibn Khaldûn chose not to write about the Machreq for lack of materials. This changed once he settled in Egypt, where he wrote the part concerning the history of the Persians and the Romans and the last part, concerning his own life. Thus, the book is composed of three parts: the *Muqaddima;* the history of the Berbers, Arabs, Persians, Romans, and other peoples; and the part usually considered biography.[23]

Each of these three parts is self-contained and appeals to a different audience. Ibn Khaldûn as an author is not considered to be the sum of what he wrote, including his early work. He is considered to be a different author depending on what portion of his work is under discussion. In other words, Ibn Khaldûn is a syncretism of authors. In the *Muqaddima,* he is an epistemic subject who evaluated the field of historiography in his time and elaborated a rigorous way of writing history that was deemed rational, modern, and in conformity with the European practice of history in the age of positivism. However, Ibn Khaldûn is another author when it comes to his historiography, in which he failed to follow his own preaching. He is researcher and a practitioner of historiography who is no different from the previous historians that he criticizes in the *Muqaddima* for their lack of a critical approach *(tamhîs, nazar).*[24] Later, even Ibn Khaldûn the practitioner of historiography was divided into two. One is the author of the history of North Africa who brought new knowledge ("an ethnographic history," as the colonial expression goes), and applied, up to a point, the epistemological remarks elaborated in the *Muqaddima.*[25] As the author of the history of the Orient, he is usually seen as less competent and less original than the authors of the two other parts. The autobiography has not drawn much attention despite recent interest in the genre.[26] However, when de Sacy drew attention to the need to translate the *Muqaddima,* he also suggested its French title: *Prolégomènes historiques,* a title that later would become the definitive title of the French translation by William de Slane, a student of de Sacy. Joseph de Hammer, on the other hand, insisted on the urgency of translating the part related to the history of the Berbers (the second book). In 1847, de Slane, the principal interpreter of the Armée d'Afrique, published under the auspices of the Imprimerie du Gouvernement (the Government Press) the Arabic text related to the history of the Berbers.[27] In 1854, he published the translation under the title *Histoire des Berbères*. In 1858, Quatremère published the Arabic text of the *Muqaddima*.[28] De Slane published his translation of the *Muqaddima* in 1863 under the title *Prolégomènes*. The two texts have had different trajectories. The *Muqaddima* was used effectively by sociologists such as Emile Durkheim[29] and Robert Montagne,[30] whereas the *Histoire des Berbères* served as the framework of the history of North Africa. In fact, it was published by the Ministry of War, and its importance for the colonial enterprise was immediately noted. Indeed, Joseph Reinaud wrote:

> The History of the Berbers of Ibn Khaldûn could not fail to draw the attention of the French government. With the establishment of the French in Algeria daily relations, contacts of friendships and war have been established between them and the tribes that occupy the interior of the country.[31]

Ibn Khaldûn as a colonial author was, therefore, born in fragments—Arabic texts for the purpose of pedagogy, summaries of the entire book addressed to draw attention to his importance to the colonial enterprise, reviews of the book, entries in bibliographies, and statements about the man, his age, and his culture. In short, a discourse on him, not of him, has emerged that cannot be separated from the translation. The analysis of Ibn Khaldûn's translated text—what Ibn Khaldûn says in French—should go hand in hand with what is said about Ibn Khaldûn. He thus appears in this discourse as a "genius," "skilful," and also "solitary," a man who contrasts sharply with his own milieu. Further, the discourse on Ibn Khaldûn is made up of two diametrically opposed views. On the one hand, he is modern and therefore represents Europe with its rationality and its historicity. On the other hand, he contrasts with the civilization from which he came: he is enlightened, and it is dark; he is rational, and it is obscurantist; he is excellent and a genius, and it is poor and mediocre. How could this be possible? He may not be from that civilization. He may be European.[32] And while he is ignored in his own country by his own people, he is discovered and given his due respect in Europe.[33] The colonial discovery of Ibn Khaldûn thus became a discovery both for Orientalism and even more important for his own people. He is "the genius who has long been ignored by his people," wrote Jacques Berque.[34] To discover Ibn Khaldûn means above all that the French scholar is a competent epistemic subject, able to evaluate and sanction an intellectual activity. This competence is lacking in Arab and Islamic traditions for they have failed to recognize the genius of Ibn Khaldûn. The myth of the Orientalist discovery of Ibn Khaldûn thus legitimizes the French interpretation of Ibn Khaldûn. Despite the fact that even a genius is the product of a historical, social, and intellectual moment,[35] this discourse continued to be produced by French scholars in the postcolonial period[36] and by "natives" and "post-natives." For instance, a French Orientalist might repeat the *idée reçue* and say that Ibn Khaldûn is a "solitary" mind that "arose all of a sudden to explain the profound causes of history" and that "it is no wonder that this mind did not have an echo in a world that was not prepared to receive him."[37] A "native" scholar echoes the judgment even more bluntly, using the language of the Enlightenment to mark his affiliation to it and his own distance from the civilization that produced Ibn Khaldûn: "Ibn Khaldûn's star shines the more brightly by contrast with the foil darkness against which it flashes out. . . . He is indeed the one outstanding personality in the history of a civilization whose social life on the whole was solitary, poor, nasty, brutish, and short."[38] Colonizing the imaginary also means that colonial judgments, whose birth and formulation are linked to a specific context, continue to be reproduced and passed on uncritically, even in the postcolonial period, carrying with them their original myths and perpetuating colonial relations.

THE TRICKERY OF THE INTRODUCTION

De Slane introduces his translation of Ibn Khaldûn's text related to the history of the Berbers by stating that

> The task of the translator is not limited to the exact reproduction of ideas uttered in the text that is the subject of his translation. There are other obligations as well. He should rectify the errors of the author, clarify the passages that offer some obscurities, provide ideas that lead to the perfect understanding of the narrative, and give the necessary assistance to make the book better understood.[39]

The translator is bilingual, but he is also a researcher who is capable of adding necessary information to the translated work. In other words, the translator is required, by the act of translation, to add his own voice to that of the author. The translator's voice is not only complementary but also a rectifying voice that corrects errors and helps to be understood. The translator contests dates, events, and interpretations, he reveals "deficiencies," and provides information. The translator transmits a message from one language to another and rectifies the errors of the message. In doing so, he converts the original text into a colonial one, for correction implies an inadequacy in the cognitive universe of the author. The correction creates an adequacy but at the expense of the author, whose voice and cognitive universe have been changed to conform to the voice and cognitive universe of the translator.[40]

In the introduction, de Slane maintains that despite its richness, the Arabic text of Ibn Khaldûn is obscure, and when it is not, it is "verbose and repetitive" (lxix). In fact, he continues, "it is a simple draft," "very badly written" (lxix). Hence, the task of the translator is to clarify what is obscure and eliminate what is repetitive. Although translators see their task as the reproduction of the same text in another language, and leaving aside whether this is indeed possible, they in fact construct another text that is alien to the original text but is nonetheless part of it. But why does a translator need to write an introduction if his goal is only to serve the original author by lending him another tongue? What function does the introduction fulfill?

An introduction usually takes the form of a preface, which is a *metadiscourse*. It is written after the translation is completed and is usually a reflection of the author on his own discourse. Algirdas-Julien Greimas wrote:

> The preface is not a part of the corpus. Along the temporal axis, it is a post-face and follows on the discourse of the research and its being put into writing. Its status is that of a *metadiscursive* thought concerning a discourse that has already been produced. This *metadiscourse* is supposed to reveal what the author himself thinks of his own discourse, its goal, and its organization.[41]

De Slane's introduction to his translation of Ibn Khaldûn reflects on the translated text, its composition, its theses, the task of the translator, his cognitive endeavor, and his translation. But the introduction to the translated text of Ibn Khaldûn is also a discursive strategy to determine the reading of the translated text. De Slane suggests an interpretation that conditions any reading of his translated text. His introduction summarizes the translated text, and this summary is a means for making the reader perceive the text in a certain way. This cognitive manipulation makes the reader understand the translated text as interpreted by the translator.

However, de Slane first gives a general description of the whole book by Ibn Khaldûn, the *'Ibar,* whose third part is the object of his translation. Thus, one finds the familiar discourse on Ibn Khaldûn as being a genius and yet attached to superstition (iii). De Slane then gives a general view of the translated book, the *Histoire des Berbères,* which, he says, is made up of the fourth section of the *'Ibar* (which narrates the history of the Arabs in North Africa), and the third book of the *'Ibar* (which contains "a genealogical history of the great indigenous race that dominated for centuries)" (viii). The translator provides a linear narrative on the different empires that succeeded one another in North Africa, beginning with the Arab conquest of the seventh century and continuing to the fourteenth century (the time of Ibn Khaldûn).

De Slane's narrative first describes a situation of lack. According to him, sectarian divisions, indigenous revolts, and a Vandal conquest weakened Roman North Africa before the Arab conquest. The Latin inhabitants abandoned their possessions to the Berbers and moved to the coast. The Vandals delivered a fatal blow to Byzantine rule in North Africa, and although Belisarius and Salomon reestablished Byzantine rule, North Africa became a fragile land, easy prey for a religiously unified and aggressive adversary coming from the Orient—Arabia. To make things worse, the Goths of Spain took over Tingitana, thus creating a more divided North Africa. One part, mainly Carthage, was still loyal to the Roman empire; the other part, the province of Tingitana, was under the Goths' yoke. North Africa was weakened and divided as a result of a Christian heresy and a European conflict. Fragile and fragmented, it was soon faced with the presence of the Arabs, unified by their new religion—Islam. The text opposes two entities. One is represented by Arab Muslims (the Orient), and the other is represented by a Christian Europe whose territory extends to and includes North Africa.

This situation of lack made the conquest of North Africa possible. North Africa was taken away from the Romans. But what about the Berbers? They appear first as an indigenous population that revolted (thus participating in the weakening of the Roman empire) and then as Roman servants (who were liberated by the Arabs). Their lives did not improve, however. Soon afterward, they joined the Romans against the Arabs, who had burdened them by religious duties and heavier taxes, taking half their harvests. This alliance between Berbers and Romans resulted in a joint victory against the Arabs and the formation of the "first Berber empire." The actors in de Slane's narrative are all distinguished from the outset—the Romans, the Arabs, and in between the Berbers. The relation between the first and the last is perfectly clear, for it is one of opposition. The Arabs were at war against the Romans because they wanted the land and also wanted to impose their religion. The Romans, the masters of North Africa, were weakened yet were defending their possessions. The relationships between Berbers and Arabs and between Berbers and Romans seem unclear. The Berbers revolted against the Romans and joined the Arabs only because they were burdened by imperial taxes. Likewise, they initially joined the Arabs and then revolted against them only because of a misunderstanding. They first saw the Arabs as liberators but opposed them once they realized the Arabs were like the Romans, if not worse. In other words, once they came to know the Arabs, the Berbers deliberately chose the Romans. Thus, they defeated the Arabs. A Berber kingdom ensued under the leadership of Kusayla. This was only transitory, for the Arabs returned and crushed the Berbers. This time there is no mention of the Romans, only of a female Berber leader called the Kahina. This is the beginning of what de Slane calls the age of "Arab domination" and the beginning of an opposition between the Arab nation and the Berber race, which was always "impatient under the foreign yoke" (xx). To show that his introductory narrative is a summary of the translated work, de Slane asks his readers to consult such and such chapters for more details about the events he has just summarized.

This narrative became fundamental in French colonial historiography. It explains how North Africa had been subjugated by the Arabs in the seventh century and shows that the country had been a part of the Roman empire. Further, the narrative contains that same imaginary structure that had been developed in Europe—the opposition between Occident and Orient. When this is reproduced in the colonial context, it suggests a specific colonial policy. This time, Arabs are opposed to both Rome and contemporary Europeans. For instance, when de Slane mentions

the great discord among Arabs that arose after the death of the
Prophet in 622, he happily notes that "the largest part of the
Arab nation was led into this quarrel that, fortunately for Europe, forever broke the unity of the empire" (xx). Thus, introducing Europe into a fourteenth-century narrative about the
conquest of North Africa in the seventh century simply reacti-
vated that same representation. Europe, along with its struggle
against the Orient, is now a part of that French text called
Histoire des Berbères.

De Slane's introduction is supposedly a summary of his translation of Ibn Khaldûn. Let us now examine the translation itself,
which is not so much the transmission of a message from the
first to the second language but rather the conversion of local
categories into colonial categories. This conversion is the result
of a passage from one culture to another and from one historical
moment to another. A speaker of a language may formulate a
fact differently from the speaker of another one. This may lead
one to conclude, using Roland Barthes' own formulation, that
"facts have only a linguistic existence." But how do these facts
change from one language to another language? Why do the
facts of a text not remain unchanged when translated to a different language?

The type of translation under consideration is what Roman
Jakobson calls "interlingual translation," which means that one
interprets a verbal sign as a verbal sign in another language.[42]
Therefore, one is removed from one cultural space to another
(from France to the Maghreb) and also from one cultural time to
another (from fourteenth-century Islam to nineteenth-century
Europe). After all, language is not only an instrument by which
a group communicates but is also a tool made up of categories
by which a group orders and signifies its world. To quote
Benjamin Whorf:

> Every language is a vast pattern-system, different from others, in
> which are culturally ordained the forms and categories by which

the personality not only communicates, but also analyzes nature, notices or neglects types of relationship and phenomena, channels his reasoning, and builds the house of his consciousness.[43]

A language does not exist only in theory. It is practiced in real situations. It is a speech-act (*parole,* as Saussure put it) and a textual practice (*language,* in the same Saussaurian terminology).[44] The type of language considered in this instance is nineteenth-century French as actualized by de Slane in his translation. Therefore, I examine the components of the translator's language or text, assuming that the translated text as a whole, including the introduction, is made up of a number of levels. The text is divided into signifier (*expression,* in the terminology of Louis Hjelmslev) and signified *(content),* and each has a form and a substance. Thus, the text is made up of the form of the expression (the linguistic system) and the substance of the expression (the phonetic system). Further, the content itself has a form (semantics) and a substance (grammar).[45] It is the content (with its expression and substance, its syntax and its semantics) that I now investigate to explain the transformation of the original text and its conversion into a colonial narrative.

Let me note at this point that translating a historical narrative presents different problems from translating a literary narrative. In addition to the difficulties of reproducing the poetics of a text, a process similar to translation in literature, the translator of historical narratives faces the tremendous challenge of reproducing the imaginary structure of the translated work—the categories by and through which an author or a community thinks, interprets, orders, and signifies the world. This may be the *intentio* that Benjamin considers as essential for translation.[46]

LOCAL HISTORY AND COLONIAL HISTORICAL CONSCIOUSNESS

The *intentio* in the historical narrative, unlike the literary one, is the question of historical consciousness. By *historical conscious-*

ness, Raymond Aron means "the consciousness of a dialectic between tradition and freedom, the effort of grasping the reality or
the truth of the past, the feeling that the effect of the social organizations and the human creations through time is zero or unim-
portant, but it concerns man in what is essential within him."[47]
This does not have to be theoretically articulated, Aron continues; even the crudest narrative implies a theory. As a practicing
translator of great literary texts, including works of Charles
Baudelaire and Marcel Proust, Walter Benjamin reflected in a
well-known essay about the task of the translator and concluded
that what needs to be reproduced in the translation is the
intentio of the author.[48] Benjamin wrote: "As regards the meaning, the language of a translation can—in fact, must—let itself
go, so that it gives voice to the *intentio* of the original not as reproduction but as harmony, as a supplement to the language in
which it expresses itself, as its own kind of *intentio.*"[49] The remark clearly pertains to literary texts but not historiography or
ethnography, whose translations have their own specificities.[50]
Several theoreticians of translation have echoed Benjamin's view
without questioning whether literary translation offers the same
challenges of other texts, such as historiography, ethnography,
and philosophy.[51] The literary *intentio* that Benjamin mentions
but does not explain is open to interpretation. The *intentio* in literary work is intentionally ambiguous; without it, a fiction
would lose one of its fundamental qualities. When asked about
his intention in one of his novels, Joseph Conrad answered that
"a work of art is very seldom limited to one exclusive meaning
and not necessarily tending to a definite conclusion. And this for
the reason that the nearer it approaches art, the more it acquires
a symbolic character."[52] Roland Barthes establishes a distinction
between writing by an author and writing by a writer. The first
makes texts out of previous ones; he integrates a "fabric of quotations" by contesting and approving and gives ultimate meaning (intent) to his writing. The second makes texts out of words,
whose function is to posit meaning in order to "evaporate it."

He offers not explanations but spectacles; he questions, and in doing so, he introduces ambiguities.[53] In other words, the text is polysemic; it contains a multiplicity of intentions.

Therefore, the *intentio* of the historical narrative does not impose the same challenge as in literature (what Barthes prefers to call *writing*). And one can see that Ibn Khaldûn makes his text out of a "fabric of quotations."[54] He argues against some, adopts others, and ultimately constructs his own text that offers explanations of the states of the Maghreb with the ultimate intention that he himself makes clear at the beginning of his work. Ibn Khaldûn initially undertook to write the history of the Berbers; that was the main lack that he wanted to fulfill. He noted that Islamic history had found its historians, especially in times of major historical transformations. Thus the historian Mas'udi (d. 928) wrote in such a time, but al-Bakri (d. 1094) did not describe any such transformation. In the fourteenth century, a transformation occurred that had not been recorded. As Ibn Khaldûn notes, the Berbers were defeated, the Arabs had the upper hand, and the plague caused great damage to civilization:

> When the situation changes completely, it is as if the whole creation has been transformed in its entirety, and the world has turned around wholly, as if it were a new creation, a continued production, and an original world. Thus, there is a need in this age for someone to record the conditions of the creation, the regions, the peoples, the customs, and the doctrines that have been changed by the change of its peoples. Following thus in the footsteps of Mas'udi in his age, so as to become a model for future historians. (*Muqaddima*, 33)

The enterprise of Ibn Khaldûn stemmed from a specific situation in North Africa, which he intended to describe in his book. The initial enterprise was, in fact, a question about the present, which was marked by the supremacy of the Arabs, the weakness of the Berbers, and the decline of civilization. The apparent intention of Ibn Khaldûn seems to be a historical one, specific to the author of the *târîkh*—to record what happened as exactly as possible. However, this recording is inscribed in a long narrative tradition made up of numerous, diverse, and even contradictory accounts that were accumulated through the ages by Muslim historians regarding the Berbers, their origins, their history, and the circumstances of their conversion.

In fact, the Arab empire—built by the eighth century almost exclusively on force of arms, like all premodern empires—faced the problem of the other only after it completed its conquests. Only then were questions about Berber origins, their place within the Muslim community, and the history of their conversion (forced or by free will) posed—mainly for fiscal reasons.[55] The Berber as an other had to be explained and integrated. The text of Ibn Khaldûn is situated within this textual tradition. By the fourteenth century, the Berbers had proved their ability to be autonomous and to build an empire that extended south into Africa and north to Europe. The Berber deserved his own discourse, known as the *mafâkhir* (an apologia that recorded glorious deeds). The text of Ibn Khaldûn was a *mafâkhir* made up of a "fabric of quotations" to prove the excellence *(fadâʾil)* of the Berber. Maya Shatzmiller wrote:

> The *ʿIbar* is only a more comprehensive examination of the theme of *mafâkhir*. It would be the most profoundly intelligent and magnificent realization of the aim that the author of *mafâkhir* sets for himself in rough terms contrary to all the authors of the fourteenth century—to prove the glory of the Berbers through their history.[56]

However, whereas the narrative of the Arab conquest in the original text of Ibn Khaldûn is part of a larger discourse that exalts the virtues and glorious deeds of the Berbers, in the colonial discourse it explained not only the present but also any other events since the Arab conquest. This narrative became a paradigm that is repeated over and over again. There is a conflict between the two races, and each time a confrontation ends, it begins again. De Slane asserts that "from then [the time of the conquest] the emirs that governed Africa had a twofold task: to fight the Berbers, a race always impatient of the foreign yoke, and to resist the ambitious Arab chiefs that were their subcommanders" (xx). De Slane then shows how the various episodes occurred, each time with different coloring. Thus, the Berbers adopted an egalitarian Islamic heresy to fight the Arabs and succeeded in becoming "masters in their own lands." At this point, de Slane gives both the genealogies of Arab dynasties and a list of the governors of Africa. He then refers to the chapters of his translation that narrate the events that he has just summed up in his introduction. The summary molds the text. The text itself affirms the introduction. Thus, de Slane directs his readers to the chapters that narrate the events in question. The first chapter has the title "The Berbers under Arab Domination." Ibn Khaldûn calls this chapter *fî dhikri akhbârihim ʿalâ al-jumla min qabli al-fathi al-islâmî wa min baʿdihi ilâ wilâyati banî al-aghlab* ("On the general history [*akhbâr*] of the Berbers before and after the Islamic era [literal translation of *fath*: opening of an era] and until the dynasty of the Banu al-Aghlab"). Each title reveals different intentions. In the original, Ibn Khaldûn intends to report narratives of the Berbers and give information about who they were and what they have accomplished. The translator wants to show the domination of Berbers by Arabs. However, the episode of "Arab domination" does not begin with the Arab conquest (*al-fath*) and end with the collapse of the Aghlabid dynasty. It has come to constitute a fundamental aspect of North Africa and continues in the present.

To make the connection between past and present as clear as possible, de Slane translated names of places. All the old towns, cities, and regions in the text of Ibn Khaldûn are given French colonial names. In other words, de Slane also translates the fourteenth-century map of Ibn Khaldûn into a colonial map, thus solidifying colonial representations.

COLONIAL SEMANTICS

*It is another property of the human mind that whenever men can
form no idea of distant and unknown things, they judge them
by what is familiar and at hand.*

—Vico

Ibn Khaldûn's *Histoire des Berbères,* as interpreted by the translator, William de Slane, is in two parts. One is about the Orient, including the non-Arab dynasties such as those of the Persians and the Israelites. The other is about the Berbers and the Arabs in North Africa. The histories of the non-Arab dynasties are narrated only for their relevance to the history of the "Arab races," and the history of Arabs in North Africa is told for its relevance to the history of the "Berber races." In short, the history of French Ibn Khaldûn is a history of two races—a conqueror race that came from the Orient and a conquered one that was indigenous to North Africa. Further, both Arabs and Berbers are not only two races but two nations as well. How does Ibn Khaldûn designate them in the original? What are the meanings of the terms he uses?

Before answering these questions, let me first attempt a definition of the terms *race* and *nation* as they were used in nineteenth-century France. In nineteenth-century Europe, the terms *race* and *nation* gained specific meanings, and with the rise of nationalism, the concepts of race and nation became fundamental to Europeans' understanding of the development of human societies. Three influential names dominate this discussion in France—Comte de Gobineau, Ernest Renan, and Hyppolite Taine.[57] Gobineau first articulated the most widely accepted discourse on race in France and in Europe. His views became most influential not because they were novel but because they were widely accepted before he even articulated them. As Hananh Arendt put it in a comparative study of race-thinking in Europe:

The Comte de Gobineau developed an opinion already generally accepted within the French nobility into a full-fledged historical doctrine, claiming to have detected the secret law of the fall of civilization and to have exalted history to the dignity of a natural science. With him, race-thinking completed its first stage and began its second stage, whose influences were to be felt until the twenties of our century.[58]

Despite their differences, the three major scholars of race in France—Gobineau, Taine, and Renan—agreed on at least two fundamental points—that the world is inhabited by races that are unequal, as are the various breeds of dogs, and that there is an antagonism between races. But what is a race? A race is marked by inherent, hereditary, permanent qualities—physical, psychological and intellectual. No matter how much a race is subjected to change and accidents of nature, it will always preserve these elements.[59] Not only are human races antagonistic and hostile to each other, but they are also unequal. As Gobineau states:

> The existing races constitute separate branches of one or many primitive stocks. These stocks have now vanished. They are not known in historical times at all, and we cannot form even the most general idea of their qualities. They differed from each other in the shape and proportions of the limbs, the structure of the skull, the internal conformation of the body, the nature of the capillary system, the color of the skin, and the like; and they never succeeded in losing their characteristic features except under powerful influence of the crossing blood.[60]

There is thus a hierarchy of races, and the world has been inhabited by various races that are unequal to and resentful of each other. But one thing is clear and certain: the Aryan race has proved its excellence throughout the ages. Excellence in a race is not only manifested in the phenotypes, which is unquestionable as far as the Aryan race is concerned, but it is also by far the most beautiful, the best shaped, and the most capable of creating civilization. Aryan civilization has always showed proofs of its excellence.[61] Civilization is thus associated with race, and a race is by definition a people with a common origin, common "blood," common "identity," and the ability (or inability) to create civilization. Civilization is, according to Gobineau, "a state of relative stability, where the mass of men try to satisfy their wants by peaceful means, and are refined in their conduct and intelligence."[62] Renan defines *civilization* differently. For Renan, it is a creation, the result of the capacity of a nation to feed as many useless mouths as possible—poets, writers, historians, artists, and even mathematicians, he says. The first definition does not contradict the second, for to be able to have "useless mouths" to feed, a nation has to ensure peace and prosperity. Europe is then the locus of civilization. A civilization is the product of a race, it is specific to this race, and it is the expression of its genius. If one wants to study a race, one studies the form of its civilization. These forms constitute Taine's work, which was mainly a study of European races, especially the Latin and German races.[63] If civilizations are expressions of races, they are therefore, like races, unequal and antagonistic to each other, and their combination results in degeneration. Gobineau writes:

> Civilization is incommunicable, not only to savages, but also to more enlightened nations. This is shown by the efforts of French goodwill and conciliation in the ancient kingdom of Algiers at the present day, as well as the experience of the English in India, and the Dutch in Java.[64]

Prior to Ernest Renan's "What Is a Nation?," the words *race* and *nation* were often used interchangeably, even in the work of Taine and Gobineau. Renan laid down the first and still authoritative theoretical conception of nation.[65] Renan read Ibn Khaldûn and the available literature about the Berbers that was synthesized in the work of Hanouteau and Letourneau, two officers of the Arab Bureau,[66] and in his discussion of the Berbers he begins with the crucial question, "What is a race?" Here is how he defines it:

> From the point of view of historical sciences, five things constitute the characteristics of race and give one the right to talk about it as a distinct entity within the human species. The five items that prove that a race still lives are: a language of its own, a literature that has particular characteristics, a religion, a history, and laws. Sometimes one can add to this a particular alphabet; but this condition is not necessary, for great races, such as the Indo-European race, have never had an alphabet of their own. They have borrowed them from other races.[67]

Few years later, during a lecture at the Sorbonne, on March 11, 1882, Renan made a theoretical distinction between the concepts of race and nation. In a classic text "What Is a Nation?," Renan laid down his concept of nation.[68] For him, a nation requires a shared experience and the will to live together, and shared experience is nothing more than historical knowledge—made both of memories and forgetfulness, of what a nation remembers and what it forgets. Nationhood is closely associated with the specificity of this historical knowledge. In the discourse of nationalism, the assumption is that we have a common identity: we were the same, we have been the same, we are the same, and we shall be the same. Although Renan also thinks in terms of race and is the first to distinguish between the Semitic and Aryan races and consider it a decisive "division du genre humain," the foundation of this distinction lies in the fact that the Semites (and by this he means Arabs and Jews) are incapable of science, creation, and liberal government, things that are produced only by the Aryan race.[69] Arendt wrote that Renan "held civilization to be the great force which destroys local originalities as well as original race differences."[70] But whose civilization does this destroying? It is done by the civilization, of those who are capable of producing a civilization. Renan does not really relativize race-thinking but shows the possibility of Europe's civ-

ilizing mission. Unlike Gobineau and because of his faith in colonization, he believes that civilization is capable of converting
other races; it is communicable. Rome did it in the past;[71] therefore, Europe can do it in the present. However, Renan shares
with Gobineau another important thesis: some races are capable
of creating civilization, and some are not because they are unable to go beyond the tribal stage.[72] Tribalism is the hallmark of
the uncivilized (who live in tribes), and nationalism is the hallmark of the civilized (who live in nation-states). Only Europe
achieved the second: "the concept of nation," Renan wrote with
pride, "is ours."[73] This view was reproduced forcefully by
Emile-Félix Gautier, who was the major historian of colonial
North Africa and had a lasting effect on North African historiography (see chapter 4). By the mid-nineteenth century, race-
thinking constituted a "subconscious culture" in which human
relations were defined essentially by inequality and antagonism.
The translated text of Ibn Khaldûn carried with it this colonial
semantics. By examining the Arab concepts that de Slane translated as race and nation, we can attempt to find Ibn Khaldûn's
explanation of human diversity.

The Arab concepts translated as *race* and *nation* are *jîl,*
umma, and *tabaqa.* Ibn Khaldûn most often uses *jîl,* which appears as a synonym for both *umma* and *tabaqa.* It has a specific
meaning, however, that the two others do not share. Etymolog-
ically, *jîl* means a generation, but Ibn Khaldûn uses it in the sense
of a tribe or a group of tribes living in a specific historical moment. Ibn Khaldûn speaks of *jîl al-'arab* (generation of the
Arabs) and *jîl al-barbar* (generation of the Berbers). Ibn Khaldûn also uses the term *jîl* to designate a specific stage in human
development: *jîl al-badw* (those who are in the stage of nature
or, in a literal translation, those with a Bedouin lifestyle), *jîl al-*
hadar (those who are in the stage of culture or, again in a literal
sense, those with an urban lifestyle).[74]

One could conclude that the concept *jîl* is temporal or chronological. *Jîl* is a human grouping clearly defined in time. Ibn

Khaldûn speaks of the *jîl al-awwal li-al-'arab* (the first generation of Arabs), *al-jîl ath-thâni li-al-'arab* (the second generation
of Arabs), and so forth. It is also defined genealogically, for a *jîl*
is linked to another *jîl* by a common ancestor *(nasab)*, real or often imaginary. The *jîl* as a unified group is differentiated from
others mainly by a representation of its origins (by history).
However, a *jîl* as understood by Ibn Khaldûn could also be otherwise defined. First, a *jîl* can be defined by its phenotypes,
which Ibn Khaldûn explains first by the climate that changes the
color of a group's skin and influences its members' mood. Second, a *jîl* can be defined by its culture as a result of its economic
activity *(inna ikhtilafa al-ajyal innama huwa bi ikhtilaf nihlati-
hum mina al-ma'ash)* (The differences among the *ajyâl* are the
result of their different ways of making their living) (Ibn Khaldûn, *Muqaddima*, 129). The term *umma* is more global. It refers
either to a religious community and its total historical experiences (the *umma* of Islam is not only Arabs but all who have
shared the Islamic religious experience) or to a historical community and its different stages (the *umma* of the Arabs and the
umma of the Persians have religious or dynastic identifiers). For
Ibn Khaldûn,

> The genealogists were led into error by their belief that the differ-
> ence between *umam* [people] is in their *nasab* [genealogy]. This is
> not so. The difference between a *jîl* or *umma* for some is due to ge-
> nealogy [*nasab*] as in the case of the Arabs, the Children of Israel,
> and the Persians. For others, such as the Zinj, the Abysinians, the
> Slavs, and the Sudanese Negroes, it is due to geographical location
> and phenotype [*sima*]. It may be caused by customs [*'awâ'id*] and
> sentiments [*shi'âr*], as in the case of the Arabs. It may be caused by
> other conditions [*ahwâl*], features [*khawâs*], and specific traits
> [*mumayizât*] of *umam* [plr. *umma*]. But to generalize and say that
> the inhabitants of such and such region in the south or in the
> north are the descendants of the well known so and so because
> they have a common *nihla* [sect] or color or phenotype of the fore-
> head is of [the order] of these errors caused by the ignorance of the

nature of beings and places which changes through generations [*a'qab*] and does not stay the same.[75] (*Muqaddima*, 91).

History, (the *târîkh* of the Arabs) is originally a religious discipline, and its development was a result of the success of the Islamic conquests.[76] Given the fact that the Arab conquest was ultimately an experience of the other, the explanation of this otherness had a religious character. In Islam, human unity is presented as an unquestionable fact. People are creatures of the same Creator and are also equal in the sense that humans are all able to receive the divine message. Human inequality occurs not on a biological level (it is not the result of the ability or inability of a group to create civilization) but rather on a moral level. Humanity is not divided into inferior and superior races but rather into believers and nonbelievers. This inequality is not irreversible. A nonbeliever is as susceptible to becoming a believer as a believer is susceptible to becoming a nonbeliever—hence, the importance of the concept of the *fath* (the transition from nonbelief to belief).[77]

Ibn Khaldûn is too much of a historian not to notice that tribes and individuals are unequal in might *(jâh)* and that although religion provides cohesion for a group (this is why he talks about the *umma* of Islam and the *umma* of Muhammad), there is also diversity and inequality within the same *umma*. An *umma* is also made up of a number of *jîls* that differ in might, in conquest, and in deeds. It is their diversity (or inequality) that Ibn Khaldûn explains. How is this inequality engendered?

Ibn Khaldûn uses his concept of *'asabiya* (tribal solidarity). For him, *'asabiya* is general but uneven in strength among tribes. The bigger the tribe, the stronger its tribal solidarity; the stronger the tribal solidarity, the more powerful the tribe. The power of the tribe, however great it may be, is not a sufficient condition for it to become a dynasty. Religion is an important factor for *'asabiya* to become operational and allows the tribe to solidify its power and go beyond itself to become a dynasty. Because one of the keys of Ibn Khaldûn's explanation of human transformation is the fact that power is provisional, the tribe dynasty itself is subject to a process of disintegration. Its power results in luxury and unjust practices, which weaken the *ʿasabiya* that provides the cohesion and strength of a group. The dynasty comes to an end and is replaced by that of another tribe, which goes through the same patterns of rise and fall. The superiority of a tribe is contingent, therefore, and that superiority is not inherent in the tribe as strength is inherent in superior races according to Gobineau, Taine, and Renan. For Ibn Khaldûn, inequality is constant and variant at the same time. It is constant in that humans are constituted of dominant and dominated. But because the material world, including humans and human conditions, is subject to dissolution, neither inequality nor superiority is inherent in a group. They are contingencies *(ʿawârid)*, and as such they are doomed to end. Ibn Khaldûn mentions the Greeks, Romans, Persians, Arabs, and Jews as people who dominated and later lost their strength. "States *(duwal)* have ages", he asserts, "like those of individuals" *(Muqaddima, 180)*.

There is also diversity within the same *jîl* because not all the members of a *jîl* are equal in terms of might *(jâh)*. How can this inequality be explained? Here Ibn Khaldûn uses a number of concepts to account for the difference in power *(qudra)* among individuals or groups within the same *jîl*. For Ibn Khaldûn, superiority is always maintained by a superiority in numbers, by a noble genealogy *(nasab sharîf)*, and by power *(qudra)* to impose religious and political order. This domination is necessary for the benefit of both dominator *(ghâlib)* and dominated *(maghlûb)*. They both benefit from the elimination of what is harmful and the pursuit of what is useful.[78] Ibn Khaldûn suggests that tribes are unequal in their *hasab* (nobility), which is not inherent in their nature but generated from their own deeds and is associated with might and conquest. However, *hasab* does not last more than four generations *(ajyâl)* *(Muqaddima, 145)*.

Consequently, there is neither progress, nor degeneration, nor racial hierarchy in Ibn Khaldûn. His historical narrative is regulated by other categories, such as *jîl, 'asabiya, qudra, nasab,* and *hasab.* In some ways, historical events reproduce themselves in the same way. Tribes become dynasties due to *'asabiya* and religion (in the form of prophecy *(nubuwwa)* or sanctity *(wilaya).* They decline after they reach their peak, only to be replaced by another tribe that follows the same patterns of rise and fall (*Muqaddima,* passim).

The text of de Slane's translation is marked by a racial ideology that sets Arabs and Berbers apart and in opposition and also by the theme of domination, which connotes a state of colonialism of the bad type (it is Oriental and therefore based on force and destruction). Even in his introduction, de Slane speaks of Arab domination, and he translates the title of the first chapter of Ibn Khaldûn as "Arab Domination." De Slane also translates the term *fath* as *domination* or *conquest,* meaning forced subordination (to other men) that is imposed by weapons. It describes the relationship of a loser to a winner on a form of colonialism in which the goal is to impose religion on the vanquished.[79] What does the word *fath* actually mean? For Ibn Khaldûn (as for any Muslim) it is a positive term that designates the opening of an area of belief (Islam) and the ending of a period of disbelief *(Jâhiliya).* Therefore, it is a divine favor for both those who join of their own free will and those who join by force. Submission, in this view, is not of men to other men but to God. *Fath* is a necessary condition for a Muslim. The first Islamic community passed from a stage of *Jâhiliya* (ignorance, disbelief, darkness) to a stage of Islam (belief, and light made possible by *fath*). This is submission *(islâm)* to God and not to men, even if the latter plays the role of instrument. People submit to the transformation.

OBJECTS OF COLONIAL DISCOURSE

In the colonial translation, the term *Arab* does not mean what it does in the original text of Ibn Khaldûn. For Ibn Khaldûn, it means the various Arab populations, either original or recently Arabized, with various generations (*ajyâl*, pl. of *jîl*) marked with different levels of cohesiveness (*'asabiya*), might (*jah*), and power *(qudra)*. For de Slane, the term *Arab* refers to the Oriental of Orientalism, whose image was familiar to European readers as someone who does not change or disappear, who is always dominant, and whose domination brings destruction. The term *Berber* in Ibn Khaldûn means the diverse Berber tribes, whose origins are mostly Oriental and whose histories and deeds are associated with Arabs. For de Slane, the term *Berber* refers to a newcomer in the field of Orientalism. He did not exist prior to the conquest of Algiers, Europe at that time, identified the other in the region as the Arab, the Moor, or the Saracen. In the nineteenth-century French imaginary, the Berber joins a category of people who had been familiar to the European since the beginning of the nineteenth century—the primitive who represents the past of Europeans. This new semantics determined the narrative syntax of the translation of de Slane—the actors, objects, and relations involved in the narrative.

Colonial historiography, based on the translated Ibn Khaldûn, is marked by two major narratives—the narrative on the Kâhina, whose significance in colonial scholarship is immense, and the episode of the Banu Hilal.[80] Both narratives explained contemporary North Africa to colonial scholars, especially how it became Arab and Muslim despite a large Berber presence and a long Roman history.[81] These two Arab invasions constitute in French colonial historiography narratives of origins and great discontinuities that changed the course of North African history and shaped it in a certain way relevant to the French presence in the Maghreb. To show how race-thinking and nation-thinking have shaped the colonial narrative, I briefly discuss the objects found in Ibn Khaldûn's original text to explain their transformations in de Slane's translation.

De Slane's introduction did not attain all its objectives of correction, rectification, and orientation. According to the translator himself, one objective was not attained: "The translator has proposed to devote a number of pages in this short introduction to examine the origins of the Berbers. His work was about to be finished when a number of items of information came to modify his conclusions."[82]

Despite the fact that one finds in Ibn Khaldûn an explanation of the origins of the Berbers, this seemed to de Slane to be unsatisfactory and needed to be corrected. De Slane promised his readers to put his text regarding the origins of the Berbers in the third volume. But he does not do so. Why does the translator judge Ibn Khaldûn's views of the origins of the Berbers as unsatisfactory? De Slane has read, interpreted, and translated the narrative of Ibn Khaldûn concerning the Berbers and judged it as untrue in relation to his own narrative. It does not correspond to it. Furthermore, he considered his own narrative to be differently untrue in relation to another one (presumably the dominant view of the Arab Bureau). It has not been published, but it is easy to find the available colonial explanation regarding the origins of the Berbers.

The early ethnographers of the Arab Bureau had already set in place a discourse on the origins of the Berbers that provided them with a European origin. By their skin color, culture, architecture, and even religious beliefs, Berbers were believed to be descended from an indigenous population (about which little was known) and Roman, Greek, and German populations that inhabited the country at the dawn of historical of time. The Arab invasion changed little in the racial landscape of North Africa. Berbers still spoke a distinct language, preserved the same skin color (white), were liberal, and were unconcerned about religion (Islam). They still observed Roman law *(qânûn)*, not Islamic law *(sharî'a)*. Further they still lived in a primitive republic with democratic principles (there was a Berber custom of electing a municipal council, *djemaa*). By the time the translation of Ibn Khaldûn was made, there was already a widely accepted discourse on Berbers, that made them primitive Europeans.[83] When Louis Léon César Faidherbe, a general in the French army and a vice president of the *Société d'Anthropologie,* summed up the situation of anthropological research in Algeria in 1874, his statistical conclusion was that the country was overwhelmingly Berber.[84] For him the inhabitants of Algeria by the beginning of the nineteenth century were divided in the following manner:

Indigenous Libyans	75%
Blonds from the North	
Phoenicians	1%
Romans, their auxiliaries, and Greeks from the Late Empire	1%
Vandals (in the East)	0.5%
Arabs (a good number of them remained pure; stronger proportions in the East and the West)	15%
Negroes of all races and sorts (the majority at the state of interbreeding in all degrees) more numerous in the South	5%
Jews (completely analogous to the Arabs)	2%
Turks from all the provinces and European renegades	0.5%

North Africa was believed to be inhabited by a predominantly Berber—that is, European—population. They constituted a little more than 76 percent of the population as opposed to the Arabs, who constituted 15 or rather 17 percent, given that at this date Arabs and Jews were still part of the same discourse. They were the Semites of Renan and Gobineau (a degenerate race, a mixture of white and black). Algeria, in French colonial ethnography, was numerically largely Berber and historically European. Such a discourse contradicts the narrative of Ibn Khaldûn on the origins of the Berbers, but it fits nicely with the translated text of de Slane, which makes the history of North Africa the history of a struggle between Arabs and Berbers.

In an influential article on translation, Walter Benjamin wrote "it should be pointed out that certain correlative concepts retain their meaning, and possibly their foremost significance, if they are referred exclusively to man."[85] Despite the translation's revised history of the relationship between Arabs and Berbers, the narrative of Ibn Khaldûn concerning the origins of the Berbers is preserved. A brief examination of Ibn Khaldûn's account of the origins of the Berbers, both in the original and in the translated text, describes the intention of the original and asks whether it was lost in the process of translation or remained the same.

"All knowledge," according to Gustave Bachelard, "taken at the moment of its constitution, is polemical knowledge."[86] The *Ibar* of Ibn Khaldûn was polemical in its time. It was a defense of the Berbers against the negative image that was created soon after the Arab conquest of North Africa in the late seventh century. Ibn Khaldûn states the goal of his book clearly. He wants to show "The strength [the Berbers have shown] through time, that they inspired fear; they are brave and powerful comparable to other nations and peoples of the world such as the Arabs, the Persians, the Greeks and the Romans" (*Ibar*, 121).

Ibn Khaldûn was not the only one who made an effort to put the Berbers on an equal footing with the Arabs and other nations. By the fourteenth century, a positive discourse had been created about the Berbers that was made up of stories of their great deeds in the past and linked them genealogically to the Arabs. Ibn Khaldûn echoes this discourse in his description of the genealogy of the Berbers:

> The truth that should be accepted regarding the origin of the Berbers is that they are descendants of Canaan, son of Ham, son of Noah, as indicated in the presentation of the genealogies of men since the Creation. The name of their ancestors is Mazigh; the Kerethetes [Arqish] and the Philistines were their brothers; their brother Casluhim, son of Mizrain, son of Ham. Their king Goliath is well-known as one of their kings. There were well-known wars between the Philistines and the Children of Israel in Syria. The Canaanites and the Kerethites were allies of the Philistines. This is what one must believe because it is the truth that must not be ignored. (*Ibar*, 6: 113)

The project of Arabizing the Berber was the culmination of a long-term effort undertaken from the ninth century onward to fuse two populations that seemed to be opposed as conqueror and conquered.[87] The conquest of North Africa by the Arabs had to be interpreted in a way that made it not seem to be a conquest—the domination of one group by another. After the establishment of Berber dynasties, the conquest of North Africa came to be seen as a reunion of two groups of the same origins. They were both Arabs: one of them came at the dawn of time, and the other came in the late seventh century to transmit the prophetic message.[88]

This discourse, which I have elsewhere characterized as inclusive and integrative,[89] would have questioned the colonial discourse that was built on the division of Arab versus Berber. Obliterating the opposition between Arabs and Berbers would lead to one of two conclusions—either that both groups are Algerians (of mixed origins) and therefore Algeria belongs to them and to them only or (if the view of Ibn Khaldûn is adopted) that both groups are Arabs and therefore not only is the French presence illegitimate but so too was the Roman presence. When the view of Ibn Khaldûn on this issue could not be converted by the act of translation, it was simply deemed incorrect and declared as such by the authority of the translator.

The Arabic text of Ibn Khaldûn reveals, as I have attempted to show, a different imaginary structure, that is not marked by racialism or colonial ideology and does not contain a plot, in which a hero and antihero pursue opposite quests. Nor does it point to a major lack that is at the heart of North African history. Instead, Ibn Khaldûn's long and complex narrative reveals a complex set of relations between tribes. It is a recording *(târîkh)* of various states of successive generations—it is an ordering of the Maghreb of the fourteenth century according to a number of categories specific to his time (tribal, genealogical, religious, *'asabiya, jâh, qudra, hasab,* and *nasab*). History happens in a cyclic way, reproducing the same pattern; with actors grouped in different polities, tribal and dynastic. This history undoubtedly implies change and transformation but excludes the notion of progress and a shared human future toward which all peoples head with different and unequal speeds.

NOTES

1. Those are related to history, geography, and law: Mohammed ibn abi-El-Raïni Qayrawani, *Histoire de l'Afrique*, trans. E. Pellissier and Ch. Remusat (Paris: Imprimerie Impériale, 1845); Al-Aiachi-Moula-Ahmed, *Voyages dans le sud de l'Algérie et des etats barbaresques de l'ouest et de l'est*, trans. Berbrugger (1846); Khalil B. Ishaq, *Précis de jurisprudence musulmane et principes de législation musulmane civile et religious selon le rite malikite*, trans. Nicholas Perron (Paris, Imprimerie nationale, 1848–52).

2. Ernest Carette, *Recherches sur l'origine et les migrations des principales tribus de l'Afrique septentrionale et particulièrement de l'Algérie;* Ernest Carette, *Etudes sur la Kabylie proproment dite.*

3. Ibn Khaldûn, *Histoire des Berbères,* 4 vols. (Algiers: Imprimerie du Governement, 1852–1856).

4. For this subject, see Aziz Azmeh, *Ibn Khaldûn in Modern Scholarship* (London: Third World Center for Research, 1981); see also Abdessalem Cheddadi, *Ibn Khaldûn revisité* (Casablanca: Toubkal, 1999).

5. Lawrence Venuti, *The Scandals of Translation: Towards an Ethic of Difference* (New York: Routledge, 1998), 81–82.

6. Paul Ricoeur, "Imagination in Discourse and in Action," in Gillian Robinson and John Rundell, eds., *Rethinking Imagination* (New York: Routledge, 1994), 118–135.

7. Antoine Berman, *Pour une critique des traductions: John Donne* (Paris: Gallimard, 1995); quoted in Venuti, *The Scandals of Translation,* 84.

8. Cornelius Castoriadis, *L'institution et l'imaginaire* (Paris: Seuil, 1975), 8.

9. Clifford Geertz, *The Interpretation of Cultures* (New York: Basic Books, 1975), 44.

10. Cornelius Castoriadis, "The Imaginary: Creation in the Social-Historical Domain," in Paisley Livingston, ed., *Order and Disorder* (Menlo Park, Calif. : Benjamin/Cummings Pub. Co., Advanced

Book Program, 1984.), 152. For the French text, see "L'imaginaire: la création dans le domaine social-historique," in Cornelius Castoriadis *Domaines de l'homme* (Paris: Seuil, 1977), 226–227.

11. Ernest Cassirer, *An Essay on Man* (New Haven: Yale University Press, 1944).

12. See also Collingwood, for whom history is a reenactment of past experiences in the mind of the historian. Robin George Collingwood, *The Idea of History* (Oxford: Oxford University Press, 1963), 282.

13. Maurice Merleau-Ponty, "The Crisis of Understanding," *Adventures of the Dialectics,* trans. Joseph Bien, (Evanston: Northwestern University Press, 1973), 11.

14. Cassirer, *An Essay on Man,* 178.

15. Ibid.

16. Said, *Orientalism,* 124.

17. Silvestre de Sacy, *Chrestomathie arabe* (1808), 2: 387, 393–401; see also Silvestre de Sacy, *Relation de l'Egypte par Abd-Allatif* (Paris: Treuttel et Würtz, 1810), 509.

18. Silvestre de Sacy, "Ibn Khaldûn," in *Biographie universelle* (1818), 21: 154.

19. Joseph de Hammer, "Sur l'introduction à la connaissance de l'histoire, célèbre ouvrage d'Ibn Khaldûn," *Journal Asiatique* (1822): 267–278.

20. Garcin de Tassy, "Suppélement à la notice de M. de Hammer," *Journal Asiatique* (1824): 158–161.

21. F. E. Schulz, "Sur le grand ouvrage historique et critique d'Ibn Khaldûn," *Journal Asiatique*(1825): 213–300.

22. Ibn Khaldûn himself narrates the history of the composition of his book in the last part, entitled *"al-ta'rif bi ibn Khaldûn."*

23. Cheddadi, *Ibn Khaldûn revisité.*

24. This view was first expressed by de Sacy and reproduced in the Arab discourse of Ibn Khaldûn. See, for instance, Taha Hussein, *Etude analytique de la philosophie sociale d'Ibn Khaldûn* (Paris: Vrin, 1919). It has been confirmed by most of the subsequent interpreters of Ibn Khaldûn.

25. Such is the view of Robert Brunschvig, *La Berbérie orientale sous les Hafsides* (Paris: Adrien-Maisonneuve) (1982), vol. 1.

26. An example of this is the collective work edited by Dwight

Reynold, *Interpreting the Self.* (Berkeley: University of California Press, 2001).

27. Ibn Khaldûn, *Histoire des berbères.*

28. Etienne Quatremère, "Ibn Khaldûn' *Muqaddima.*" in *Notices et extraits des mss de la Bibliothèque impériale,* vols. 16–18 (Paris: 1858), trans. William de Slane, *Prolégomènes,* vols. 19–21.

29. See Ernest Gellner, *Muslim Society* (Cambridge: Cambridge University Press, 1981). However, Gellner does not investigate the relation between Ibn Khaldûn and Durkheim. The work of Ibn Khaldûn was available by the mid-nineteenth century, and Durkheim also had an Egyptian doctoral candidate, Taha Hussein, working on the *Muqaddima.*

30. See Hannoum, "L'auteur comme autorité en ethnographie coloniale," 249–264.

31. Joseph Reinaud, "Ibn Khaldûn," in *Nouvelle biographie générale* (1861), 25: 746.

32. Emile-Felix Gautier, *Les siècles obscurs* (Paris: Payot, 1927); Franz Rosenthal, *Muqaddima* (Princeton: Princeton University Press, 1967).

33. Jacques Berque, *L'intérieur du Maghreb* (Paris: Gallimard, 1978), 1.

34. Ibid.

35. See especially the work of Michel Foucault, *The Archeology of Knowledge* (New York: Pantheon Books: 1972).

36. Régis Blachère, "La place d'Ibn Khaldun dans l'humanisme arabo-islamique," *Revue des Deux Mondes* (October 1972): 70–79.

37. Ibid., 79.

38. Charles Issawi, *An Arab Philosophy of History: Selections* (Princeton: Darwin Press, 1987), ix. Issawi is quoting Thomas Hobbes, who considered the natural propensity of man to violence as resulting in a life that was "solitary, poor, nasty, brutish, and short." Hobbes was describing a life without constraints—without what he calls a "common power."

39. De Slane, *Histoire des Berbères,* i.

40. Algirdas-Julien Greimas, "Le savoir et le croire: un seul univers cognitif," *Du Sens II,* 115–133.

41. Algirdas-Julien Greimas, "On Chance Occurrences in What We Call the Human Sciences," *On Meaning,* trans. Paul J. Perron and

Frank H. Collins, foreword by Frederic Jameson (London: Pinter, 1987).

42. Roman Jakobson, "On the Linguistics Aspects of Translation," *Language and Literature* (Cambridge: Harvard University Press, 1987), 429–430.

43. Whorf, *Language Thought and Reality*, 242.

44. Ferdinand de Saussure, *Cours de linguistique générale* (Paris: Payot, 1985).

45. See Louis Hyelmslev, *Prolégomènes à une théorie du language* (Paris: Minuit, 1968), trans. Una Canger (from Danish). Also see the contribution of Algirdas-Julien Greimas, "A Text," in Algirdas-Julien Greimas and Joseph Courtès, *Dictionnaire raisonné du language* (Paris: Hachette, 1979).

46. Walter Benjamin, "The Task of the Translator," *Illuminations* (New York: Schocken, 1969).

47. Raymond Aron, "De l'objet de l'histoire," *Dimensions de la conscience historique* (Paris: Plon, 1961), 87.

48. Benjamin, "The Task of the Translator."

49. Ibid., 78–79.

50. For more details, see Abdelmajid Hannoum, "Translation and the Imaginary," *Anthropology News* 43 (8) November, 8–9.

51. Among those are Paul Ricoeur, "Les paradigms de la traduction," *Esprit* (1999): 8–19 ; Paul de Man, "'Conclusions' on Walter Benjamin's *The Task of the Translator*," *Yale French Studies* 97 (2000): 10–35; Talal Asad, "The Concept of Cultural Translation in British Social Anthropology)," *Genealogies of Religion*, 171–199.

52. Cited by Franklin Walker in his introduction to Joseph Conrad's *Heart of Darkness* (New York: Bantam, 1981), vii–viii.

53. Roland Barthes, "Authors and Writers," *A Barthes Reader* (New York: Farrar, Straus and Giroux, 1982) 185–193; see also Barthes, "The Death of the Author," ibid., 49–55.

54. For a general view, see Walter Fischel, "Ibn Khaldūn's Use of Historical Sources" *Studia Islamica*, No. 14 (1961), 109–119

55. Abdellah Laroui, "Les Arabes et l'histoire," *The Crisis of the Arab Intellectual* (California: University of California Press, 1976), 13–32.

56. Maya Shatzmiller *L'historiographie mérinide: Ibn Khaldûn et ses contemporains* (Leiden: E. J. Brill, 1982), 132.

57. John White, "Taine on Race and Genius," *Social Research* 10 (February 1943): 76–99.

58. Hananh Arendt, "Race-Thinking before Racism," *The Origins of Totalitarianism* (New York: Harcourt, Brace & Wold, Inc., 1966), 165 ; see also Théophile Simar, *Etude critique sur la formation de la doctrine des races au 18è siécle et son expansion au 19è siècle* (Brussels: Lamertin, 1922).

59. See Joseph Arthur de Gobineau, *Essai sur l'inégalité des races humaines* (Paris: Firmin Didot, 1853–1855). *The Inequality of Human Races,* trans. Adrian Collins, (New York: H. Fertig, 1967); Taine, *Histoire de la littérature anglaise,* vol. 1.

60. Gobineau, *The Inequality of Human Races,* 133.

61. Ibid., 92–93.

62. Ibid., 91.

63. Hyppolite Taine was a dominant figure in nineteenth-century Europe. Among his admirers was Nietzsche. After studying philosophy, he turned to art and literature and wrote many well-known works, including *La Fontaine et ses fables* (Paris: Hachette, 1861), *Histoire de la littérature anglaise,* and *De l'intelligence* (Paris: Hachette, 1861).

64. Gobineau, *The Inequality of Human Races,* 171.

65. Ernest Renan, "Qu'est-ce qu'une nation?," in *Oeuvres complètes* (Paris: C. Levy, 1947), vol. 1.

66. Hanouteau and Letourneau, *La Kabylie et les coutumes kabyles.*

67. Renan, "La société berbère," 323.

68. Renan, "Qu'est-ce qu'une nation?," 887–906.

69. Ernest Renan, "De la part des peuples sémitiques dans l'histoire des civilisation)," *Mélanges d'histoire et de voyages* (Paris: Calmann Levy, 1878), 1–25.

70. Arendt, "Race-Thinking," 59.

71. Renan, "La société berbère."

72. See Gobineau, *The Inequality of Human Races,* 30.

73. Renan, "Qu'est-ce qu'une nation?," 000–000.

74. Jacques Berque, "Ibn Khaldûn et les bedouins," *Maghreb: histoire et sociétés* (Algiers: Duculot, 1974), 18. Berque too translates *jîl* as "race." Ibid.

75. I depart from the English translation of Franz Rosenthal and its colonial discourse. He, too, translates *jîl* and *umma* as "race" and "nation," respectively.

76. See Tarif Khalidi, *Arabic Thought in the Classical Period* (Cambridge: Cambridge University Press, 1994).

77. The transition from *belief* to *disbelief* is also possible—it is *murtadd* (apostate)—but this possibility is to be eliminated.

78. See Cheddadi, *Ibn Khaldûn revisité.*

79. In a nineteenth-century French dictionary, domination means: "Autorité qui, accepté ou non des subordonnés, s'exerce pleinement" (Littré). The word *autorité* means "pouvoir de se faire obéir" (ibid.). Whereas Ibn Khaldûn always mentions *fath* as "Islamic" (*al-fath al-islâmî*), de Slane mentions it as "Arab conquest." The word *conquête* means to "conquérir par les armes" (Littré).

80. See A. Hannoum, *Colonial Histories, Post-Colonial Memories* (Portsmouth: Greenwood, 2001).

81. Ibid, 29–69

82. De Slane, *L'Histoire des Berbères.*

83. See chapter 1, above.

84. Louis Léon César Faidherbe, *Instructions sur l'anthropologie de l'Algérie* (Paris: Hennuyer, 1874), 12. More on these numbers in chapter 4.

85. Walter Benjamin, "The Task of Translation," *Illuminations,* 70.

86. Quoted in Johannes Fabian, *Time and the Other* (New York: Columbia University Press, 1983), 143.

87. For more details, see Hannoum, *Colonial Histories, Post-Colonial Memories,* 1–28.

88. Ibid.

89. Ibid.

· THREE ·

Colonial Violence and Its Narratives

This atmosphere of violence and menaces, these rockets brandished by both sides, do not frighten nor deflect the colonized peoples.
—Frantz Fanon

And because the man who rebels is finally inexplicable; it takes a wrenching-away that interrupts the flow of history, and its long chains of reasons, for a man to be able, "really," to prefer the risk of death to the certainty of having to obey.
—Michel Foucault

Even with a highly impressive modern machinery of governance—an army of soldiers, administrators, agents, and servants that reduced people to objects to be observed and studied—French colonialism did not reign supreme in Algeria. Despite the colonial machinery of knowledge, the population was not always caught by the intricacies of colonial discourse. Knowledge is a representation of its agents—a system of meaning and the product of imagination—and as such, it accounts for experiences but does not substitute for them or even mirror them. The knowledge on which colonial policies were made was subject to errors and thus to failure. Although it was a strong means of governance, the colonial agents themselves were caught in the webs of representations—for knowledge often produces belief, and belief, action, and action, reaction. The first victims of a knowledge set may be its own producers.[1]

French colonialism engaged in the conquest of knowledge from the earliest stages of its long history, and it turned soldiers into scholars and administrators into historians and ethnographers. It became a machine of thought despite its sustained and violent physical practices. In only a few decades, 1830 to 1871, France's reservoir of knowledge about Algeria grew to a colossal size. Colonial scholars did not neglect any region, city, or time period. Monographs, reports, maps, statistics, journals, and magazines were produced with amazing speed and efficiency to tackle each issue related to the colony. By 1871, the French knew Algeria, and their knowledge became the foundation for guiding their policies toward their colony. This body of knowledge—despite its heterogeneous texts, contradictory statements, and conflicting representations—constituted the system of meaning that became Algerian reality. When French soldiers were sent off to fight Prussia and the war with Prussia ended with a crushing defeat of the French army (which caused the fall of the empire and the disintegration of the structure of the state), a massive uprising against the French was launched in the Great Kabylia area. It was clearly well calculated and well organized by the population, and the colonial administrations used their body of research to respond to the revolt.

The texts of the Kabyle revolt (as it is known in both Arabic and French texts) are all colonial texts. They cannot be thought of outside colonial semantics, for the event itself is a colonial narrative construction: this narrative is an expression of the culture of colonial society in Algeria. The colonial narration of the event does not tell what happened in the field for over a year but explains what colonial agents, soldiers, politicians, administrators, and settlers thought was happening, how they accounted for it, and how they took part in it. Therefore, any positivist attempt to reconstruct what happened in the colonial period regarding this event will at best create a narrative of failure (i.e., "this is a movement for liberation that failed") and, at worst, will reproduce the colonial narrative (i.e., *this is an irrational, irresponsible act that led to disaster"*). Instead of seeing these texts about the uprising of 1871 as a record of what happened in the field, I consider them as discursive practices that colonialists used to account for local resistance, to give it meaning, to control it, and to find reasons for the political divisions within colonial society. This approach allows us to go beyond the clear-cut opposition between colonizer and colonized, elite and subaltern. Such an approach also shows that the uprising of 1871 is a narrative that is the object of struggle among various groups in colonial society. This chapter shows how the local population created, caused, and sometimes even determined colonial political discourse and the actions informed by it.

Frantz Fanon once wrote, "Colonialism is not a thinking machine, nor a body endowed with reasoning faculties. It is violence in its natural state."[2] Anthropologists and historians of colonialism seem to focus on showing the thinking behind the colonial machine by analyzing the colonial discourse—its genealogies, its links to power, its strategies, and its functions of subjugation and governance. But they have neglected how colonialism practiced its violence and how it made narratives part of these violent practices. The violence directed against the population is inseparable from the writing about violence. Colonialism *acts* on others—physically, symbolically, and discursively—and *thinks* of its actions simultaneously. Colonial violence resides in its thinking and acting. It reveals itself as both a military and a thinking machine; each operating violently and each side is part and parcel of the other. To examine how colonialism writes its violence is not to write a history of "rebellion" or "insurgency" but to look at the texts that explain why, how, and under what conditions the population resorted to arms and how their actions were crushed. The logic of colonialism can be found in the violence and specificity of colonial writing on violence. Such an approach shows that colonial knowledge was not a peaceful work of erudition completed in libraries or an ethnographic activity carried out among complicit natives. It was the product of violent encounters. The chapter also shows that colonial politics were often dictated, transformed, and changed by the masses of people who were thinking and acting under colonial oppression, and the dynamics of this relation is examined here through narratives of violence and the violence of narratives.

EVENTS, NARRATIVES, AND ARCHIVES

In his book *La mémoire, l'histoire, l'oublie,* published in 2000, Paul Ricoeur returns to one of his favorites topics—the writing of history—and he draws on an entire literature on memory. He asserts that history begins with witnessing and therefore with memory: "With witnessing, an epistemological process opens. It departs from declared memory, passes through the archives and the documents, and ends with the documentary proof."[3]

In other words, before archivization, there is a witnessing phase, which is complex and has different uses but whose fundamental characteristic is that it is a narrative. As such, it is separate from the narrator. Ricoeur contends that between the saying and the said, there is a gap that allows what is said about things to have a life of its own. In the archives, the historian finds witnessing converted into writing. The historian is thus a reader. To say *archive* is to refer not only to masses of witnessing, Ricoeur continues, but also to a physical and social space. The place where both the inclusion and exclusion of discourses happen provides the framework for what Michel de Certeau calls "the historiographic operation."[4] For Ricoeur, this is the domain not of history or historiography but of a distinct discipline called *archiving*. Whereas the document of the archive (the document being the witnessing fixed in writing and placed somewhere) does not have a specific receiver, the witnessing has one and is addressed to someone particular. The document of the archives is, in Ricoeur's words, both "silent" and "orphan"; it is detached from its authors.[5] Thus, in the historical culture of the age, archives are believed to provide objectivity. The archive, Ricoeur contends, is nothing more or less than archived memory. The archives are based on witnessing and therefore on memory. But unlike memory, which establishes a fiduciary contract between sender and the receiver, archives are made of multiple sources and voices. One could borrow Bakhtin's expression and say they are *polyphonic*. The historian is a "judge." For Ricoeur, "He is put in real or potential situation of contest and tends to prove that such explanation is better than another."[6] The historian—who is therefore a judge—does not come to the archives innocently but with an agenda and with a set of questions that affects the constitution of the "evidence" on which historical knowledge is always based, according to Ricoeur. The matrix of historical knowledge is memory, and that memory becomes institutionalized as it goes through channels of power and through the intricacies of making historical knowledge.[7]

In July 2004, I entered the archives at the chateaux of Versailles (Les Archives d'Outre Mer), not only with an agenda (as Ricoeur would say) but also with a story in mind. I had read colonial and national literatures and knew what the archives held (letters sent and received by leaders and colonial administrators, reports written by the latter during and after the event, the report on the leaders' trials, and so forth). I entered with the call numbers of the boxes where the documents were archived. Ricoeur is right. I entered with an agenda and a set of questions: Why and how do these documents end up in the archives? How are they archived? Do archives have a nationality? Do archives have politics? Why? And what does it mean to have "my documents" in "your archives"?

On March 10, 2004, the president of the French republic, Jacques Chirac, declared: "The archives constitute an intrinsic element of our identity. Place of memory and source of our history, they are an irreplaceable treasure."[8] Chirac here echoes the official mission of the archives, as published on October 23, 1979: "To manage or control the public archives that constitute the memory of the nation and are an essential part of the historic heritage."[9]

The archives are a French place of memory (not an Algerian one). With young soldiers handing me boxes of different sizes, I immediately noticed a young black soldier who reminded me of the "symbol of the empire" analyzed by Roland Barthes.[10] Probably from Martinique, he reminded me of a French empire that may not have completely vanished (as say, the Ottoman empire has).

I sat down and read letter after letter. They were all handwritten—sent from officer to officer, from a spy to an office, or from a native to a Frenchman during the 1871 uprisings. Although these letters provided many details about the uprising, they did not change my general knowledge of what happened, which I had obtained by reading colonial and national literatures. My initial understanding of the uprising was colonial because there is no alternative to the colonial narrative. Even the letters from local leaders have a meaning that is consistent with the colonial narrative. All traces of the uprisings—letters, memos, telegraphs, and so on—are archived by the French Ministry of Defense (formerly called the Ministry of War). The archives are set up to tell the story in a specific way, so the archivists must know the story before they organize the documents (the document comes before the archives, and the archives are essentially a place for documents). The 1871 uprising was first constructed by the French colonial administration in Algeria before it ended up in the French archives in Versailles. It was appropriated, both figuratively and literarily, as a narrative and as an archive.

Within this space called *archives* are stored thousands of this multitude of documents and each is an event that was written in one place and at one time. A true history of their writing, if possible to create, would make an endless narrative and still not be comprehensive. In this section, I examine the process by which the early narratives of the 1871 events came into being and by which the uprising has been constructed as a narrative.

The location of the event—the Great Kabylia—is examined in

chapter 1. The Kabyles had come to be seen as so different from the Arabs, and so close to the French that they were expected to fill the role of European settlers—be removed from the mountains to the plains and thus consolidate colonization.[11] By 1870, a colonial political and epistemological order was already in place, yet something undermined that order, an event: "Something happens, explodes, breaks an established order. Then an imperious quest of meaning is made clear, like an exigent need to establish order. Finally, the event is not only taken back to order but, in some ways, remains to be thought. It is recognized, honored, and exalted like a crest of meaning."[12] How was this quest to establish order through meaning carried out and by whom?

In his study "The Prose of Counter-Insurgency," Ranajit Guha attempts to categorize what he calls "historical writings on peasant insurgency":

> The corpus of historical writings on peasant insurgency in colonial India is made up of three types of discourse. These may be described as primary, secondary, and tertiary according to the order of their appearance in time and their filiations. Each of these is differentiated from the other two by the degree of its formal and/acknowledged (as opposed to real and/or tacit) identification with an official point of view, by the measure of its distance from the event to which it refers, and by the ration of the distributive and integrative components in its narrative.[13]

Although the division of such a discourse on the principle of time may seem useful at first glance, there are complexities associated with the category of time. First, the order of narratives surrounding an insurgency's appearance is itself a colonial order of time. François Hartog wrote about the writing of history and the conception of time:

> All history, whatever its mode of expression, presupposes, refers to, translates, betrays, magnifies, or contradicts one or several experiences of time. With the regime of historicity, we thus touched on one of the conditions of the possibility of the production of

histories—depending on the respective rapports to the present, to the past, and to the future. Some types of history are possible, and not others.[14]

The archives on the uprising reveal the existence of a specific colonial order of time that Hartog calls *présentisme*. The incidents that happened in the present, including the most gruesome, were explained in relation to a future that would unavoidably bring progress. In the archive, all of the narratives are assembled in boxes under the title "the Kabyle revolt of 1871." In the logic of colonial time, something has happened and was doomed to end by the reestablishment of the colonial order. In this perception of time, the future eliminates the present. What counts is the horizon, which brings what is best. This perception marks modernity, according to Hartog.[15]

If the events of 1871 had resulted in the collapse of the colonial order, they would have been called a war or revolution, which happened with the events of 1954.[16] One cannot take the "identification with an official point" as a criterion, for such identification is common to all discourses, not only those of insurgency. The primary discourse is characterized by an instantaneous perception, and the old categories are immediately used to make sense of an event that breaks the old categories and results in a crisis of knowledge—what Taussig calls "an epistemological murk."[17] In this instance, old categories are applied to a new situation—and challenged. The primary discourse is always characterized by ambiguity and contradictions, signs of its crisis. In the secondary discourse, the epistemological crisis is solved, and ambiguity and contradictions disappear (or are minimized), giving birth to a new order of categories. This new order is nothing but an adjustment that tries to make sense of what happened while preserving the previous body of knowledge from falling into bankruptcy. The tertiary discourse is marked by a conflict of interpretations in which what is usually at stake is not the event itself but the event as a means to address the present situation. In other words, the event enters the realm of historical memory, is manipulated for political reasons and becomes either forced or repressed. One can argue that any discourse beyond the secondary one is tertiary, no matter how close or far it is from the event itself. The discourse of the analyst historian is also a tertiary one.[18]

No narratives account for what was happening in the moment. Instead, the archives contain telegraphs, memos, brief reports, and letters intercepted by the French administration at various times during the fall of 1871 and even before September 4, which is usually considered the beginning of the "revolt." These colonial textual traces signal interruptions in their localities—for instance, an attack against a caravanserai,[19] the cutting of the telegraphic line,[20] an unusual "disturbance,"[21] or some "agitation" about news of France's defeat by the Prussians.[22] The archives indicate events and narratives (things were happening here and there, and these things were worthy of report) but do not signal that this was "the rebellion of 1871." The French newspapers in Oran, Constantine, and Algiers reported the troubling events of the defeat of the French army in great detail. The news of the capture of Napoleon III and the defeat of what Marx had sarcastically called "the heroes of Africa"[23] left little room for any other news reports in colonial Algeria. As late as March, there was no indication that something major was happening in Algeria.[24] On March 6, 1871, the general commander of the south of Dellys wrote a report addressing the situation. It was still not an uprising but a situation where France seemed to have lost respect in the eyes of the population:

My General,

The defeats that France has suffered in its fight with Prussia have greatly undermined our military prestige in the eyes of the indigenous population and, as a consequence, weakened the respect that our authority had before this unfortunate war.[25]

This report suggested delaying the return of the native Algerians who took part in the Prussian war so they would not report stories of French defeat.

In the fall of 1871, French newspapers published telegraphs and short narratives, and there was a sense that there had been an "insurrection." But nothing that looked like the grand narrative of Louis Rinn (1891) or like any of the narratives published after 1871 (analyzed in the third section of this chapter). For instance, on September 19, *L'Echo d'Oran* published a telegraph from the general of the region of Constantine stating that the activities of the insurgents were bothersome—but that these activities consisted mainly of taking 300 camels and making the roads dangerous. This type of news conveys something more like brigandage and theft than systematic warfare for a political cause. It makes the events seem like petty crimes and not directed against the colonial state with the aim of challenging it. Another telegraph, reassuring, follows: "All the tribes of Bougie have entered into obedience."[26] During the week of October 14th, 1871, the news about General La Croix and his "successful campaigns" reported in *Le Courrier de Mostaganem* appeared reassuring. The situation seemed, according to a telegraph, well under control, and the native who delivers some of the "news" gives it credibility: "An indigenous man of this region said that it plunged the entire region into fear and terror. The Kabyles have begun to understand that we are no longer pleased to follow the old traditions and that we seriously want to suppress the revolt."[27]

Even on March 17, 1871, the fragments of news about pieces of events (but not the event) continued to arrive and convey brigandage, theft, and intertribal conflicts. They began to have the form of reports, covering a day or more of events, and thus start to be endowed with a narrative form, with the situation disturbed by the presence of an antihero.

Around this time, other reports began to articulate narratives of insurgency. Corneille Trumelet was familiar with such events and was already the author of a book narrating the uprising of Ouled Sidi Cheikh in 1864.[28] In 1871, at the beginning of the uprising, he was asked to give a fuller meaning to numerous "incidents" that were communicated to the French authorities in fragments.[29] In this report, the word *war* is used to describe the incidents for the first time. Trumelet finds it necessary to "remind [the reader] of the facts that preceded" the incidents of March 16 to March 18. This time, a beginning is indicated: "The first symptoms of agitation were declared among our neighbors of the east, the Beni Abbas, around February 8. As usual, disorder begins with a *nefra* [mass agitation] in the market of Arbaa of the tribe we just indicated."[30]

Narratives have beginnings (this beginning is necessarily one of "disorder," when order is disturbed and awaits normalization) and must have a cast of actors organized in a specific way. The author of the disorder is the Bach-Agha, Mokrani, who by this time has not declared war but is prepared to "lift the mask"—meaning that the antihero (the one who disturbed the colonial order) is hidden. This tactical ploy makes it appear to be an act of one person—Mokrani. Lifting the mask is a trope that indicates that this is an individual movement (despite its mass appearance) and an individual treason. Mokrani appeared to be on the side of the French, but he plotted the event.[31]

With Trumelet, the narrative structure of the uprising is set in place. The narrative of insurgency thus seems a colonial narrative of an antihero. This narrative carries in itself the heroic narrative, when the French hero, motivated by civilization, tries to restore order against a villain. But this is not explicit. This narrative exists in other fragments. Thus, by January 3, 1872, telegraphs announce a narrative of successful quests:

Sir the Minister,

The political situation of this region continues to be satisfactory. The spirit of the population is good; the most complete security reigns throughout all the roads and in our markets.[32]

By this date, the narrative existed but in fragments that were awaiting a unified narration. Such narration was an effort to make sense of the event for the colonial administration and to identify what went wrong with the colonial project—to put the responsibility of what happened on someone. I shall return to this point later.

In the archives (the physical place where these documents are now deposited), it is possible to construct a narrative of insurgency. The archives contain documents by which colonial authors, agents, and administrators constructed the event after the repression of the local uprising. These documents allow the national historian to construct a narrative of failed liberation and the postcolonial historians to point out the fragmentation of the archives. Such fragmentation is given a visible unity in the archives, which are a physical and a social space regulated by rules invisible and unknown to the historian. Only the ethnography of such archives reveals the politics of archiving.

LOCAL KNOWLEDGE AND ITS FORMS

In the French archives, there are many documents written in Arabic by qaids who are loyal to the French, others who are hostile to them, and religious and tribal leaders of the uprising. These documents contain local knowledge. Colonial interest in what the population thought of the French, the motives for the revolt, and the intentions of the insurgents—and their whereabouts, tactics, and alliances—significantly increased during this period. Colonialism set out to comprehend this local knowledge, but this "local knowledge" is also colonial. In essence, it does not only say, "This is what the native knew"; it also says, "This is what the French knew that the native knew." It shows the process and the mechanisms by which the subjugated people observed the French, studied them, guessed or knew their intentions and motives, categorized them, and eventually used that knowledge to throw off that domination and again take control of their lands and their lives.

Nevertheless, local knowledge was not necessarily a strategy directed against the colonial machine. In some instances, it was a discourse that was in the service of the colonial machine—part of the structure of domination. This type of discourse, native in its form and colonial in its function, was intended to end the uprising and perpetuate domination and subjugation. Letters, many of them written by locals, often the elite, were secretly sent to the French administration to inform it about those who joined "the rebellion," who killed or were killed, who deserted, for what reasons, and so forth.[33] The qaid of Oulad Bulbul wrote:

> To the respectable, honorable Colonel, governor of the division of Sour Al-Ghizlan. May peace and the blessing of Allah be on you. I bring to your knowledge the fact that I heard that you are in doubt regarding the death of the Hajj Mokrani. Sir, he undoubtedly died; it was no illusion. He was killed by a soldier of yours. All the tribes were defeated and have dispersed as a result of his death. His brother Abu Mezrag wrote to all the tribes asking for advice regarding the war, and they presented him with condolences on his brother [Mokrani]. After their defeat, however, they received a note from the qaid Ben al-A'waad, who told them that most *al-mahallah* had been killed and that those who were left surrendered to the general. Thus, he relieved them. I [should also] inform you of the army located in Dra' al-Mizan. They went outside of the Borj and dug meters [around]. They began to watch from there and to kill whomever rode around from the tribes. They [the army] are under the safety of Allah. They have whatever they need from outside the Bordj. There is no need to worry about them. This is my information, and [I have] no more to offer except respect for your high honor. Written by the order of Sayyid Muhammed Ben Mansour, qaid of Oulad Bulbul.[34]

Local knowledge also shows the conflict that existed among the people themselves. Even in the area of the uprising, the opposition was not only between the colonizer and the colonized (even though this was the fundamental one that articulated others) but also among the colonized, who were divided.

In local narratives, the French are seen as infidels who are to be fought not because they are Christians but because they occupy the land and seek to divert people from their religion *(dîn)* and their way of life.[35] Another group of people called *mturnîn* have turned from being Muslim into being French and have "sold out."[36] War was waged equally against both French and *mturnîn*. From the day of the declaration of war, Mokrani directed many letters to heads and leaders of other groups and leaders. Attacks against the *mturnîn* seem to have been frequent. Complaints to the French were often received: "We want to tell you about Boumezrag. He launched the Bedouins against us. He cut the roads and ways. We cannot find any way to use them."[37]

Historians and anthropologists have noted that, in times of war, there is a proliferation of what are usually referred to as rumors.[38] But rumors of war are peculiar because they are elemental to the violence. Rumors thus become narratives of struggle. They are used to misinform the enemy, mobilize fighters, lift spirits, and inform one party about another's movements, intentions, and locations.

Rumors are narratives themselves, and as such, they can be interpreted by the receiver as either false or true, depending on the receiver's cognitive universe. Because rumors are often the result of ambiguous situations, they have a specific function (to solidify a group seeking social control) and a meaning contingent on the contexts in which they were formed. Rumors are a type of news that serves as the basis for people's actions.[39] They are not necessarily fabricated with the intent to deceive or incite. They are formed through a "collective transaction, involving a division of labor among participants, each of whom makes a different contribution."[40] Rumors are marked by circularity, a process through which they are enriched, changed, and transformed. At the same time, there is something paradoxical in these narratives. On the one hand, they are generally viewed as false reports; the very word *rumor* (even its Arabic equivalent *isha'a*) connotes falsehood in its common usage. On the other hand, in their own contexts, where they are formed, rumors have considerable credibility and are received as true, particularly because the process of oral exchange relies on trust.[41]

In a number of local uprisings in Algeria, people first started talking about the coming of the man of the hour *(mûl al-sa'a)*.

Such prophetic messages were always interpreted literally by colonial sources, an interpretation that was consistent with—and
reinforced—a view of native primitiveness.[42] Such an interpretation is also adopted by some historians of these uprisings.[43] But
the story of the man of the hour is a metaphor inspired by the
Qu'ran: "the hour is undoubtedly coming" *(inna al-sa'ata
atiyatun lâ yarba fîha).* The hour (or rather Time) brings its
agents. The agent of change comes in his time. Thus, he is the
man of the hour. Colonial and postcolonial historians often
adopted literal interpretations of local metaphors and tropes,
which is common in colonial readings of native discourse, as
Gananath Obysekere once noted, "this problem of literalizing
tropes is endemic to ethnography because very few outsiders can
pick up the nuances of utterances.[44]

In the uprising of 1871, there were no narratives about "the
master of the hour" because the uprising was not the work of a
religious, charismatic leader—although it was represented as
such by colonial authors. For them, the uprising was understood
to be the work of a leader who succeeded in allying the support
of the religious order of the Rahmaniya.[45] But the uprising itself
remained associated to Mokrani, who had no claim to a religious title.

In the eyes of the population, the uprising did not have the
character of a "charismatic adventure" as had some previous
uprisings, such as that of 1864.[46] Indeed, the rumors preceding
the uprising of 1871 were not of a religious character. Some examples of these rumors may be telling about the conditions and
the characteristics of the uprising.

First, colonial sources report that, at the outbreak of the uprising, rumor of the French defeat at the hands of the Prussians
spread all over the country: "The French lost all the power to
harm or to serve."[47] This rumor expresses a local understanding
of the events of 1870 and shows that the population was somewhat informed about what was happening in Europe. This rumor (or information) was brought by returning native soldiers.

Local French newspapers also reported it. So the local population had information that helped it plan the uprising.

Other rumors spread the information that in Algeria, "all the cities of the west were destroyed and pillaged and Islamic government has been established." This is of particular interest. It was not related to the uprising of Great Kabylia but refers to another uprising initiated in western Algeria on the Tunisian border, by Mouhy el-Din, the grandson of the well-known Abdel Qadir, who, against the will of his father, came to organize the "liberation of Algeria."[48]

Louis Rinn, the author of the most comprehensive work on the 1871 uprising, cites other rumors. For instance, "France is going to take the land of the indigenous and give it to the French of the metropole who are deprived and ruined by the Prussians. It will [also] give it to the Algerian settlers, and, finally, to the Jews, who have become the chiefs and important agents of the new government."[49]

For Algerians, these were not rumors but information about the consequence of the fall of the French empire, the change of the status of the Jews, and the rise of a civilian regime in Algeria. In fact, the civilian regime was always clear and extremely militant about its plans to establish the right of conqueror in Algeria—that is, to take land and expand colonization by abolishing native, collective ownership. This narrative about France taking land for its settlers was more than a piece of information; it was a narrative that made the struggle worthy and even necessary. Such a narrative was a means of mobilizing people by convincing them of something familiar—the proverb "a man dies for his children or for his land" *(al-rajil kaymout ʾla wladu walla ʾla bladu).*

Rumors were expressed orally and also in writing. A general rumor at one point could later be revealed to be a form of knowledge of colonial politics. When the uprising was gradually oppressed, for example, a local leader created and spread rumors about the intentions of the French in writing: "Ali-Oukaci

wrote and said everywhere, that there is no pity or generosity to
be expected from the French, that the retributions and conditions imposed on those who surrendered were excessive, and
that it was better to die [fighting] than to surrender [to the
French]."[50] Even though initially written, this rumor circulated
orally, and the writing was only an auxiliary to its propagation.

Rumors are not always false information. They are a form of
knowledge, in the sense that they are interpretations of events
and experiences, and they tend to dictate or guide actions. In
times of war, rumors contain information that expresses an
identity with a political position. Rumors are not neutral. Guha
believes that rumors are "a *universal* and *necessary* carrier of insurgency in any pre-industrial, pre-literate society."[51] This Euro-
centric view suggests that Europe, because of its industry, has
knowledge (correct, precise, and informed), and others have rumors (false, incorrect, and misinformed). Rumors are found in
preindustrial societies as well as in industrial ones. In both situations, they take an oral form as well as a written form.[52]

Thus, colonial texts about the uprising paid special attention
to rumors, seeing them as extremely dangerous and as a force
behind the actions of the insurgents. But the word *rumor* is not
neutral; it is dismissive. It contains a judgment that categorizes
other people's news as false. In the context at hand, it is a colonial term. In Arabic, the term for *rumor* is *isha'a*, but this seems
to be a translation of the French term. The term is from *sha'a*
(propagate, to divulge). But it does have a nuanced meaning of
"it is known, but it is not true." There is also a *sha'a al-khabar*
(who propagates the narrative or the news), which may or may
not be a "true" narrative (depending on the recognition of the
receiver). In fact, rumors are always someone else's narratives,
never our own. Still, much rumor is established as truth and
never suspected as such.

Rumor was not the only form of narrative that proliferated
during the uprising. Letters were circulated. In the archives and
in colonial secondary sources, astonishing numbers of local letters were sent by notables to each other and to the high officers

of colonial administrators. These letters state the reasons for the uprising, show the alliances and enmities between notables and tribes, and reveal a local system of knowledge specific to the time period. One letter is believed to be a declaration of war and is thus systematically cited by colonial sources as the beginning of the revolt. It is written by Mokrani. His letter, addressed to General Augeraud, is itself an event:

> Thank you for the excellent things you said to me. I thank you for the goodness you have shown me. I will remember it fondly. However, I have only one response: I have given Marshal MacMahon my resignation, and he accepted it. If I have continued to serve France, it is because it was at war with Prussia and I did not want to worsen its difficult situation. Today, peace is concluded and I want to enjoy my freedom. You know this, for I have said it to you [before]: I cannot accept being the agent of a civil government that accuses me of partisanship and has already designated my successor. We will see later whether they were right to act this way or whether it was I who was wrong. My servants have been arrested in Setif and in Aumale, and everywhere they claim that I have rebelled. Why? Because they want my condemnation. So this is it! With these people I will exchange nothing but gunpowder, and I will wait. I write to Mr. Olivier to say that I refuse my tenure as of February and that he should watch out. For I am ready to fight him.[53]

This letter shows that Mokrani is well informed about colonial politics and is part of it—an actor who contests it first discursively and then violently when the discourse has failed. He is not satisfied with the establishment of the civilian regime. He expresses his deep frustration, even anger, against colonial policy. But there is the unsaid in this letter. This letter can be understood only in relation to the larger context of colonial politics. Even before the 1870 French defeat to the Prussians, the rise of the settlers as a cogent political force was uncontested. The settlers were opposed to the politics of the Arab Bureau, which defended a colonial policy of coexistence (albeit a colonial one) and for that reason was seen as pro-Arab. The settlers championed the politics of colonization—of settlement, which required more expropriation of native lands. Mokrani's letter shows that he was happy with the Arab Bureau but ready to fight the civilian regime.

The letter of Boumezrag, who succeeded his brother Mokrani, does not contradict the above letter but mentions the reasons for the uprising and propels another leader to join the fight. In this letter, the settler again seems to be the enemy:

> You are aware of the weakness of the Christian State [*al-dawlah al-nasrâniyah*] and the dissolution that was inflicted on it by God. You know that its army and its soldiers lost much ammunition and that the settler is now with no strength or willingness for war.[54]

All of these local letters contain explanations that differ from those offered by the colonial administration. The uprising is described as a *jihâd*. The term, in this context, describes a fight against the Christian state to reestablish the doctrine *(madhhab)* of Allah and his Prophet. Colonial interpretation states the local reason, only to refute it. Thus, in the letters exchanged by the leaders, they discuss other reasons. Boumezrag, the brother and successor of Mokrani, wrote to other notables—including Mohammed ben Chennane, Saad ben Hamida, Ben Belkhir, and other "Muslim brothers." The letters remind them that "Islam is your religion. We know your previous promises." The goal is given: "We should return to God with willingness and fervent ardor."[55] While this is presented as the goal, the circumstances are noted as convenient—"the great weakness of the French government" and "the absence of soldiers and military troops; there is only the civilian" who is not "a fervent [fighter] in combat." Thus, "If you are with us, if you are our sons, you should join our camp, reach our hand in the name of the holy war."[56]

Yet the local letters are part of colonial knowledge and are trapped in their colonial interpretations. Colonial authors always comment on the letters as expressing "fanaticism" and as the work of leaders who were inventing excuses to serve their personal cause. These colonial historians seem to believe that "fanaticism" (the exhortation of the masses using religion) was used for merely personal reasons by some leaders.[57] Thus, from the outset of his comprehensive and authoritative book, Rinn determines the mindset of his reader:

> The insurrection of 1871 in Algeria was neither the revolt of the oppressed against the oppressor, nor the demand of a nationality, nor a religious war, nor a racial war. It was but the political uprising of some unhappy nobles and one skeptic and ambitious man. He was the executive chief, by birth, of a large religious Muslim congregation.[58]

The colonial discourse imposes its own explanation even on local discourse. When local narratives repeatedly mention that the reason for the uprising is the ascension of the settlers to power, colonial discourse considers this to be only an excuse and provides its own explanation. When local narratives speak of the defense of the homeland *(watan)* and of religion *(dîn)*, Rinn dismisses their explanations, stating that the real reason is the personal ambition of a leader "who has war and peace under his thumb."[59] The local discourse of the population may also be echoed in colonial literature about the event. Rinn reports on a peasant who speaks of the abuses of colonial administrators. But Rinn is dismissive because the peasant has no understanding of what is happening: "He always misses the historical truth." ("Why?" one might ask.) Rinn continues: "This [is] a judgment reported by a peasant regarding facts he had witnessed, however, he did not have the ability to understand them." ("What should be done, then?" one may still ask.) Rinn recommends that readers "use circumspection" when considering information provided by natives. How should the circumspection be observed? Rinn provides the solution: "add footnotes, address certain affirmations, and indicate the means by which to reestablish denaturalized facts."[60]

What Rinn suggests and practices is that in the process of interpreting local knowledge, any statement that does not correspond to the colonial interpretation should be converted by forceful linguistic procedures that make it fit. This colonial procedure—also practiced in other types of translation—was believed to be corrective. It is *reason* that turns denaturalized facts (products of local *un*reason, which *experiences* but is unable to *interpret* or *understand*) into natural facts. No matter what, the case against the uprising should be defended discursively.

However, the same colonial discourse that depicts the uprising as a revolt—a work of ambitious, unmodern leaders leading masses of people—betrays the fact that what was happening was not a riot. A defining characteristic of a riot, in the views of Nathalie Zemon Davis, is the presence of the crowd without leaders.[61] In the early modern era in France, according to Davis, a riot is the result of a failure of leadership. The Algerian uprising of 1871 was not a riot precisely because it was an organized reaction against France as a colonial power. Indeed, the French and Arabic texts show the presence of political leaders who are guiding an organized group of men. Their target is colonial occupation. Therefore, the Algerian uprising of 1871—because of its organization, the clarity of its goals, and the people's determination to achieve them—resembles the uprisings that France witnessed at the time of the French Revolution, when peasants allied with the monarchy and resisted the revolution that epitomized the triumph of modernity.[62] Modernity had to fight wars at home and abroad to become modernity at large.

THE VIOLENCE OF NARRATIVES

Even colonial texts clearly show the challenge that the population posed to the colonial order. Again, colonialism has never reigned supreme. It has paid a high price for its presence (even though the local population paid a higher one). Its gigantic machinery of governance was always obstructed—sometimes even made obsolete and forced to change—by local reactions. Those reactions consisted of armed struggle but also used forms of knowledge (historical narratives, tales and stories, poems and letters) to produce local knowledge about the French. The French were made the object of a local discourse. They were categorized and turned into discursive objects to be circulated among the local population. Power was not symmetrical, but there was not the colonial power on the one hand (with absolute force and sophisticated intelligence) and, on the other hand, the natives (submissive, subjugated, powerless, deprived of their will and their initiative, or endowed with an irrational will as ineffective as it was disastrous). If anything, colonial knowledge is the product of these interactions between two peoples with similar wills but different and unequal power—the French colonial machine and the local population.

This unequal power relation is first expressed in the colonial appropriation of the event. Colonial administration constructed, named, defined, and even translated the entire experience into its language. Even local rumors and Arabic texts written by local leaders were incorporated into the general meaning of the event and conserved as such in colonial archives. The colonial power consisted first in naming the event: "it is a revolt, and it is a revolt of Mokrani" (despite the fact that Mokrani lived through only three of the twelve months of the uprising). *Révolte* (in the nineteenth-century French dictionary *Lettré*) means *"soulèvement contre l'autorité établie"* (uprising against the established authority). The name given to the event itself is *révolte*. It is an uprising—not an action against a colonial enterprise with no authority at all but rather a process, a movement, a happening against order. The word *revolt* consecrates the authority of colonial power (as opposed to a system of brute and illegitimate occupation), and quelling revolt is the natural action of established order against a movement that seeks to upset that order.

The numerous uprisings that French colonialism had known in Algeria from the time of its landing in Algiers in 1830 to the time of the uprising of 1871 (and even beyond) show that colonialism had no authority in the eyes of the population. It was contested from beginning to end. It was imposed on the population, also by brute force, but not accepted. Therefore, to describe and better understand local resistance to colonialism, one needs to avoid colonial naming.

One does not need to be a "native" to be shocked by the violence of colonial narratives. Narratives of violence can also become the violence of narratives. This is when the colonial author imposes colonial reason on local reason, thus subjugating the event in the way that the military machine seeks to subjugate the people. The colonial author tends to describe coldly—sometimes even jubilantly—the acts of violence inflicted against the local population. This coldness sharply contrasts with the passionate condemnation of local acts of violence, and the jubilation contrasts with the feelings of sadness and grief that appear in descriptive narratives of violence inflicted on the settlers or the French army. Consider, for instance, this simple description of a killing: "Around the village, solitude seemed complete. We only saw a miserable *indigène,* who, surprised ransacking in the middle of ruins, was executed."[63]

This description conveys the image of a stray animal in the midst of ruins, most likely searching for something to eat. The narrative coldly describes the arbitrary execution. The narrative is indifferent to the criminality of the executioners in a way that makes it complicit with the execution. It is also indifferent to the executed native in a way that makes it a violent narrative in and of itself. The violence displayed here is twofold: one is described, which is the colonial criminal execution of a miserable native; the other is the descriptive narrative itself, which does not mourn the executed native and does not denounce the executioner. Consider, on the other hand, narratives about the violence inflicted by local people on the settlers and colonial soldiers. Not only are those Europeans humanized, but their actions are described as heroic, especially when their actions produce local victims—the more the merrier:

> Settlers and soldiers fight bravely, defending the field foot by foot, and kill a great number of rebels. But they cannot stand any longer against these masses that keep renewing themselves and increasing [in number] at each moment.[64]

Alone, the native is portrayed as a miserable animal, lacking human individuality. His death, consequently, does not warrant sadness. When natives are in groups, they are described as a herd—without individuality. They do not decrease in numbers. The death of some does not affect the entity, as far as the colonial observer is concerned. Dead, they are only "corpses"; captured alive, they are burdens to be disposed of:

> The field is all covered with corpses, the prisoners have become burdensome, two dozen people were arrested, weapons in hand. They were executed by the firemen, who refused to stay and guard them while the fight was going on nearby.[65]

But what if the native is the author of a magnanimous act that is carried out for the benefit of the French? In the colonial discourse, this is a contradiction and does not happen. Whatever magnanimity is showed by the natives, colonial perception is there to translate it into colonial language. The colonial French term *indigène* is a category charged with meanings of savagery and primitivism and thus implying a lack of rights. Consider this instance, when settlers are saved by a group of natives:

> Of 23 Europeans who were here, 12 were killed while defending themselves; 11 succeeded in running away and finally escaped, thanks to the more or less disinterested protection of some natives whom they met at the wood, [only] meters away from the place of aggression.[66]

The protection is noted not as a good act but rather as a "more or less disinterested" one—meaning not entirely disinterested. It is interested to a degree, but in what? The colonial narrative does not say. But the act is interpreted as dictated by motives that are not clear; lack of clarity is suspicious. Mistrust is one of the invariant themes in colonial thinking about others. The native should not be trusted. He is never innocent even when he appears magnanimous. Consider also this instance, when the colonial narrative states that a group of *indigènes* are "innocent," meaning they were not part of the uprising. They brought the *gooms* (native soldiers) provisions and left. On their way back, they were arrested by a militia of settlers, who immediately set up a tribunal for their judgment. They were declared guilty by a unanimous vote. ("Guilty of what?" one might ask.) The primary sources—the letter sent by the lieutenant-colonel and the process-verbal—do not say what the natives were guilty of. In the absence of any charge in the reports, one can only conclude that in times of uprising a native is not innocent.[67] Thus, they were executed, and Rinn describes the execution with typical indifference:

> A line of execution was ordered. A good number of militia refused to take part in it. Volunteers were requested, and they were in sufficient number to undertake the sinister task. For in this detachment there were men who belonged to the "walking army"; they were incorporated a bit randomly. The miserable indigenous [men] were tied two by two. They collapsed when shot by these ferocious [volunteers], who finished killing them by beating them with big sticks.[68]

Three months after the beginning of the uprising, Mokrani was accidentally shot dead. Considering that the uprising was believed to be the result of his personal ambitions, one would expect his death to be its end. But the uprising went on without showing any signs of waning. How to explain it? Colonial discourse finds epistemic solutions within its own contradiction. The leader who launched the uprising was the only one who could stop it. That was why it went on after his death. Indeed, Rinn writes:

> This death [of Mokrani] was an unfortunate accident for us as well as for the rebels. It deprived the insurrection of a leader who

was already disabused and, in fact, disposed to enter dialogues to compromise or to put en end to a hopeless fight.[69]

In any case, the uprising went on unabated, despite the increase in colonial repression. At this point, colonial documents speak of the reaction of the local people, who resort to drastic measures to fight on. These measures were believed to be a specifically Kabyle tactic, used only in exceptional cases and only against outsiders in times of foreign occupation, never in inter-tribal feuds and conflicts. One is tempted to call these the tactics of "suicide fighters." In fact, it involves the selection of young men who will be sent in a mission to fight the enemy without the chance of coming back. It was called *msebleen,* a term that colonial authors thought was a Kabyle one but was not. The *msebeel* (singular) is the one who is sacrificed for the cause. Indeed, the *amseebel,* once chosen, is already a dead man who witnesses the ritual of his funerals before he is sent to the enemy. The *imessbelen* are carefully chosen by members of the *djemaa* (local council). Once selected, they go through a death ceremony. Funeral prayers are organized for them. This means they are dead, and the villagers witness their one death.[70]

Colonial sources mention such practices during the uprising of 1871. The Kabyles prepared 1,600 *amessebel* (Rinn, who reports Robin verbatim, mentions 2,280). The goal was to launch a "suicidal attack" against Fort National to weaken French attacks against the mountains of the Great Kabylia. The plan was set up earlier, in great secrecy, and yet betrayed, Nil Robin reports, by a native who communicated to the French. Unaware, the *imsseblen* were sent to accomplish the task. Robin, a French lieutenant-colonel Marechal participant, describes the attacks:

> The night of 21 to 22 was very calm, unlike what happened in the previous days. No shouting from outside was heard, no rifle shot. When we lit the stoves of the bulwark that we used during the dark nights, a deep silence reigned outside and inside the city. Around 2 a.m., a religious song was heard coming from the hills of Tablabalt. A quarter of an hour later, the same sound was re-

peated at Ourfea, followed by a morn silence that lasted a few minutes. Suddenly, thousands of savage screams rose in the gulches, the shouting started, a rain of bullets passed over the fort. The enemy was under the wall with ladders to climb. At this moment, the fort was wrapped by a cordon of fire. It was the defendants who, in rare cold blood, were shouting randomly [*à bout porant*] at everything that moved while the artillery was shooting in all directions, and chased them to the bottom of gulches, where they backed off. The fire continued for an hour and, by day, the enemy disappeared, leaving behind ladders under the wall. Other ladders were abandoned around and were gathered by the agents of the *makhzen* [local policemen] and brought to the Arab Bureau. Long files, following the road to Algiers, were carried by the dead and the wounded. The enemy had suffered enormous loss. We counted one dead *sphahis* [a native soldier in the French army], nine wounded, among them was an officer.[71]

One can see how episodes of the uprising were written in total consistency with the colonial ideology. On the other side, there is darkness, savagery, and animality portrayed as geographically low (beneath the wall) and posing imminent danger. It is the world of the native. On this side (high), there is fire, which spreads light on the inside and bullets of defense into the outside, where danger lies. The two spaces are thus diametrically opposed in the colonial discourse—civilization versus barbarism. The result is the victory of the first against the second, as the "enemy had suffered enormous loss" while the French had suffered none—for the *spahis* is an *"indigène."* Even among the nine wounded, only one is French.

In her well-known essay on violence, Hannah Arendt writes that "violence appears as a last resort to keep the power structure intact against individual challengers."[72] But there is another way to look at this: violence is also the last resort for undermining and even destroying the power structure. Colonialism did not only engage in violence; it *was* violence. It was modern power expanded and fully exerted elsewhere. Yet its expansion was always justified. Colonialism did not think of itself as violence but rather as a humanitarian enterprise that brought civilization and peace to others, even if the means to achieve this was war. For colonialism, violence was a price worth paying for progress. Rinn reports numerous horrific episodes of violence against the people—dispossessions, executions, imprisonments, and exiles that shocked even him at times. Yet he calmly writes: "French colonization and civilization came out triumphant from this battle that representatives of another age waged against modern law. Despite the terrible crushing of the revolt, the *indigènes* too benefit from this victory."[73]

Twenty years later, Alfred Rambaud applauded the outcome of the repression of the uprising and considered it a victory that gave birth to a "democratic society." He writes:

> The old patriarchal, aristocratic, theocratic society has gradually been replaced by a democratic society that will soon take consciousness of all that it has similar or in common with us. In 1871, French domination was proven to be strong enough for the Muslims to despair of destroying. [Now] it has to show that it is also just enough so that the firm will of keeping it for and against all may emerge.[74]

Physical force, with its brutality and its ruthlessness, at times reminded the colonials, such as Rinn and Rambaud, that the work of and for "civilization" was not civil and required inhumane and bloody practices. But there was a solution for this. The solution was to remind oneself of the narrative that makes progress redeem violence. For the anthropologist-historian, this violence is modernity in action.

THE POLITICAL USE OF EVENTS

Once the 1871 Algerian uprising was repressed and the French political colonial order was reestablished, this important event needed more explanation. The primary discourse made sense of the actions of the colonized people for the colonial society. Once the uprising was narrated with a beginning and an end, the question asked by colonial administrators and settlers was, "Why and how did this happen?" Surprise was an important part of the uprising, and an important part of this surprise was the fact that the local inhabitants were considered friendly and close to the French by race, origin, culture, and even religion. Why, then, did the Kabyles "revolt"? In their attempt to explain why and how the uprising broke out, colonial scholars were faced with a great riddle that caused a serious crisis in the colonial body of knowledge. Observing habits, customs, beliefs, and world views and translating written knowledge no longer seemed to be sufficient to know the natives. Colonial scholars attempted to find answers: "They are similar to us and we bring them civilization to become fully part of us. Why then do they hate us?" The answer was clear but unconvincing: "They hate us because they hate Christians." But in the colonial discourse of the period before 1871, the Kabyles were Muslim converts and were historically Christian. The colonial discourse of the period before 1871 shows European Berbers who were close to the French even in an indifference to religion and were so established in a Christian heritage that Islam could not touch them. With this in mind, the explanation that the uprising was motivated by the Kabyles' hatred for Christians is not convincing.

It usually takes time to solve riddles and paradoxes in systems of perception. As time passes and more narratives are developed about an event, we seem to know about it, even though it would seem that the closer one is to the event, the more one should know about it. How can such scarcity at the bottom and proliferation at the top be explained? Arthur Danto once explained that what he calls a *narrative sentence* is made of two events—an explicit event (which the narrative refers to and attempts to communicate) and an implicit event (which makes the first one possible).[75] But we could go beyond the positivism of Danto and maintain that the implicit event (and correlatively the explicit one) is ever-changing in space as well as in time—and so is the narrative. The multiplicity of the implicit events (that is, the series of events produced across time) increases the meaning of the first narrative event. At the beginning when the 1871 events were happening, the meaning was somehow restricted to a specific goal—how to make sense of a local uprising by a people who are supposed to adhere to the colonizers' civilizing works because of their history with Europe.

After meaning was made despite ambiguities and contradictions and an official version of what happened was finally articulated, this version itself had to be defended (by making more copies of it) and challenged by other versions that disputed earlier interpretations of what happened. A narrative of an uprising is marked by a political position that is made by selecting and omitting semantic elements. A narrative of an uprising includes the silence and absence of other narratives, especially those of competitors—for no narrative reigns supreme, even the most dominant one.

Narratives of violence are pieces of colonial historiography but also weapons used in the colonial conflicts that divided colonial society. They express the unequal power relationships between colonizers and colonized and the conflicting political positions among various groups within colonial society itself. Those who initially constructed the events (such as Robin and Rinn) were mainly soldiers who participated in the repression of the uprising. They had the authority of eyewitnesses and a monopoly over knowledge. As officers of the Arab Bureau, they ruled the country directly and indirectly for decades. Because of their status, they were responsible for repressing the uprising, accounting for it, and submitting reports about it.

The first consequence of the uprising was the disturbance of colonial knowledge. In the colonial discourse, the Berbers should not revolt because they were originally European and had cultural, historical, and kinship ties to Europe. How could they now be revolting? After an interpretation has been proven wrong by the people it represents, one cannot immediately invent an epistemological solution. Instead, one first looks at one's old stock of information. The French went back to theirs: the inhabitants of Algeria were not Arabs and Berbers but rather they were Muslims. A year after the end of the uprising, Ernest

Waterbled, an army officer, wrote, "The Muslims obey and accept, like an expiation of their sins, this sacrilious domination of infidels, but this domination is odious to them."[76]

The Kabyles are no longer artificially Muslim or historically Christian: they are fully Muslim. As if the description of the Kabyles as Muslim was not enough, Waterbled makes them Arab: "Arabs cannot understand our good intentions, the feelings of justice and humanity that guide us. Indifferent to our advances, disdainful of our generosity, they remain always hostile to us and consider our benevolence a weakness inherent to our race."[77] A year after the end of the uprising, the explanatory contradiction persists. It does so more bluntly in the report of the National Assembly of 1871, which, on one hand, repeats the older discourse on the Kabyle:

> The Kabyles or the Berbers, descendants of the Christians and old owners of the soil, take refuge in the mountainous regions that make it easy for them to defend their independence; more sedentary than Arabs, they practice agriculture and even industry. They are grouped in small tribes that are organized in almost a democratic manner, for power is effective and revocable. They themselves are grouped in confederations. They offer a populated area that is almost as rich as one of the regions of France.[78]

On the other hand, it describes the uprising as the work of Arabs:

> What is worth noting from the outset of this report is that a long and cruel experience ought to teach us that all our sacrifices of men and money could not assure our domination over Arabs. They are subject to it, but they do not accept it.[79]

Of the numerous writings about the event, one claims anteriority to the event and deploys a strategy based on a narrative device that can be summed up as "we knew it all along." In this type of narrative, the event is supposed to have been known either because of historical precedents or because of visible signs that supposedly announced it. Sometimes, two tactics are deployed: "we knew it," and "it was clear that this was happening." An example of such a narrative is a brochure published by the end of 1871 and entitled *The Truth about Algeria*,[80] which Ducrot, a senator and a former general of the Arab Bureau, claimed to have written it in 1868.

The brochure begins by narrating the history of North Africa from ancient times to the present. This history seems to be one of continual struggle and disaster for the colonial forces, Roman and Turk. For Ducrot, the uprising of 1871 is not new because the population has always revolted. But this is not the ultimate message he wants to convey to his readers. The officers of the Arab Bureau were blamed for the uprising because of their lenient policies toward the natives, but Ducrot is saying that this is not the fault of the Arab Bureau. In his opinion, the country and its people have always been "unwelcoming to strangers." The people are rebellious, he asserts, and their land is of "mediocre fertility." What should be done? At a time when the civilian regime was in charge in Algeria and the Arab Bureau still held responsibility for the uprising, even a former officer of the Arab Bureau would not openly ask for its reinstitution. Yet Ducrot wanted to give credibility to the institution and regain trust in its role. For him, the Arab Bureau was an institution with a colonial vision of Algeria. It undoubtedly believed in colonization but wanted to ensure its success by balancing the settlers' desire for more land and the rights of conquest and the local people's need to keep their land. Ducrot, who speaks from within the discursive tradition of the Arab Bureau (whose authorities he quotes liberally), preaches what seems to be a new solution: colonization should be achieved through the cooperation of the Kabyles, a population of European origin. But this is the old policy of the Arab Bureau. Ducrot defends both:

> It is the military administration that in the midst of numberless difficulties, founded, created, and organized the centers of the European populations and put at the disposal of the settlers, often too inexperienced, the knowledge of the officers [of the Arab Bureau], the arms of its soldiers, and the varied sources of its

storages. Everywhere, the isolated colony has found the material and moral support of the military authority.[81]

Ducrot also addresses the issues of the uprising:

During the last years of the empire, our colony has never been so calm and never has our power been so firm. . . . Algeria has become a French territory, and it was with real national spirit that the sons of the Berbers marched against the men of the North [meaning the Prussians during the 1870 war], our enemies.[82]

But how should one explain the uprising of the Kabyles against the French? The answer is simple, in the opinion of Ducrot. They did not want the civilian regime. In the same footnote, he writes, "Mokrani, officer of the *legion d'honneur, bachagha de la Medjana,* whose family had always been an ally of France, gave his resignation, writing, 'I do not want to obey the civilian government.'"[83] But there was another reason, according to Ducrot, which added "fire to everything":

The Decree Crémieux, by which the Jews were granted French citizenship, was a cause of the uprising. "What?" the indigenes said, "the Jews do not pay taxes, do not know the smell of gunpowder [meaning they do not engage in combats], [yet] they become equal to the sons of the French, and we, who give all our gold and our Beylich [a region administered by a bey, who was a Turkish governor], we are treated like losers.[84]"

Ducrot repeats and defends the argument of the Arab Bureau. According to him, Algeria was well governed, became French, and enjoyed calm and tranquility, and its Berber population was integrated into France to such an extent that it was part of the French army against Prussia. This considerable work was interrupted by the dismissal of the Arab Bureau and the establishment of the civilian regime. This is why the Kabyles revolted. Nonetheless, Ducrot repeats the idea about the rebellious nature of the Kabyles.

This brochure by Ducrot was part of an intense and even virulent debate over the 1871 uprising that followed its repression.

But here again, the discourse of the Arab Bureau, as articulated by Ducrot, was repeated and defended with vigor, despite the uncontested reign of the civilian regimes.

Immediately after the publication of the brochure, Edouard Ducos, a former high administrator for the civilian labor in Algeria, wrote a quick response in a brochure titled *Algeria*.[85] Ducos attacks Ducrot's brochure and its foundational text, the letter that Napoleon III wrote after his three-day visit to Algeria in 1865. Ducos attacks the two main points of the brochure. The population resisted previous occupations because those used force to rule—the same method preached by Ducrot. French occupation is something else because it is a work of civilization, not exploitation. He maintains that French ideas, customs, justice, and humanity are not the same as those of the Romans or the Phoenicians. Thus it is not force as much as ideals supported by force that will achieve the work of civilization, which he equates—as is the norm in colonial literature—with colonization. But is this worth France's efforts? For Ducrot, the land is too arid to deserve any sacrifice. For Ducos, the land of Algeria is similar to that of southern France; it had been known since the time of Sallustre (whom he quotes) for its fertility. Hence, the hope that Algeria—what he calls the France of *outre mer* (overseas)—will help restore the French economy after the disasters of the 1870 war with Prussia. The main point that one gets from the Ducos brochure is that the event was caused by the Arab Bureau, for it did not happen in the areas under civilian control where there is assimilation and prosperity. The solution seems to be clear: the civilian regime is able to carry out the work of colonization, and the Arab Bureau should stay out of it.

In an article on the definition of *event*, Louis Mink maintains that events are "descriptions," that is narrative, and thus "they are not raw material out of which narratives are constructed; rather an event is an abstraction from a narrative."[86] In 1871, the narratives (taken to be the event) were changing constantly, depending on political contexts. Further, one event becomes another, meaning new narratives were added to old ones, and thus transformed the original ones. An important narrative that became part and parcel of the narratives of 1871 was the Frenchification of the Jews by the Decree Crémieux. This combination of two narratives (or two events) resulted into a discourse that the officers of the Arab Bureau used against the civilian regime. The narrative of the uprising became a narrative of native anger, a specific anger caused by the Frenchification of the Jews, thus it was a matter of internal native politics, triggered by reckless politics of civilian authorities. In a meeting with Captain Olivier, Mokrani allegedly said the following:

> I beg you to come and find me because I cannot come to you, the merchants will assassinate me in town, and you will be unable to protect me, for you have no authority. I sent my resignation as a *bachaga*. I no longer want to serve France and even though I don't want to revolt against you, one day I will take on arms if my resignation is refused. Because for me such a refusal would be a death sentence, and they will not have my head. How do you want me to serve your government? I don't want to accept your republic because, since it was proclaimed, I have witnessed horrible things. You see what, Captain Olivier? You are a high commander, and they sent a chief to command the troops at the Bordj. They [thus] offend you, and as if it were not enough to take away your military command, they also sent a civilian commissioner to watch your administrative acts. I used to listen to your advice. To whom shall I listen now? To you, to the commander, or to the civilian commissionaire? For God's sake, I no longer understand. They insulted your generals, toward whom we showed submission and respect. They replaced them with merchants and Jews, and we cannot accept this. For my part, I will never accept it, and this is why I am proffering my resignation. I don't know if I will see you before long. Be well, peace be with you, and may God protect you.[87]

The question whether the Jews were the cause of the uprising was repeated by the officers of the Arab Bureau and used to defend themselves against the accusations of the civilian regimes.

This is despite the fact that the above quote refers to a group of people that both Jews and merchants were part of—civilians. The importance of this cause was such that a tribunal was set up in Algeria to discuss the allegation and examine whether the Decree Crémieux of 1870, by which all Jews of Algeria became automatically French, was the cause of the uprising. Crémieux himself was summoned and interrogated in court. His testimony included the following: "In the religious views of the Muslims, the Jews and the Christians are the object of the same disdain. Why would they care about the French status [granted to the Jews]? They want to remain who they are."[88]

Crémieux displays here the familiar but at the time relatively new colonial dichotomy of Muslims versus Jews and Christians. While the dichotomy of Christians versus Muslims was old, only Crémieux put Jews with Christians. This might have been the earliest attempt to rethink the dichotomy of East versus West, whose variant was Muslims versus Christians. For the settlers, the Jews were indigenous. In racial theories of the time, the Jews were part of the East and were impossible to integrate into Europe. Yet with Crémieux, a legal and epistemological break was introduced. The dichotomy of Orient versus Occident changed. The Jews moved from the first to the second. This move was not responsible for the uprising. In the minds of the Muslims, Jews were on the other side of the dichotomy.

Louis Forest wrote a book entitled *The Naturalization of the Algerian Jews and the Insurrection of 1871.*[89] As Crémieux did, he makes the Jews French before the naturalization. It is a small group of 38,000, he says, who, unlike the Muslims, did not numerically threaten the French. In addition, they have successfully assimilated: "They show a vivid taste for French education. They filled up our schools, primarily colleges and high schools, and they excel."[90]

The Jews also participated in the work of conquest by providing interpreters and soldiers who gave their lives to France, he continues. With great conviction, he adds: "The Israelites have assimilated with the French in almost everything, and the Muslim is, at best, able to assimilate. The Israelite is a Frenchman almost accomplished; the Muslim is a Frenchman who has barely begun."[91]

Such assimilation was not only cultural, according to Forest, but also legal. The Jews were granted citizenship in 1865. If one thinks that the Decree Crémieux was the direct or indirect cause, it was issued. The uprising happened in 1870, where there was no Jewish presence. But for Forest, before 1871 there were revolts, and after 1871 there were also revolts. It is thus impossible that the Decree Crémieux was a cause for the uprising. Who is then responsible for the uprising? For Forest too, it is the Arab Bureau. He writes:

> The officers of the Arab Bureau are imbued for the most part by the purely military spirit. They certainly had more sympathy for the *djouad* [local notables], men of the sword, the great lords of the *burnous,* than for their compatriots, whom they treat as merchants.[92]

Having heard about the defeat of France by Prussia, he continues, and been informed of French civilian discords, the "Arabs" believed that France was destroyed. The responsibility of the Arab Bureau was that they encouraged the insurrection.

The event thus becomes the means by which colonial society is now divided. It also becomes a thermometer of patriotism. The officers of the Arab Bureau joined the camp of the enemy. They were considered "blind and sold out," wrote Albert Lavigne, a high officer and convert to the civilian cause.[93] They had come to be seen as a hindrance to colonization and thus to civilization and freedom. Lavigne argues:

> Do you want to know now why every year 500,000 Europeans emigrate to the United States and why in forty years we have been unable to attract more than 230,000 emigrants, [only] 135,000 of whom are French? It is because in America they find what they look for: freedom. You don't know [what it means] and you cannot, or you do not want to give it.[94]

Lavigne here refers to the freedom to colonize, to take the land, and to settle Europeans in it. Lavigne, then, maintains that there are only two solutions for Algeria:

> Either that the government will entirely dissipate the Arab race by massacring them or pushing them out to the desert, beyond the high plateaus of the Tell. . . . or it will need to assimilate the Arab race to our political life. In this case, it needs to purely and simply annex Algeria to France.[95]

Because of the Algerian uprising, French colonial society was more divided than it ever had been. The uprising brought local divisions to the surface, both on the level of discourse and on a practical level. The event had become a discourse involving numerous ideological conflicts in the colonizer and colonized, and it remained the primary political discourse of Algeria for many years.

Twenty years later, in 1891, when Rinn published his comprehensive book on the uprising, there were still contradictions in his narrative. The people involved in the uprising were rarely called Arab, but their name was Arabized. The word *Qbaïls* (the Arabized name of the Kabyle) means "tribes," which suggests that the most characteristic aspect of the Arab was tribalism and its primitivism, disorder, and anarchy, which Europe had long left behind for the nation-state. The rebels in Rinn's narratives are referred to often as "the enemy." They were no longer distant relatives of Europeans. But despite the explanations that were given at the moment and twenty years later, the fact that the Berbers opposed French rule in a serious uprising was still an unsolved enigma. By the turn of the twentieth century, contradictions within colonial knowledge cried out for explanations. New knowledge soon emerged in a context of a significant colonial transformation.

NOTES

1. Later, when the colonized people were exposed to colonial knowledge, they too became caught in colonial webs of significance de-

spite their agency. On this specific point, see Abdelmajid Hannoum, "Notes on the (Post)colonial in the Maghreb," *Critique of Anthropology* 29, no. 3 (2009): 324–344 .

2. Frantz Fanon, *The Wretched of the Earth* (New York: Grove Press, 1963), 48.

3. Paul Ricoeur, *La mémoire, l'histoire, oubli* (Paris: Seuil, 2000), 210.

4. Michel de Certeau, "L'opération historiographique," *L'écriture de l'histoire* (Paris: Gallimard, 1975), 63.

5. Ricoeur, *La mémoire, l'histoire, oubli, 213.*

6. Paul Ricoeur, *Temps et récit* (Paris: Seuil, 1983), 1: 247.

7. Ricoeur, *Histoire, mémoire et oublie, 201;* see also a review by Abdelmajid Hannoum, "Paul Ricoeur on Memory," *Theory, Culture, and Society* (2005): 128.

8. *Le Monde,* March 10, 2004.

9. Krystztof Pomian, "Les archives," in Pierre Nora, eds., *Lieux de mémoire* (Paris: Gallimard, 1992), 162.

10. Roland Barthes, *Mythologies* (New York: Hill and Wang, 1972).

11. Auguste Ducrot, *La vérité sur l'Algérie* (Paris: E. Dentu, 1871), 31.

12. Paul Ricoeur, "Evénement et sens," *L'événement en perspective* (Paris: EHESS, 1991), 41.

13. Ranajit Guha, "The Prose of Counter-Insurgency," *Subaltern Studies* (Oxford: Oxford University Press, 1988), 47.

14. François Hartog, *Régimes d'historicité* (Paris: Seuil, 2003); Reinhart Koselleck, *Future Pasts* (Cambridge: MIT Press, 1986), 27–28; see also, Abdelmajid Hannoum, "What Is an Order of Time?" *History and Theory* 47, no. 3 (October 2008): 458–471.

15. Hartog, *Régimes d'historicité.*

16. This was the Algerian war for liberation. It was referred to by the French as the events of Algeria, until 2005, when the French government called it a war.

17. Michael Taussig, "Culture of Terror-Space of Death: Roger Casement's Putumayo Report and the Explanation of Torture," *Comparative Studies in Society and History* 26, no. 3 (1984): 467–497.

18. Such as the narrative of Eric Wolf who wrote about the 1871 Kabyle uprising in his 1973 book *Peasant Wars of the Twentieth Century,* he called it a peasant revolt. Eric Wolf, *Peasant Wars of the Twentieth Century* (New York: Harper Colophon, 1973), 219.

19. Archives, Carton H

20. Archives, Carton H 375.
21. Archives, Carton H 375.
22. Achives, Carton H 375.
23. Karl Marx, *The Eighteenth Brumaire of Louis Bonaparte* (New York: International Publishers, 1935).
24. Archives, Carton H 375.
25. Archives, Carton H 375.
26. *L'Echo d'Oran,* "Nouvelle de l'insurrection," Tuesday, September 26, 1871.
27. "Nouvelle de l'insurrection" in *Le Courrier de Mostaganem,* "Nouvelle de l'insurrection," Saturday, October 14, 1871.
28. Corneille Trumelet, *Histoire de l'insurrection des Ouled Sidi Cheikh de 1864 à 1880* (Algiers: Jourdan, 1880).
29. Rapport du Lieutenant Colonel Trumelet. Commandant de la subdivision sur les combats et expéditions qui eurent lieu pendant l'année 1871, Carton H375.
30. Ibid.
31. Ibid.
32. Archives, Carton H 193.
33. Archives, Carton H 375.
34. Archives, Carton H 191.
35. Asad, *Genealogies of Religion.*
36. Louis Rinn, *Histoire de l'insurrection de 1871 en Algérie* (Algiers: Jourdan, 1891), 278.
37. Ibid.
38. Ranajit Guha, *Elementary Aspects of Peasant Insurgency in Colonial India* (Durham: Duke University Press, 1999), 251; Ann Stoler, "In Cold Blood: Hierarchies of Credibility and the Politics of Colonial Narratives," *Representations* (Winter 1992): 151–189; Julia Clancy-Smith, *Rebel and Saint* (Berkeley: University of California Press, 1994), 99–104.
39. Tamotsu Shibutani, *Improvised News: A Sociological Study of Rumor* (Indianapolis: Bobbs-Merrill, 1965), 17.
40. Ibid., 13.
41. I owe this remark to Deborah Kapchan.
42. See Gananath Obeysekere in his discussion of the European narrative on Captain Cook, in *European Mythmaking in the Pacific: the Apotheosis of Captain Cook* (Princeton: Princeton University Press, 1992, 1996).

43. Clancy-Smith, *Rebel and Saint.*
44. Obyesekere, *European Mythmaking,* 175. Obeyesekere discussed examples from the Pacific and several others from Sri Lanka (171–176).
45. On the Rahmaniya see Julia Clancy Smith, Rebel and Saint, 57–59 and passim.
46. See examples in Julia Clancy-Smith, *Rebel and Saint,* 99–104.
47. Rinn, *Histoire de l'insurrection de 1871 en Algérie,* 421.
48. Yaha Bou Aziz, *Thawrat 1871: Dawr al Muqrani wa al Haddad* (Algiers: Al-Sharika al Wataniya, 1978).
49. Rinn, *Histoire de l'insurrection de 1871 en Algérie,* 202.
50. Ibid., 436.
51. Guha, "The Prose of Counter-Insurgency."
52. Jean-Noel Kapferer, *Rumeurs: le plus view media du monde* (Paris: Seuil, 1987), English translation, *Rumors: Uses, Interpretations, and Images* (New Brunswick: Rutgers University Press, 1990).
53. Rinn, *Histoire de l'insurrection de 1871,* 153.
54. Archives, Carton H.
55. Bou Aziz., *Thawrat 1871: Dawr al Muqrani wa al Haddad,* 123.
56. Rinn, *Histoire de l'insurrection de 1871 en Alterie,* 175–176.
57. Alfred Rambaud, "L'insurrection algérienne de 1871," *Nouvelle Revue* (October 1–15, 1891): 34.
58. Rinn, *Histoire de l'insurrection de 1871 en Algérie,* 1.
59. Rambaud, "L'insurrection algerienne de 1871," 34.
60. Rinn, "Deux documents indigènes sur l'histoire de l'insurrection," *Revue Africaine* (1891): 22.
61. See Nathalie Zemon Davis, "The Rites of Violence," *Society and Culture in Early Modern France* (Stanford: Stanford University Press, 1975), 152–187.
62. Arno Mayor, *The Furies: Violence and Terror in the French and Russian Revolutions* (Princeton: Princeton University Press, 2000), esp. chapter 9, "Peasant War in France: The Vendee," 323–370.
63. Rinn, *Histoire de l'insurrection de 1871 et Algerie,* 311.
64. Ibid.
65. Ibid.
66. Ibid., 325.
67. Not only in the time of uprising, but in any time of colonial rule, which is also always a rule of uncertainty. This is what Fanon noted: "Confronted with a world ruled by the settler, the native is

always presumed guilty. But the native's guilt is never a guilt which he accepts; it is rather a kind of curse, a sort of sword of Damocles, for, in his innermost spirit, the native admits no accusation." Fanon, *Wretched of the Earth*, 42.

68. Ibid., 335.
69. Ibid., 354.
70. Nil Robin, *"Les imessebelen," Revue Africaine* 108 (November 1874): 401–412.
71. Ibid., 410–411.
72. Hanah Arendt, *On Violence* (New York: Harvest Books, 1969), 47.
73. Rinn, *Histoire de l'insurrection de 1871 en Algeries*, 1.
74. Rambaud, "L'insurrection algérienne de 1871," 50.
75. Arthur Danto, "Narrative Sentences," *Narration and Knowledge* (New York: Columbia University Press, 1986).
76. Waterbled, "L'insurrection Kabyle," 625.
77. Ibid.
78. *Rapport fait au nom de la commission d'enquête sur les actes du gouvernement de la défense nationale* (Versailles: Imprimeurs de l'Assemblee Nationale, 1872), 6.
79. Ibid., 11.
80. Ducrot, *La vérité sur l'Algérie*.
81. Ibid., 48.
82. Ibid.
83. Ibid.
84. Ibid., 49.
85. E. Ducos, *L'Algérie: quelques mots de réponse à la brochure, La vérité sur l'Algérie par le général Ducrot* (Paris: E. Dentu, 1871).
86. Louis Mink, *Historical Understanding* (Ithaca: Cornell University Press, 1987), 201. But does he mean to say "an abstraction from a narrative?" since the abstraction is meaning and since the meaning and narrative form are one and the same, why not say: "an event is a narrative?" This is the idea that comes up from reading Mink. And one can conclude that events have only a narrative existence. For more on the concept of event, see footnote 3 in chapter 5.
87. Francine Ducheron, *Bordj-bou-Arreridj pendant l'insurrection de 1871 en Algérie* (Paris: Plon, 1873).
88. Cited in Louis Forest, *La naturalisation des Juifs algériens et*

l'insurrection de 1871 (Paris: Société française d'imprimerie, 1897), 36.

89. Ibid.
90. Ibid., 9–10.
91. Ibid., 13.
92. Ibid., 51.
93. Albert Lavigne, *Le régime du sabre* (Paris: Lacroix, 1871), 6. This was a common civilian charge against the officers of the Arab Bureau. They sold out to the local notables because they enjoy partaking in local activities, horse races, and festivities. They are "blind" for they are soldiers inexperienced in politics.
94. Ibid., 11.
95. Ibid., 7.

FOUR

The Historiographic State

I employed the word state: it is obvious what is meant—some pack of blond beasts of prey, a conqueror and master race which, organized for war and with the ability to organize, unhesitatingly lays its terrible claws upon a populace perhaps tremendously superior in numbers but still formless and nomad. . . . their work is an instinctive creation and imposition of forms; they are the most involuntary, unconscious artists there are— wherever they appear something new soon arises, a ruling structure that lives, in which parts and functions are delimited and coordinated, in which nothing whatever finds a place that has not first been assigned a "meaning" in relation to the whole.

—Nietzsche

Before 1870, ethnography was the predominant mode of knowledge in French colonial Algeria, for it was the instrument by and through which tribes could be located politically, geographically, and socially. The ethnography of the Arab Bureau had a dual function. On the one hand, it organized the colonial conditions, so that the colony's administrators could rule in a way that was less onerous and more profitable for France. On the other hand, it represented the Berbers as primitive Europeans who were opposed—like Christian Europeans—to the Arabs by race, religion, and culture. The scholarship of the Arab Bureau was noticeably statistical and concerned with taking inventories and categorizing native people and their land to order what an unknown world for the French. The colonial state was investigating its new territory, intending to open it up to colonization. Yet by 1871, following the crushed Kabyle uprising, there was a sense that ethnographic knowledge had failed. It had depicted the Kabyles as close allies, when in fact they were no different from the Arabs in their hostility to the French. The crushing of the Kabyle uprising in Algeria, the fall of France's Second Empire to Prussia, and the rise of a civilian regime in Algeria allowed the champions of the "Frenchification" of Algeria to state their case.

This had an important effect on colonial forms of knowledge. From 1871 on, historiography became the dominant mode of colonial knowledge, and historical knowledge became the means of integrating new territories into the colonial state. I would call such a state a *historiographic* state is different from the ethnographic state of colonial India (as described by Nicholas Dirks), which relied heavily on recording habits, customs, religions, and so forth to form and validate itself.[1] Given the difficulties associated with the concept of the state,[2] I analyze not the nature or the legitimacy of the French colonial state but rather its practices—how certain institutions of the state became more operative at certain times, what kind of practices they undertook, and with what types of effects. What I intend to do is see how a state operates through its institutions to create the "what to be" and the "what to do." Michel Foucault called this operation *governmentality* and drew attention to the artistic, creative, and productive practices that the state used to make subjects be and behave.[3] The goal is to explore the shift to the institutional production of historical knowledge in Algeria to Frenchify the country—to transform a land that was foreign and "theirs," into a land that is "ours" and French.

This chapter focuses on the period immediately following the full formation of the settler society and after the political decision to make Algeria French. The cultural policies put in place were to make Algeria French in the minds of French people, both in Algeria and in France. My argument, different from the one put forth by David Prochaska[4], is that to have a settler society—to have the settlers settle and not move—Algeria needed to be French, and this truth needed to be articulated and made persuasive and credible by state institutions. Only then would settlers be convinced that they were settling in their own land. In other words, only once Algeria was made culturally French could the French settle there.

Even though the body of historiographic work analyzed here is gigantic—found in enormous volumes and numerous articles—it is authored by no more than a handful of men. The terms *author* and *authoring* here are meant in a sense used by Foucault. The author is not only the producer of his or her own work but also the author of "the possibility and the rule of the formation of other texts."[5] Foucault gives the examples of Freud and Marx, but such authors can be found in any discursive formation. This concept focuses the analysis on discontinuities and on ruptures rather than on continuities and repetitions. Such discontinuities interest me here, not only because they are rarer than continuities but especially because they generate continuities. A novel interpretation becomes common through repetition,[6] and repetition reinforces the *verdiction* of ideas, meaning it creates more mechanisms by which a text becomes more authoritative and thus more "true." My analysis is focused on a handful of authors—Ibn Khaldûn (whom I have called Ibn Khaldûn the Orientalist), Ernest Mercier, Stéphane Gsell, and Emile Felix Gautier.

EVENTS AND KNOWLEDGE

How do events affect knowledge? What is an event? Paul Ricoeur defines *event* as something that happens, creates a disturbance in our mode of knowledge, and cries for an explanation. To eliminate the disturbance, a meaning must be assigned.[7] The event of 1871, which was a serious uprising of local people against the French governing presence in Algeria, became the marker of a new phase of politics, policies, and epistemology (understood as an ideology of knowledge). Before 1871, Algeria was inhabited by Arabs and Berbers, whose European reality was constructed mostly—but not exclusively—by French ethnographic work. After 1871, France needed to rethink the opposition and the historical place of French settlers in Algeria. Algeria was Arab and Berber, and both were in subordination to a more politically important actor—the settlers. After 1871, what became most important for French civilian administrators, scholars, and their sympathizers was history as the means of generating a new understanding of what Algeria was and how its inhabitants were created. The settlers needed to find themselves in a past that seemed only Arab and Berber. The settlers championed a policy of colonization—that is, of settling the land—so there was a need to make this settlement legitimate and real.

After the great uprising of 1871, the civilian regime in Algeria soon developed its own institutions and produced its own intellectual authorities to make a narrative that explained, ordered, and accounted for the colonial situation. Within one of the most respected, and productive of these institutions, the Société Archéologique de Constantine, Ibn Khaldûn's *Histoire des Berbères* (translated by William de Slane) was transformed into another colonial narrative to produce a version that was supposedly more accurate about Algeria and its inhabitants. Founded in 1853, the Society was initially under military control but gradually came to be dominated by civilians. Its motto was *Collecter, préserver, décrire* (gather, preserve, describe). But what the society intended to gather, preserve, and describe were the Roman characteristics of North Africa.[8] It intended to make North Africa a historically European territory. The institutional organ of this society was devoted more to historical writings than to ethnographic research and more to the Roman antiquity of Africa than to its Arab or Turkish past. Almost 80 percent of the society's writings were devoted to antiquity, especially Roman, and only 10 percent were devoted to the so-called indigenous population.[9]

The other important institution of historical research, the

Société Historique Algérienne, was founded for similar reasons soon afterward in 1857. It was established by a group of scholars who were aware of the importance of historical research for a country that had been considered politically part of France. Its publication was the *Journal Revue Africaine*. Among the founders were Adrian Berbrugger, who was elected journal president, and William de Slane, the translator of Ibn Khaldûn, who was vice president. Officers of the army also offered their support and were listed as founders. So historical institutions—societies, journals, and publishing houses—were present, active, and at times prolific in an area dominated by officers of the Arab Bureau. But their political importance was overshadowed by what was deemed most important for the young colonial enterprise—ethnography (then termed *military science*). It was practiced mainly, if not exclusively, within the institution of the Arab Bureau.

After 1871, the year when the civilian regime was set up, historical institutions (the Société Archéologique de Constantine and the *Journal Revue Africaine*) gained wider significance and became principally civilian institutions. The *Revue Africaine* had an editorial committee of civilian scholars, and its cultural production was historiographic. Its president, Ernest Mercier (mayor of Constantine), was a historian and the author of a major history of North Africa that was the first and most significant narrative produced by the civilian regime. The cultural production of the Société Archéologique de Constantine was focused mostly on the past, but the Société Historique Algérienne was devoted entirely to historical matters. "The epistemological murk" that emerged during and immediately after the uprising of the Kabyles in 1871 was soon followed by an epistemological, historical clarity.

Having a civilian regime in Algeria meant that the land (not the people) was an extension of France. Whereas the military regime saw Algeria as a colony (with a population to control, rule, and protect against the avidity of the settlers), if necessary, against itself—the civilian regime saw Algeria as a French *terri-*

tory (not a colony, not an Arab kingdom, but an inseparable part of France). The conquest gave France this right, but so did history. This is why history became—with the establishment of the civilian regime—an important means by which France could build a colonial state. As Bernard Cohn put it, "states" depend a great deal on "determining, codifying, controlling, and representing the past."[10] Indeed, the goals of the civilian colonial administration were to know the region, to inventory and categorize its peoples and its goods, and also to dismiss the idea (so resented and resisted) of Algeria as an Arab kingdom and replace it with the idea of a Roman (and therefore European and specifically French) North Africa. The point was to let the past show that Algeria and by extension North Africa were neither Arab nor foreign to France. The region was part of French history and territory precisely because it was Roman.

In this chapter, I analyze the historiography of the civilian regimes to see how this view of history was articulated to conform to the needs of the new colonial policy. I argue that historiography (such as the transformation of the text of Ibn Khaldûn as translated by de Slane) was the strongest means by which Algeria was integrated into France. Yet integration was meant for the land, not the people. The policy of integrating Algeria into France also employed techniques of exclusion. Although the land was made French, its local populations were set apart by their different relations to France—the Arab in relation to enmity and the Berber in relation to subordination and inferiority.

In the following section, I examine the work of one of the major architects of French colonial policy in and knowledge of Algeria. Ernest Mercier was undoubtedly the region's most prolific and authoritative author post–1871. The historiographic hegemony of his work makes him one of the most quoted authors in colonial scholarship and beyond. Mercier also was a well-regarded politician and scholar. As previously stated, he was a mayor of one of the most important cities of colonial Algeria—Constantine. In addition to three volumes on the history of

North Africa, Mercier was a regular contributor to both the *Revue Africaine* and the Société Archéologique de Constantine.

COUNTERHISTORY: THE NARRATIVE OF THE RACE STRUGGLE

The primary author, especially in the period that followed the fall of the military regime in Algeria, had an Arab name—Ibn Khaldûn—but the text attributed to him is a French colonial one. *The History of the Berbers,* translated by William de Slane in 1852, gained substantial significance from the beginning of the civilian regime.[11] The text itself was translated by a French-Irish man who was a student of the well-known master (for some, the founder) of Orientalism, Silvestre de Sacy. But because translation is fundamentally an act of conversion or even appropriation,[12] the French text, *L'histoire des Berbères,* is regulated by colonial categories not found in the Arabic text, *Kitab al-ʿibar.*[13] While the Arabic text seems too full of events and has too little structure to suit the reading habits of modern French historians and anthropologists, the French text has a distinct narrative structure. In fact, it recounts the history of the Maghreb as a racial struggle between the domineering Arab and the dominated Berber.

Ibn Khaldûn's original narrative is a typically Muslim one. The events, at least metaphorically, happen under the eyes of God. The deeds recounted are of a people referred to as *al barbar* (the Berber). Events unfold in a way that may seem chaotic but no less so than in "real" life. The narrative is not regulated by Aristotelian divisions: there is no beginning, no plot, and no ending. Greimas's actantial model does not apply: there is no hero, no villain, no opponents, no helpers, no sender, and no receiver. There is not a quest or the object of a quest.[14]

The Muslim historiographic discourse, in its Khaldûnian form, celebrates the glory of the Berbers and is inscribed in a narrative tradition called *mafâkhir* (glory).[15] It glorifies a suzerain (in a line of suzerain that were Berber from the ninth to four-teenth centuries, which is Ibn Khaldûn's time). In this narrative tradition, the leader is identified with his people, and the glor-ification is ultimately his. In the Arabic text written by Ibn Khal-dûn, there is no opposition between Arabs and Berbers; there is no divided race. Rather, there are Berber tribes, Arab tribes, Arabized Berbers, and Berberized Arabs—all of whom share Arab origin.

One can see why a colonial historian would be lost—and not only in the Arabic text. The translation offers some guidance, di-viding Arabs and Berbers by race and setting up their opposition in these terms—and taking the form of a European narrative. Foucault notices a change in form, function, and meaning in Eu-ropean historical discourse in the early to late nineteenth cen-tury:

> The history, the counterhistory that was born with the narrative of the struggle of races, will speak from the side of shadow, from this shadow. It will be the discourse of those who have no glory, or those who lost it and who found themselves now, for a time per-haps, but doubtless for awhile, in obscurity and in silence.[16]

This narrative had to be transformed and introduced in the colonial discourse. De Slane initiated such a transformation with his translation. Ernest Mercier needed to transform this translated text, which still bore the name of Ibn Khaldûn, into the discourse of the colonial state that established itself after 1871.

Mercier's project is to transform Ibn Khaldûn's work into a European narrative that introduces race. About Ibn Khaldûn, he writes,

> His work is a veritable and precious mine of information. Unfor-tunately, the historian was subject to the literary influence of his time, albeit to a lesser degree than his contemporaries, and his book is deficient in organization. By giving separately the annals of each tribe, he takes away from his history the unity of views

and wholeness that are indispensable. Thus he breaks the chronological chain and is forced to fall into tedious repetitions.[17]

Mercier restructured de Slane's French translation and transformed it into a book whose title clearly reveals the agenda of the author: *L'histoire de l'établissement des Arabes dans l'Afrique Septentrionale: d'après les auteurs arabes et notamment Ibn Khaldûn* (a title taken from the translation). Mercier's book intended to show

> the transformation of North Africa from a Berber land into an Arab land. To this end, one has to specify the period or the periods when the Arab entered the country, follow the trajectory of the invaders, indicate the resistance they faced from the indigenous populations, and finally recognize particularly how they have been grouped, how they compare in proportion with the indigenous population, and what places they occupy today.[18]

Mercier divides his book into three narratives, each occupying an entire volume—the history of northern Africa in ancient times, the story of the Arab conquest of the seventh century, and the Arab invasion of the eleventh century. From the outset, Mercier speaks about northern Africa as the stage for racial conflicts between the Phoenicians and the Romans, with the Berbers caught in the middle. Orientalist categories of Semites versus Aryans and East versus West are also articulated (the Phoenicians, Semites from the Orient, dispute the region with the Romans). The Berbers, in Mercier's view, are a mixture of races, including Iberian and Celtic races, a "blond population"[19] (the Kabyles), and the rest are the product of intermarriage with previous Asian immigrants to the area. In Mercier's later work, Berbers themselves are presented as a blond race.

Mercier shows the misfortune of the region and the misery of its people as different conquerors chase one another. The Romans chased the Phoenicians and were chased by the Vandals, who were ousted by the Byzantines. In the midst of this conflict, the Berbers are not passive, but their role is reduced to that of helpers. They helped the Romans chase the Phoenicians, but they were unable to fight for their own land until the seventh century, when another conqueror arrived, the Arabs:

> Such was the state of Africa in the time when the Arabs erupted. The Berbers, one can see, had almost regained their independence. It was against them that the invaders had to fight. However, the disunion of the indigenous population, the absence of patriotic feelings among these people who were not unified yet, would allow their temporary enslavement to the Muslims of the Orient, who were unified and disciplined by a strong religious idea.[20]

For Mercier, this is the beginning of Arab domination, which is both the theme of his work and its objective. Racial opposition is clearer and more articulate in his narrative than it is in the work of de Slane. The Arab is presented as different from all previous conquerors that succeeded one another in the region. All were colonialists (in Mercier's time, the term was associated with civilization and prosperity), but the Arabs were nomads and destructive and ruthless conquerors who lived on pillage and brigandage. Their inner taste for them was furthered by Islam.[21] Mercier introduces for the first time the theme of nomadism to the colonial narrative. Nomadism is made the defining characteristic of Arabs. Civilization is absent, and disorder and anarchy rule. But in Mercier's narrative, nomadism does not have the meaning it has in the works of Mercier's successors (especially Gautier, whose work I later analyze). Mercier focuses on the race struggle and the political opposition between Arabs and Berbers.

In Mercier's narrative, the Berber is caught in a tragic conflict, and despite heroic struggles, he ends up being subdued and dominated by the Arabs. The two actors, Arab and Berber, stand in sharp contrast: Arabs are nomadic Muslims who impose their will by conquest, and Berbers were originally Christians and Jews from Europe. The Arabs are motivated primarily by religious ideology, and the Berbers are motivated not by religion but by a primitive form of nationalism.

In this narrative, the Berbers fail to achieve their goal for the same reason as before—their nationalism is not mature. But the Arabs also do not achieve their goal. Although Islam is introduced to North Africa, a series of revolts drives the Arabs out of the country. At this juncture, Mercier concludes that the conquest was "a failure."[22] This history is presented not only in relation to European history but as European history. The French presence in Algeria is justified because the history of North Africa is the history of the Romans, the Vandals, the Greeks, and the Berbers and also the history of Spain and France. Here, Mercier makes the history of Spain and France part of the history of the Arab conquest of the seventh and eighth centuries. The Arabs assaulted not only the Berbers but also the Christians of Spain and France. And the Arabs relied on the Berbers for their invasion of Europe. The history of the Berbers explains the history of Europe, and the Arab invasion of Europe was stopped. It was not because Charles Martel defeated the Arabs in the Battle of Poitiers in 732, as had been commonly believed but, as Mercier argues, because Berber emigration to Spain stopped after numerous revolts against the Arabs in North Africa.[23] The shortage of Berber emigrants to Spain weakened the Muslim presence there, giving the occupation a fatal blow.

In his third narrative, Mercier tackles what he deems to be the most important change to the landscape of the region—the "second Arab invasion," which happened in the eleventh century. At this time, hordes of Arab tribes (the Banu Hilal and the Banu Sulaym) left the deserts of Arabia, wandered into northern Egypt, and plundered the region. Their huge number drastically modified the demography of North Africa. Mercier writes:

> To fight their neighbors or the people of their own race, the Berber sovereigns used the Arabs who were always ready for war. To recompense them for their service or to maintain loyalty, the Berbers granted them the land of the losers. Thus they were engaged in putting down the aborigines, whose independent character made it difficult for them to obey. Thus, the Berber element was crushed, put down, removed for the benefit of the foreigners.[24]

In this part of the book, Mercier argues his case forcefully. Because of the second Arab invasion's success and deep impact on the region, it ended in what Mercier calls Arab settlement in northern Africa. The Arabs were nomadic herders and spread across the region, occupying the best lands. If northern Africa is Arab, it is because it has been occupied. Yet in Mercier's view, the occupiers are still identifiable as nomads who live on the plains, not in the mountains. And occupation is not possession, especially in colonial times, when the heir of Rome (France) returned to where it rightfully belonged.

This significant narrative, provided to the colonial state post–1871, gave a different meaning to Algeria. The short-lived argument of the "Arab Kingdom" of Napoleon III as well as the "Arabophile" policy of the Arab Bureau fell apart and lost whatever sense it might have had before 1871. Mercier's argument, in line with the then-dominant policy of colonial settlement, presents itself as a "scientific" discovery. The perception is simple, but the mechanism of its textual possibilities and the dynamics of colonial power that govern it are complex. The narrative convinces the colonial public that something they were already convinced of—the Frenchness of Algeria—was true. Yet the narrative's contemporary viewpoint refers to a past that the present corroborates. This viewpoint became the official narrative of the colonial state. It was repeated in all textbooks[25] and had the rare power to transform and even convert the previously authoritative narratives of officers of the Arab Bureau, such as Henry Fournel.[26] Until 1929, it was the sole narrative that explained Algerian demographic landscape. The region was now Berber, and the Arabs were simply alien descendants of destructive conquerors. If the Berbers were originally Iberians and Celtics, then the French presence in the region had a double legitimacy. France, as heir of Rome, had a legitimate claim and a historical right to the region. In addition, the settlers were mostly from southern Italy and southern Spain, so the natural conclusion of Mercier's narrative is that the French presence marked the end of Arab domination and a new beginning for

Western civilization in Africa. The origins of the population and the unfolding of history were evidence of the French character of Algeria, and Western civilization was grounded in the region, its claims proven by archeological sites.

ARCHEOLOGY AS A TRACE AND AS A NARRATIVE

French colonial historical discourse at this time was not only a transformation of local Algerian knowledge and a reversal of categories. It was further enriched by European civilizations Greek, Roman, and Christian heritage. Someone like Mercier converted local knowledge into colonial knowledge, but the journal of the Société Archéologique de Constantine brought antiquity into the French discourse on Algeria—and, by extension, North Africa. The most authoritative and most prolific author was Stéphane Gsell. Even though he was a scholar, his work could not have been possible or had the importance it did without the power of the colonial administration which provided the resources (excavations of antique monuments, colonial libraries, institutions and chairs for research, funds, publishing houses, and journals) for the practice and dissemination of knowledge. Archeology with him was revealed to be an important instrument for the colonial enterprise. It provided services that no other form of knowledge could provide. As Michael Dielter put it, "Archeology provides for the popular imagination tangible connections to an identity rooted in the awe-inspiring past. Places and objects can be made into powerfully evocative symbols that serve to authenticate constructed tradition."[27] Because of the important role that archeology plays in the authentication and even creation of national identity in modern nations, it is a tool to be both used and abused,[28] "given that the state is the major owner of the means of production for archeological excavation, and museum displays has been conditioned by national mythologies for identity."[29]

Gsell provides a narrative that solidifies the colonial discourse and changes French understanding of North Africa. In addition to the meaning bestowed on the colony by someone like Mercier (who made Algeria Berber, not Arab), Gsell gives the colony a significance that makes it incontestably Western with historical foundations that are Greek, Roman, and Christian.

Unlike the historical discourse, the archeological narrative was based on what Abu El-Haj has termed in a similar context "facts on the ground." Archeology "reflects and mediates larger sociopolitical interests, its results often harnessed for identifiable political ends."[30] When new sites such as Roman stadiums, Christian churches, and even entire cities were excavated, they became tangible evidence of Algeria's Western past and narratives themselves. Whereas historical discourse consists of making something absent present through the techniques of writing,[31] archeological discourse is in fact a referee that is present, tangible, and concrete. The archeological fact is a material trace, and "in the material trace there is no absence. Everything in it is a positivity and a presence."[32] Therefore, archeology operates in two ways. Similar to historical discourse, archeology makes the past speak and is credible because of reference to the past. Moreover, archeology makes the past bear witness to the present or shows how the past has survived into the present. It creates a system of meaning that requires ruling according to a logic of legitimacy and normalcy.

The work of Gsell, as well as that undertaken by many members of the Société Archéologique de Constantine, consisted of both numerous excavations (undertaken to locate, bring to bear, revive, and present) as well as narratives (describing what was located, brought to bear, revived, and presented). There were objects found, and meanings were ascribed to them. I seek here to examine how Gsell's archeological findings were transformed into a narrative that contributed to making Algeria a part of France that shared its civilization and culture.

Archeological work was done in Algeria years before Gsell wrote his works, and the findings were published systematically in various reviews that include journal of the Société Archéologique de Constantine and the *Revue Africaine*. Gsell synthesized this research, and his monumental work *Histoire ancienne de l'Afrique du Nord* (1914–1930) gave it a forceful and eloquent articulation that assured its longevity.[33]

In 1901, prior to the publication of *Histoire ancienne de l'Afrique du Nord*, Gsell published an interesting book, *Les monuments antiques de l'Algérie*.[34] This synthesizes the tremendous work undertaken by archeologists, including Gsell himself, to unearth sites and monuments from Algerian soil and give them what Gsell calls "interpretation." He endows them with meanings not unrelated to the larger colonial enterprise. This archeological interpretation is consistent with colonial discourse on Algeria in the following way.

Like the narrative of Ernest Mercier, in this book Gsell shows the past presence of the "indigenous" (meaning the Berbers). But they are shown through monuments such as "primitive drawings of animals," graves, caves, and "bracelets and jewelry mostly made of iron, some bronze, and few of them imported from Italy." There are also skeletons buried with jars. From the description of these objects, Gsell suggests a state of "primitiveness" of the "indigenous," a lack of political organization, and a contact with Egyptians reflected in some of the inscriptions. Less numerous are traces of the Phoenicians and the Libyan Phoenicians. Only 106 pages of the book are dedicated to the indigenous (54 pages) and Punic cities (52 pages), while 175 pages are devoted to Roman cities. From the outset, Gsell writes about the Phoenicians, "The traces of their civilization are quite rare in Algeria: their work was almost everywhere covered by that of the Romans."[35]

Indeed, the part of the book devoted to the "traces" of Phoenicians is almost as thin as the part devoted to the indigenous people. The indigenous traces are more significant than the Phoenician (mausoleums and graves), but the indigenous traces are mixed with those of the Phoenicians, so that the identity of the few monuments left are unclear.

What is left of the Romans contrasts sharply with the traces of the Berbers and Phoenicians, both in quantity and majesty. As did Mercier, Gsell reproduces the idea of the civilizing mission of Rome:

> We know what good results the Roman conquest had for this country called today Algeria. It was especially in the second century and the first third of the third century that this region could develop, thanks to the peace that reigned. The old Punic and indigenous cities were transformed and became bigger. Elsewhere, especially at the foot of the Aurès, new cities were founded and became prosperous.[36]

This statement is supported by numerous photos of majestic Roman artifacts that are part of the narrative. One can only imagine the landscape in Algeria at a time when every part of the country was marked by a powerful Roman presence (fortresses, temples, arches, markets, aqueducts, and so forth), which conveyed the uncontested French character of Algeria. The archeological discourse has claim to the past and also is the present itself. It does not re-represent; it presents. It does not argue; it shows. Yet in the narrative, it silences and conceals present traces, geographies, and people more than anything else. In the artifacts, it hides what is visible—houses, cities, towns, all that signifies the life of those who live under occupation. The power of the archeological discourse is such that their absence in literary works is seldom noticed.

Gsell suggests that the traces of Roman majesty would have been even more apparent had the indigenous population—Vandals and Arabs—not destroyed many of them throughout the ages. Yet these memories *(souvenirs)* of the Romans are now rescued by the French, who came "to collect their heritage."[37]

But Gsell was not only interested in objects and traces of the past in the present. He was also interested in the dead and the living, in the language, religion, cultures, and origins of the population of Algeria. His work combines impressive data from various disciplines—anthropology, history, linguistics, and religious studies. Whereas Mercier makes the Arab presence infinitesimal in Algeria, Gsell obliterates it altogether.

The work of archeologists was limited to excavating material objects to show their consistency with the colonial present or to interpreting these objects to make narratives that cancel the effects of conquest and colonial rule. The living tradition of the indigenous culture itself became an archeological site from which, through which, and by which to show the European past continuing into the local present. Even though Gsell forcefully managed to undertake this project in his monumental work, no one completed the project as succinctly and convincingly as did Emile Masqueray in his *La formation des cités chez les populations sédentaires de l'Algérie.*[38]

Masqueray, whose work is in the tradition of the Arab Bureau and who repeats many of the ideas put forth by Adolphe Hanouteau and Aristide Letourneau in their work on the Kabyles, defends what seems to be a new thesis. Now that the Roman character of Algeria had become, with the work of colonial archeologists, a tangible present, Masqueray develops an idea that seems implicit in the work of the colonial archeologist. If the Algerian past is recovered and is now made present, then the present is that same past. If the Roman past is now present, the present is undoubtedly Roman.

Thus, Masqueray makes the Roman past something that was never interrupted. On the contrary, it was always predominant and continued to be so in the time of the French. Africa (Masqueray thinks this is a more Roman and thus more correct name for the region) repeated Roman history even during its brief and superficially "Muslim" or "Arab" episode of the seventh century: Khajism is Donatism, "and the small Aghlabid state of antique Africa . . . greatly resembles Byzantine Africa."[39] The African city provides the strongest evidence of the region's Latin character.

Archeology—through the efforts of many people, the most authoritative of them being Gsell and Masqueray—established in the minds of the French the Roman character of Algeria. Not only was Algeria once an occupied Roman territory and is now back in the hands of those who have a right to it, but the entire region itself is part of a discursive formation inseparable from that developed about the French nation. What has been said by colonial authors about Algeria is nothing more and nothing less than discursive avenues to link the parts of France—the hexagon—with its other piece across the Mediterranean.

THE NATION AND THE IDEOLOGY OF NOMADISM

By the early twentieth century, French colonization in North Aftica extended to Algeria (1830), Tunisia (1881) and Morocco (1912). Its future seemed certain, for its present was unquestionably triumphant. North Africa was henceforth known as French North Africa. In 1920, Emile-Felix Gautier, whose work I discuss here, joyously wrote: "It has been acquired then definitively. France has now a colonial empire in its backyard, only twenty-four hours away from Marseilles."[40]

The formation of this portion of the French empire appeared to be an uncontested success, and it was accompanied by the acquisition of a massive body of knowledge, mostly historiographic. Colonial knowledge—the primary function of which was to give meaning to the still recently conquered colony of Algeria—was not added smoothly, piece by piece, like bricks of a house, to form a valid and canonized work. It was constantly corrected, changed, and transformed to find consistency and coherence. Some authors were ignored, others were marginalized, a few were modified, and fewer still were canonized. What I have described thus far are attempts to acquire knowledge about the colony to give it meaning and significance. Narratives were revised according to the new politics, contexts, and dynamics of colonial society, the changing epistemology of mainland France, and transformed modes of thinking about others and the self.

The period following 1871 was marked by what Foucault calls the "counterhistory"—the introduction of the narrative of race struggle into European discourse. After 1888, as evidenced by an influential lecture about nations that Ernest Renan gave at the Sorbonne, the narrative of race struggle became less operational as the nation narrative emerged. Nationhood became the hallmark of civilization and of Europe. Other people lived in different polities, such as tribalism, which is better, in civilizational terms, than nomadism. Tribalism, which remained ill-defined for the entire colonial and even postcolonial period, connotes savagery and primitiveness but does not exclude a transition to nationhood. Nomadism, on the other hand, is the antithesis of civilization. It refuses progress and destroys civilization and nations. Nationhood is a state of peace and tranquility under the rule of law. Nomadism is permanent war and chaos.

The narrative of race struggle articulated by Mercier and constantly repeated by historians, anthropologists, and literary writers lacked explanatory force by the early twentieth century, when nationhood became equated with Europe, civilization, and modernity. Renan, who previously theorized about the concept of race, wrote his most authoritative piece on the nation. Historical knowledge then had to account for the political, colonial, and epistemological transformations that came with the turn of the twentieth century. The task fell to members of the University of Algiers, a colonial state's institution whose acting president was the governor of Algiers. Within this institution, a novel narrative was written about the Maghreb to better explain its position, especially now that Algeria was no longer the only French possession, in North Africa.

Les siècles obscurs (The Obscure Centuries) by Emile-Félix Gautier was published in 1927, by a notorious Parisian publisher to signal its importance. Its discursive significance lies principally in its transformation of the narrative of race struggle, as articulated by Mercier and Ibn Khaldûn/William de Slane. Because the Arab Ibn Khaldûn functioned as an intellectual authority (creating a paradox in the opposition between "us" and "them," between rationalism and the lack thereof, between science and superstition), Gautier immediately gets Ibn Khaldûn out of the way: "The Orientals are incredibly historically void. It is obviously self-evident. For one cannot be interested in the absolute, the afterlife, and at the same time be interested in the things of the real world."[41] He then adds: "There is an obvious exception. Ibn Khaldûn is a genius, and he left us a history of the Berbers. But he wrote it at the end of the fourteenth century. Plus, even though he is a genius, his mind is Oriental. It does not function like ours."[42]

This colonial judgment is Gautier's way to gain independence from "local knowledge," which was often associated with bias and lack of science. Civilians often accused the Arab Bureau of depending on natives for its information.[43] After Ibn Khaldûn and Muslim historiography are disqualified, Gautier could formulate his nation narrative about the Maghreb. About this he is clear:

> It is sufficient to remember that the Berber in the twentieth century, as in the seventh century, has no idea of a nation. He does not even conceive the Maghreb as a whole toward which he has obligations. He is not more interested in the smaller nation of the Numidians or the country of Zaïan. He does not have any idea of this. The only thing for which the Berber has passion and is ready to sacrifice his life is his clan, his family.[44]

The entire area now known as the Maghreb was defined principally by its lack of nationhood. But this definition does not negate the narrative of race struggle. For Gautier, there are still Berbers and Arabs, and they do not like each other. But the Berber of Gautier is different from the Berber of his predecessors, including the officers of the Arab Bureau. The Berbers of Gautier are exclusively city dwellers, yet with a lifestyle marked by tribalism, not nomadism. As the anthropological discourse entered the narrative of explanation, the Berbers of Gautier are originally Europeans, from specific locations in Europe: "Anthropologists agree that Berbers, in bodily structure and the shape of their skull, are connected with southern Italians and southern Spaniards rather than African and Oriental races."[45]

However, despite the use of the concept of race, the concept of lifestyle and culture becomes a reliable way of explaining differences and thus justifying rules. Berbers and Arabs are fundamentally different because of their lifestyles: one is a city dweller, and the other is a nomad. Berbers are the real inhabitants of the Maghreb, and Arabs are occupiers. Yet there are three phases of migration to the Maghreb. Historians before Gautier note only two. The first was during the seventh century, when Arabs arrived as conqueror. Here is his portrait:

> Having left Mecca and Medina, the Arab did not care a bit to organize his native country. He settled only in the thousand-years-old centers of Oriental civilization—Syria, Mesopotamia, and Egypt. Aside from the religious domain (and even here not much should be expected), he is a predator incapable of creating. He needs something already made, an organization created by others. This animal does not construct his shell; he lives in those of others.[46]

There is also the infamous Arabs of the eleventh century, about whom Mercier also wrote in disparaging terms. Gautier describes them in the following manner: "The Hilal and the Sulaym are pure nomads, the best ever representatives of nomadism. Born enemies of any government and of all civilizations, they are mere agents of pillage and destruction."[47] There is one characteristic that unifies the first conqueror and the second invader—nomadism.

The narrative of race struggle is not absent from this discourse; but it is slightly changed to introduce a "culture struggle." What opposed the Berbers and Arabs in the seventh century is undoubtedly race, but it is also two opposing modes of living—city dwellers and nomads. Gautier maintains that the opposition was not only between outside Arabs and inside Berbers but also among nomadic Berbers and city-dwelling Berbers, a conflict that contributed to the fall of the Maghreb to the Arabs.

Those inside Berbers are nomads. But Gautier maintains that nomadism is the defining character of the Orient and that nomadic Arabs were present in the Maghreb long before the arrival of their conqueror brothers of the seventh century. Gautier describes the intrusion of the nomad in a narrative about two animals—the elephant and the camel. He maintains that an archeological investigation of the area showed that a number of animals had disappeared at a specific time in the history of the region, while others appeared late. The most notable and significant animals were the elephant and the camel. The first disappeared at the end of the Roman empire, and the second appeared around that time. The elephant was an African animal used during wars against the Romans. The camel was typically an Arab animal that was initially introduced to Egypt and then to the Maghreb. Gautier stresses the social meaning of each animal. The Phoenicians ceased to use African elephants in their wars, especially because of their inefficiency when confronted with the Indian elephants used by the Romans. The African elephant flourished abundantly in the fields, according to Greek and Roman authors. As the Phoenicians are defined by their inability to create civilization, the Romans not only create civilization but also introduce it wherever they settle. The disappearance of the elephant from North Africa by the end of the third century is explained by the prosperity of the country. Large areas were colonized and then civilized by Rome, and the inhabitants developed the jungles and the fields where elephants had lived. But what about the appearance of the camel?

The disappearance of the elephant marks the first narrative sequence that one can interpret as the infringement of man on nature. The second narrative sequence is marked by the presence of the camel—the encroachment of people on culture and on civilization. Rome introduced the camel to the Maghreb in the period of its prosperity in the third century. By introducing this animal, Rome signed its death sentence. Camels are high-maintenance animals. They do not migrate alone but with men who are in charge of them. These people characterize the Orient. They are ferocious enemies of the Occident and of civilization in general.

For Gautier, Rome brought prosperity to the region, and the nomad, an intruder, put an end to the work of civilization. Here is the same situation that Mercier portrayed—the reverse of one order (marked by prosperity, well-being, and ultimately civilization) and the implementation of another order (introduced by the nomad and marked by disorder, scarcity, and destruction). But there is a significant difference between Mercier and Gautier. In the narrative of Mercier, the antiheroes (the Arabs) arrive at the end of the Byzantine empire, when the heroes (the Berbers) are close to achieving their national independence. In Gautier's account, Roman rule by the third century had brought prosperity, generated a demographic increase, and led to a change in social well-being that culminated in the arrival of the antihero—the nomad with his camel, his auxiliary of domination. In this second instance, the nomad obstructs the goal of the Roman; in the first, the Arab impedes the progress of the Berber.

The problem of Algeria, which is the same for the Maghreb, is thus not the absence of nationhood or the problem of race struggle. Nationhood is a stage of human development in colonial ideology that may or may not be reached by others. But Europe could help. Race struggle can be overcome by the will for nationhood, as Renan himself told Europeans. The problem that cannot be overcome is the one of nomadism—for nomadism is opposed to nationhood the way barbarism is opposed to civilization. There are nations (one of which is France), and there is nomadism (a defining character of the Orient).

Nomadism is tribalism with a plus. Tribalism was perceived in colonial situations as threatening to the European way of life because of its ability to claim autonomy in a number of ways. Mahmood Mamdani notes that such autonomy was "multifaced" and wrote that "the tribal economy was a source of livelihood, tribal ideology a source of identity and common purpose, and tribal institutions as potential locus of peasant resistance."[48] Nomadism had all of the attributes cited by Mamdani except institutions (or so it was believed), and the nomadic tribe was not "a potential locus of resistance" but rather a war regiment by its nature. Here lies exactly the "plus" of nomadism, which is also a plus in the danger that it represents to

the colonial state. Whereas tribalism can be conquered and subdued and even forced to be "civilized," nomadism cannot. Consider, for instance, Gautier's description of the greatest threat to
Western civilization throughout the history of the Maghreb
since Roman times:

> This man is the nomad—the great nomad, the camel rider,
> grouped in fearful tribes. Each is in itself a sort of a born regiment,
> without preliminary training. Quick, elusive, capable of emerging
> at any moment, unexpected, like a catastrophe of unwatched
> loneliness. A powerful military tool. This great nomad hardened
> by the privations of the desert is by natural consequence ardent, of
> deep desire, thirsty for pleasures. In his terrible poverty, this wild
> animal [*fauve*] pursues inside himself, in a confusing manner, a
> dream of plundering and domination.[49]

The ideology of tribalism is not the same as the ideology of
nomadism. Whereas tribalism can be an alternative to racism
(people can be defined even within a colonial setting in terms of
tribes), nomadism includes tribes yet asserts and reinforces racism. Arabs are nomads, and nomads are Arabs (even if they are
Berbers), and nomadism had proven itself to be fatal for civilization. The narrative of Gautier does not eliminate the narrative of
the race struggle but reinforces it. In doing so, however, it introduces the narrative of the nation and a new struggle—nation
versus nomadism, civilization versus barbarism, our will to live
together versus their will to destroy us, our history versus their
history. Gautier argues that this was the problem of France in
the twentieth century as it was also the problem of Rome before
that. France ought to avoid the fate of Rome. The narrative of
the nomad provided the nation with the element of the "foreign
inside enemy," which is common in all narratives of nationhood.

But the narrative of nomadism also provided the historiographic state with a new and needed division. Algeria and by extension North Africa were no longer divided only into Arabs
and Berbers but also into city dwellers and nomads. This division created further divisions within the local populations and

sets them against each other in racial terms—Arabs versus Berbers versus Arabized Berbers versus Arabs. Tribalism is inherent in all these divisions. In addition, the narrative of nomadism solves a paradox in the race struggle narrative when the Berbers revolted en masse against the French in 1871. In Gautier's narrative, there are Berbers who are not Berbers, but are disguised Arabs, and therefore are hostile against "us." Finally, such a narrative further licensed the appropriation of more land as colonial capitalism made further advances in colonial society.

In 1930, when France celebrated the century of its occupation of Algiers, a group of distinguished colonial scholars, including William Marçais, Stéphane Gsell, and Fernand Braudel, published a book that assessed the state of French knowledge of North Africa. The argument of Gautier was widely shared.[50] The following year, in 1931, Charles-André Julien reproduced most of Gautier's ideas.[51] Braudel, who reviewed the book in *Revue Africaine*, considered a "synthesis" of the existing literature, especially the work of Mercier and Gautier, whose work Braudel applauded in the review as "historical imperialism," along with the "great things that we have done there."[52] By "historical imperialism" Braudel refers to the practice of history that went, with Mercier and Gautier, beyond the hexagon of France's that escorted political and military imperialism. The "great things we have done there" may be simply this magical transformation of the land now called, narrated, and mapped as French Algeria.

Because of the tremendous importance and power bestowed on it, Gautier's text was able to reorder the colony in a way that was revealed to be everlasting. People are now defined differently in terms of race and in terms of their potential (or lack thereof) to constitute a nation. Colonial policies were based on this kind of discourse.[53] In fact, this historiographic text of Gautier became the dominant interpretation that other historians reproduce more or less faithfully. It was also reproduced in colonial textbooks as the official discourse of the state,[54] and appeared in novels and plays. Because the text was of such authority that it survived into the postcolonial period. The entire national historiography of the Maghreb is mostly a response to Gautier, the national discourse of the Maghreb is formulated argumentatively, especially negatively against the colonial discourse.[55]

MAPPING, NUMBERING, AND RENAMING

The French state in colonial Algeria did not use only narratives to substantiate itself as real and legitimate. It also endowed itself with a character that used mapping, numbering, and renaming as substitutes for the objects being represented. These methods are often auxiliaries of modern historiography. Since the Enlightenment, states have used these techniques to substantiate themselves. Thongchai Winichakul writes:

> In terms of most communication theories and common sense, a map is a scientific abstraction of reality. A map merely represents something which already exists objectively "there." In the history I have described, the relationship is reversed. A map anticipated spatial reality, not vice versa. In other words, a map was a model for, rather than a model of, what it purported to represent.[56]

Yet maps have a different semiotic status, for they do not operate with what Emile Benveniste calls "transphrastic" organization. They rely not entirely on language but rather on a special drawing that also aims not at representing the real (like paintings) but on being the real (thus having a status similar to photography). The map is an image of a country, a nation, or a region of the nation. The part also refers to the whole. Maps are thus images. As the photograph is the image of an individual or an object, the map is the image of a territory. Hence, it is powerful as a persuasive device. It is hard to argue with a map, even though maps get contested and can be the object of conflict between rival groups. Maps depend on narratives, without which they cannot be explained. In this sense, maps are devices of modern historiography. They reproduce the narrative visually but depend on the narrative to be intelligible. A map reproduces the narrative with its subject, objects, and their relations—but to understand it, one needs the narrative.

Mercier visualizes the situation of North Africa by providing two maps—one showing the situation in 1050 when the Berbers were close to achieving their national independence and the other showing the fourteenth-century situation after the spread and the establishment of the Arab nomadic tribes who arrived in the eleventh century. In the first map, the Berbers occupy all of North Africa, from Tripolitania (Libya) to the extreme west (Morocco). They occupy the plain, the plateaus, and the high plateaus. Most of the desert is unoccupied, but the Moroccan desert is inhabited by the Berbers of Guedala, Sanhadja, Lemtouna, and Messoufa. The map of the fourteenth century illustrates a discourse based on Ibn Khaldûn. In it, the Arabs occupy all the plateaus, the high plateaus, and the plains. More Berber tribes, especially in Algeria, had moved or been removed to the desert (such as the Houara). Berber nomads also were removed to the desert. As Mercier mentions in his narrative, the Arabs have drastically (and dramatically) changed the demography of North Africa, and whole Berber tribes have disappeared and been replaced by Arabs. Such is the case of the Maghraoua in the southern Grand Atlas, who were replaced by the Doui Mansour.

Yet French colonial historical narrative has not relied only on maps, as important as they are. Numbering is a state strategy of survival and of social control.[57] If the colonial map makes the Berber visually dominant, such domination must correspond to a number. How many Berbers and Arabs have lived in North Africa?

Ernest Carette, the author of one of the most detailed works about tribes in North Africa, gives exact numbers. In his *Recherches sur l'origine et les migrations des principaux tribus de l'Afrique septentrionale et particulièrement de l'Algérie* (1853),[58] an important book for the civilian regime despite the fact that it was written during the military regime, Carette indicates the locations and the population numbers of each Arab tribe. He suggests in numerous synoptic tables that nearly all of the regions of Algeria are inhabited by both Arabs and Berbers. The number of Berbers is always higher than the number of Arabs. Thus, his final estimate of the population of Algeria is 12,790,450 Arabs and 13,900,960 Berbers—an estimate that makes Algeria both Arab and (slightly more) Berber at once. But such numbers do not upset the narrative of Mercier or even Gautier. Given these interpretations, especially of the latter, Carette has simply consolidated the view of Gautier. The number of Arab conquerors is higher, which means that the benefit of land reform—which really means the dispossession of the enemy—will be even greater for colonization. Yet other numbers were also given.

In 1874, in the first years of the civilian regime, statistics on the population of Algeria were given by Louis Leon Cesar Faidherbe, a general in the army and a vice president of the Société d'Anthropologie.[59] North Africa was then believed to be inhabited by a predominantly Berber (that is, European) population. Berbers were said to constitute a little more than 76 percent of the population, and Arabs constituted 15 or 17 percent (at this date, Arabs and Jews were still the Semites of Renan and Gobineau, a degenerate race that was a mixture of white and black). In French colonial ethnography, Algeria was numerically largely Berber and historically European.

Yet the European character of the North African past contradicted the Arabic names of the present. A name is an important part of an identity.[60] As Derek H. Alderman puts it, "naming is a powerful vehicle for promoting identification with the past and locating oneself within wider networks of memory. . . . Naming is a noteworthy cultural practice not only because of its ability to create a sense of continuity over time but also through its capacity for changing and challenging lines of identities."[61] Names may even function as the signifier of the named. Consider the name *France* for France and *England* for England. Algeria was called an Arab kingdom despite its European character in the colonial discourse. It also had an Arabic name, Al-Jazâ'ir (the islands). Its cities had Arabic names. Thus, an entire strategy of naming and renaming was deployed to assert the Frenchness of Algeria. First, the name Algeria itself was invented or rather Frenchified to refer to Al-Jazâ'ir. Then, there was a systematic Frenchification of Arabic names (such as Algiers for Dzâyir, Bougie for Bjaia, and Oran for Wahran). Through colonial usage, those names have become French, and in colonial times, the old names were obliterated. But the Frenchification of local names was deployed conjointly with the invention of new names for old cities, such as Affreville for Khemis Meliana, Geryville for al-Bayadh, Courbet for Zemmouri, and Fort National for Larbaa Nath Irathen. Other French names were intended to wrap local cities with a French history and endow them with colonial memory. For instance, Chlef was named Orleansville in memory of the Duke of Orleans, Skikda was named Philippville, and Sour El Ghozlane was named Aumale. The politics of naming was extended even to small villages. For the colony to be integrated into France, colonial inscriptions (naming) should cover large and small areas. For the colony to become part of the whole, its own parts should refer to memory (such as Orleansville and Philippville), the military heroes of the conquest of the colony (such as Mac Mahon and Aumale), and also to the cultural figures of France—so that the colony will only appear to be the product of politicians and military men. Even small villages were given French names that represent French culture. For instance, the very French name of Victor Hugo was given to the village of Hamadia. The small city of Ain el-Hammam was given the name of the French historian Michelet. The name of the greatest historian of Latin Africa, Stéphane Gsell, was given to the village Hakimia. The village of Baghai was renamed after the philosopher and sociologist Auguste Comte.

In every Algerian city, French names were given to old and new streets, plazas, and big and small corners. Such is the case of street names in colonial Algiers[62] and in colonial Constantine.[63] For example, in the case of Bone, David Prochaska writes:

> The Algerians are virtually absent—only two streets are named after Jewish personages and places. No streets at all are named after Europeans who are not French, that is, Italians or Maltese. Rather, the overwhelming number of streets commemorates the presence of France in Bone, especially the early years of colonization and colonialism. Moreover, street names which refer to Bone's past before 1830 skip over the Arab and Turkish periods entirely to highlight instead the Romans and the world historical figure of St. Augustine. . . . All this mirrors clear-cut French colonial policies in Algeria, namely to resurrect the Romans as imperial progenitors of the French in Africa, to reassert the now defunct Christian past, and to divide Arabs and Berbers in order to rule them both more effectively.[64]

Such names were not only signifiers to locate and relocate but were a crucial part of the politics of the historiographic state. These names were engraved in villages, towns, and cities. They were what they referred to—French cities, towns, and streets. Consequently, they were also inscribed in colonial historiography. To narrate the history of Algeria—either in its remote past, its Arabic past, or its recent past—is to reproduce these French names. All point to the fact that Algeria is now France and France is also Algeria.

Its people are clearly categorized and numbered, and their relations to each other and to France are established. The new part is now part of the whole, a history of the first tells about the second, and vice versa. For the French, whether living in the hexagon or in Algeria, everything—historiography, archeology, city names, and street names—proclaims French Algeria.

NOTES

1. Nicholas Dirks, *Castes of Mind* (Princeton: Princeton University Press, 2001), 43–60.
2. For an idea on such difficulties, see Philip Abraham, "Notes on the

Difficulties of Studying the State," in *Journal of Historical Sociology* (1986): 58–89.

3. Michel Foucault, "Governmentality," in Graham Burchell, Colin Gordon, and Peter Miller, eds., *The Foucault Effect* (Chicago: University of Chicago Press, 1991), 87–104.

4. David Prochaska's, *Making Algeria French* (Cambridge: Cambridge University Press, 1992).

5. Foucault, "Qu'est-ce qu'un auteur?," 804.

6. See Greimas and Courtès, "Véridiction," *Dictionnaire raisonné du language,* 417–418.

7. Ricoeur, "Evénement et sens," 41.

8. See the editorial in *Journal de la Société Archéologique de Constantine* (1853) : 13–20.

9. For a discussion of the journal of the Société Archéologique de Constantine, see James Malarkey, "The Dramatic Structure of Scientific Discovery in Colonial Algeria: A critique of the Journal of the Société Archéologique de Constantine (1853–1876)" in Jean Claude Vatin, ed., *Connaissances du Maghreb* (Paris: CNRS), 137–160.

10. Cohn, *Colonialism and Its Forms of Knowledge: The British in India,* 3.

11. de Slane, *L'histoire des Berbères d'Ibn Khaldûn.*

12. See, for literary translation, Benjamin, "The Task of the Translator," *Illumination;* see also Lawrence Venti, *The Scandal of Translation* (New York: Routledge, 1998). For translation in historiography and in ethnography, which pose different challenges, see Abdelmajid Hannoum, "Translation and the Imaginary," *Anthropology News* (November 2002): 78.

13. Ibn Khaldûn, *Kitâb al-ʿibar was dîwân al mubatadaʿ wa al khabar fî ayyâmi al ʿarab wa al barbar wa man ʿâsarahum min dhawî al sultân al akbar,* 7 vols. (Beirut, Dar al-Kutub al-ʿIlmiya, 1959).

14. See Algirdas Julien Greimas, *Structural Semantics* (Lincoln: University of Nebraska Press, 1983).

15. Shtazmiller, *L'historiographie mérinide: Ibn Khaldun et ses contemporains,* 132.

16. Michel Foucault, *Il faut défendre la société* (Paris: Hautes Etudes, 1997), 63.

17. Ernest Mercier, *L'histoire de l'établissement des Arabes dans l'Afrique septentrionale* (Constantine: Marle, 1875), v–vi.

18. Ibid., ii.
19. Ibid. Also see Ernest Mercier, "Ethnographie de l'Afrique septentrionale: notes sur l'origine du peuple berbère," *Revue Africaine* 15 (1871): 420–433; Ernest Mercier, "La race berbère, véritable population de l'Afrique septentrionale," *Société Archéologique de Constantine* 39 (1905): 23–59.
20. Mercier, *L' histoire de l'établissement*, 40.
21. Ibid.
22. Mercier, "La race berbère: véritable population de l'Afrique septentrionale, 23–59.
23. Ibid. See also Ernest Mercier, "La bataille de Poitiers et les vraies causes de recul de l'invasion arabe," *Revue historique* 7 (1878): 1–13.
24. Mercier, *L'histoire de l'établissement des arabes,* 13.
25. E. Cate, *Petite histoire de l'Algérie* (Algiers: Jourdan, 1889), was designed specifically as a textbook. G. Fure-Biguet, *Histoire de l'Afrique septentrionale sous la domination musulmane* (Paris: Charles-Lavauzelle, 1905), was a vulgarized version of Mercier designed for the larger public, not scholars.
26. Henri Fournel, *Les Berbères: études sur la conquête de l'Afrique par les Arabes* (Paris: Imprimerie Nationale, 1875), which was a revision of his previous *Études sur la conquête de l'Afrique par les Arabes* (Paris: Imprimerie Nationale, 1857). See also, Henri Verne, *La France en Algérie* (Paris: Challamel, 1869).
27. Michael Dielter, "Our Ancestors the Gauls: Archeology, Ethnic nationalism, and the Manipulation of Celtic Identity in Modern Europe," *American Anthropologist* 96, no. 3 (September 1994): 597.
28. See Nadia Abu El-Haj, *Facts on the Ground* (Chicago: Chicago University Press, 2001); Bettina Arnold, "The Past as Propaganda: Totalitarian Archeology in Nazi Germany," *Antiquity* 64 (1990): 464–478.
29. Dielter, "Our Ancestors the Gauls," 597.
30. Abu El-Haj, *Facts on the Ground,* 9.
31. Ricoeur, *La mémoire, l'histoire, l'oublie,* see also Hannoum, "Paul Ricoeur on Memory."
32. Ricoeur, *La mémoire, l'histoire, l'oublie,* 552.
33. Stéphane Gsell, *Histoire ancienne de l'Afrique du Nord* (Paris: Hachette, 1914–1930).

34. Stéphane Gsell, *Les monuments antiques de l'Algerie* (Paris: Thorin, 1901).

35. Ibid., 55.

36. Ibid., 107.

37. Ibid., 108.

38. Emile Masqueray, *La formation des cités chez les populations sédementaries de la Algérie* (Aix-en-Provence: Edsud, 1983).

39. Ibid.

40. Emile-Félix Gautier, *L'Algérie et la métropole* (Paris: Payot, 1920), p. 245.

41. Ibid.

42. Emile-Félix Gautier, "Le cadre géographique de l'histoire en Algérie," *Histoire et historiens de l'Algérie* (Paris: Felix Alcan, 1930), 17–35.

43. Ernest Mercier, *Questions algériennes* (Paris: Challamel, 1883).

44. Ibid.

45. Ernest Gautier, "Native Life in French North Africa," *Geographical Review* 13 (1923): 29.

46. Gautier, *Les siècles obscurs,* 257.

47. Ibid., 388.

48. Mahmood Mamdani, *Citizen and Subject* (Princeton: Princeton University Press, 1996), 91.

49. Gautier, *Les siècles obscurs,* 184.

50. William Marçais, "Comment l'Afrique du Nord a été arabisée," in *Annales de l'Institut d'Etudes Orientales, Algiers* 4 (1938): 1–21.

51. Charles-Andre Julien, *L'histoire de l'Afrique du Nord* (Paris: Payot, 1931).

52. Fernand Braudel, "A propos de 'l'histoire de l'Afrique du Nord de Ch. Andre Julien'" *Revue Africaine* (1933): 37–53.

53. Gautier does so by political treatise in which he uses his authority of a historian. Gautier, *L'Algérie et la Métropole.*

54. To mention just two notorious colonial historians of the Maghreb, see Alfred Bel, *La religion musulmane en Berbérie* (Paris: Paul Geuthner, 1938); Brunschvig, *La Berbérie orientale sous les Hafside.*

55. This is the case of the notorious *L'historie du Maghreb* by Abdallah Laroui (Paris: Maspero, 1973). For a discussion of some aspects of it, see Hannoum, *Colonial Histories, Post-Colonial Memories,* 126–129.

56. Thongchi Winichakul, Thongchai *Siam Mapped: A History of the Geo-Body of a Nation* (Honolulu: University of Hawaii Press, 1994), 133.

57. Appaduri, "Numbers in the Colonial Imagination," *Modernity at Large,* 117.

58. Ernest Carette, *Recherches sur l'origine et les migrations des principaux tribus de l'Afrique septentrionale,* 476. See detailed statistics of each region of Algeria and North Africa at 436–476.

59. Faidherbe, *Instructions sur l'anthropologie de l'Algérie,* 12.

60. Barbara Bodenhorn and Gabriele Von Bruck, *The Anthropology of Names and Naming* (Cambridge: Cambridge University Press, 2006).

61. Derek H. Alderman, "Place, Naming and the Interpretation of Cultural Landscapes," in Brian and Peter Howard, eds. *Ashgate Research Companion to Heritage and Identity* (Burlington: Ashgate Publishing, 2008), 195–214.

62. Zynep Celik, *Urban Forms and Colonial Confrontations* (Berkeley: University of California Press, 1997).

63. Michele Biesse-Eichelbrenner, *Constantine: la conquête et le temps des pionniers* (Honfleur: Marie, 1985).

64. Prochaska, *Making Algeria French,* 213.

FIVE

Coming Round: Transgression, Sacrifice, and the Nation

To save the nation (or to found its state) in confronting a dangerous enemy, it may be necessary to act without being bound by ordinary moral constraints.

—Talal Asad

Colonial culture creates attitudes, visions, and thoughts, and the culture of colonial modernity is generative of events in contemporary Algeria. This book has demonstrated how the culture of modernity was imported from France to Algeria, and how it transformed local cultures. But it continues to operate in the present—shaping it, changing it, remaking it, and marking it by violent events. Events are not only "culture in action" (in the phrasing and thinking of Marshal Sahlins)[1] but are also narratives—cognitive attempts of individuals and groups to account of what is happening (or has happened) using specific cultural categories. The analysis of events cannot properly be undertaken without taking into account individual and group perspectives, which arise within institutions with specific politics, strategies, and contradictions.

To engage in this perspective, I had to apply my analysis to a series of events. Because the Algerian Revolution (1954 to 1962)

171

was a series of events that was marked mainly by the clash of French colonialism and Algerian nationalism, I opted for the present moment, when cultures generated by modernity have clashed and resulted in a continuing series of brutal events (1992 to the present). My goal is to show the continuity of colonial modernity in the present, and the Algerian revolution belongs to the colonial era. Although it is relatively easy to explain events of the Algerian revolution by the dynamics and contradictions of colonial culture, explaining Algeria in the 1990s seems more complicated. It is interesting to see how nationalism in Algeria, once ferociously opposed to colonialism, became closer, in expression and content, to colonial culture. How and under what circumstances the culture of colonial modernity was inherited and constitutes the political present deserve a new investigation. Positing the problem this way is positing the question of nationalism.

In January 1992, the Algerian government canceled parliamentary elections to avert the imminent victory of the Front Islamique du Salut (FIS). From then on, Algeria was world news. An outburst of violence erupted and was interpreted as a civil war between the ruling party—Front de Liberation National (FLN)—and the FIS. Until 1994, FIS attacks were directed against the army and other state employees, and FLN attacks were directed against the militant. For the state, this violence was the preferred means of "eradication," while for the FIS, violence was a means to gain what it was denied by way of the ballot.

In this chapter, I address a series of violent events that defy easy interpretation. They are anonymous, brutal attacks against civilians that were not claimed by any party. Each party accused the other of killing men, women, children, and even babies. The characteristics of these aggressions—their timing, methods, and locations—made them appear to be calculated elements of transgression.

By examining narratives about these violent events of Ramadan (that began on Dec. 31, 1997), I seek an anthropological understanding of the violence that raged across Algeria in the 1990s and that continues today less intensely. Because they are what Dominic LaCapra may call "extreme events"[2] and because these violent acts are highly calculated transgressions against something important in the Algerian imagination—the sacredness of the nation—their analysis will clarify the complex dynamics of nation making and the politics of the sacred in a postcolonial era. The violent events in question are narratives that use specific categories and translate specific visions and understandings.[3] I examine the categories by which the actors attempt to understand and explain—to themselves and others—events that otherwise might seem absurd. Cultural modes of understanding have a history and dynamic all their own, and this history and dynamic can be brought to bear on the events called the Algerian civil war or the Algerian tragedy.

ANONYMOUS TRANSGRESSIONS

Beginning on December 31, 1997, the first night of the holy month of Ramadan, awful news appeared in the pages of Algerian and international newspapers:

> December 31, 1997; 34 people were slaughtered and their bodies mutilated in a village at Ain Boucif, west of Medea, an attack against a train near Saida: 3 wounded. (*Liberté*, January 1, 1998, p. 4)

> January 1, 1998 a bloody night in Relizane, 78 deaths (*Le Matin*, January 2, p. 1)

> The villagers of Ouled Sahrine, Al-Abdel Kheraba, and Ould Mohamed Ben Tayeb were surprised at the time of the break of fasting by a group of terrorists wearing Afghan clothes. Official death toll: 78 deaths and 64 injured including 25 in a serious condition. According to other sources and other local testimonies, the death toll is far higher. (*La Tribune* estimates the toll of the massacre of December 31 to be 350 deaths.)

Scene of barbarism: beheaded bodies, women's breasts cut off, heads of babies fractured against the wall (*Liberté,* p. 1)

A group of young men executed after the *ftour* [breaking of the fast] in Frais Vallon, Algiers, 1 death and 4 wonded (Ibid.)

A family of 4 people slaughtered and 2 girls kidnapped near Bousaada (*La Tribune,* p. 4)

Numerous other attacks followed on that first day of Ramadan in Algeria, and two weeks later, the death toll exceeded 1,000.[4] Responsibility for the deaths was not claimed by anyone. The FLN and FIS accused each other. The atrocious nature of the attacks became a discursive weapon for each party. But these anonymous acts of horror were not unprecedented. Several months earlier, on September 22, 1997, similarly brutal attacks were launched against two villages in the Algiers suburbs of Bentalha and Sidi Mousa.[5] But the massacres of December 31, 1997, happened on the first night of Ramadan and precisely when the day's fast was to be broken—6:15 p.m. The timing, the day, and even the minute were designed to highlight their transgressive nature. They violated—spectacularly—the spaces defined by the sacred. These acts clearly targeted Muslim men, women, and children on a holy night. The month of Ramadan marks the birth of Islam because during this month the Qu'ran was revealed to the Prophet Muhammad. The month of Ramadan created a rupture in time between *jahilya* (the time prior to revelation, which was marked by disbelief, ignorance, and darkness) and the time of Islam (marked by belief, order, and light). This rupture in time also created a rupture in space—between the sacred space touched by revelation *(Dar-al-Islam)* and that not yet touched by Revelation *(Dar al-Harb,* the abode of war). As such, the month of Ramadan is supposed to be a month of piety *(shahr al-ʿiffa),* and additional prohibitions and taboos mark its sacredness. Various behaviors (such as uttering obscenities, curses, and lies or sensual touching) become illicit and risk of negating one's fast. But the month of Ramadan is marked by festivities from sunset to sundown, so it is a time when piety and joy are mixed. In Islamic countries, even those who do not pray and indulge in practices that are considered non-Islamic often observe the fast of Ramadan. Although the violation of other Islamic rules is tolerated by the state and can be overlooked by the community of believers, violating the fast is prohibited and punishable by imprisonment.

Given this context, the massacres of December 31, 1997 were intentional transgressions of the sacred. These multiple acts also constituted what might be called the *limits of transgression* or *extreme transgression*. Transgression is what is prohibited but also possible. It violates the sacred—the collective system of symbols that, in Emile Durkheim's view, bind society or constitute society itself.[6] Transgressing the sacred is an attack against society and its constitutive system of symbols and beliefs.

There are degrees and varieties of transgression. Killing a fellow member of society or publicly eating lunch in Algeria during the month of Ramadan constitute transgressions, but the latter is a light transgression (although still punishable by imprisonment). This happened during Ramadan in 2005, when three men were arrested in the town of Bejaia, some 260 kilometers east of Algiers, for eating lunch in public. The restaurant manager was sentenced to six months in prison, and the patrons were sentenced to three months. The transgressions of these men were scandalous in their communities and underscored the domain of the sacred. Their transgressions had to be punished to uphold the priority and privileged status of the sacred. Light transgressions might be punished differently but still severely. The transgression of the social code of modesty by Moroccan women performers (called *shikha*) is a transgression that results in their rejection by society, as Deborah Kapchan shows in her study.[7]

The transgressions I intend to examine are multiple, deep, and extreme. And my examination takes Michael Taussig's claim seriously when he writes, "Indeed, here we are forcefully made aware that transgression necessarily finds terrible application in the study of the sacred dimensions of violence in our time."[8] The attacks of Ramadan were directed, first, against Muslims; second, against civilians; and third, against women and children. All of these parties are protected by Islamic law. In addition, the acts violated the holy month of Ramadan, when even the slightest verbal obscenity constitutes a transgression of the sacred. Furthermore, the attacks against civilians happened within the territory of a nation-state, which is supposed to guarantee the security of its citizens and all who live within its territory. I say "is supposed to" in light of Max Weber's claim that the state monopolizes the means of violence but exercises its right to violence "within its territory"—that is, against its own citizens[9] (more on this later).

These terrible transgressions against fellow Muslims and fellow citizens during the month of Ramadan—and the competing interpretations by various actors in the public domain—illustrate how the sacred in contemporary Algeria contains heterogeneous elements that are the product of a historical formation involving both colonial and postcolonial experiences. I explore how the sacred (shown especially at the moment of transgression, as noted by Georges Bataille)[10] does not fall neatly under the category of religion or secular. Instead, a set of social and political actors competes to define what is sacred, and this competition involves the fundamental task of establishing the (legitimate) language of definition.

VIOLENCE AND ITS (POST) COLONIAL INTERPRETATIONS

What was happening in Algeria since the emergence of the FIS to political prominence in October 1989 was of great concern to France for a number of reasons. France has never been indifferent to its former colony, to which it is attached by both colonial experiences and a postcolonial condition that finds Algeria still dependent on France culturally, economically, and politically. The FIS used colonial memories in its political strategy. FIS leaders often called for opening up the dossier of colonialism. Further, because of its anticolonial rhetoric and its demand for the end of continued French cultural hegemony, the FIS appeared to restore the wounded dignity of the nation. The French language was a strong symbol of France's continuing domination, and the FIS called for replacing French with English as Algeria's second language after Arabic. The cancellation of elections in Algeria relieved French observers, although in Algeria, the view was that the coup was orchestrated in France by its *harkis* (former Algerian officers who joined the FLN in the late stages of the 1954 to 1962 war for liberation). For Algerian supporters and sympathizers of the FIS, liberation from France still needed to be achieved.

Indeed, in France the FIS was seen as an enemy fundamentalist movement that sought to establish an Iranian-style regime on the doorstep of France. The Islamist critique of colonialism was taken seriously by France. In October 1989, mass protests led to the Arabic being declared an official language in Algeria for the first time. In France, even the so-called antiracism organization SOS Racisme announced that making Arabic the official language of Algeria put the country on the road to "obscurantism."[11] French media and politicians argued that if the FIS were elected and an Islamic state established, France would see a deluge of Algerian immigrants running away from an Islamic state. In public debates, comparisons with 1930s Germany were made, and the slogan "no liberty for those who are against liberty" was maintained in public and private discussions. The FIS was presented as an antidemocratic, populist force that would democratically take power and end democracy. This was clear even in *Le Monde's* extensive coverage. A cartoon shows a veiled woman asking a bearded and mean-looking man: "Whom do you want me to vote for?" *(vous voulez que je vote pour qui?)* His answer: "You vote for *the last time*." (vous votez pour *la dernière fois*).

The specter of violence was there—crystal clear and deadly. Opinions of experts and intellectuals on the risk of a civil war were voiced over and over. Few made the case for democracy.

But civil war seemed less important than the specter of an Islamist state *à la Iraniènne*. Civil war would happen only there in Algeria, "between themselves." An islamist state would affect "us" here in France.

Not having faced its recent colonial past, France had only the older categories inherited from the colonial era to understand what was happening. The events in Algeria were covered in French newspapers as news and generated political and intellectual events. In January 1998, forums, debates, lectures, and public consultations with experts on Algeria took place almost daily. France's intense interest showed its deep interest in its former colony. Algeria is crucially important to the entire Maghreb, and the Maghreb is the backbone of France's political, cultural, and economic interests in North Africa. In some ways, the dependence, while unequal as far as power is concerned, is mutual.

After the horrific, anonymous attacks of January 1998, another forum was held to discuss the events. Pierre Bourdieu, who witnessed the discussions, wrote a short piece denouncing the dominant French understanding of what was happening. He called the forum a gathering of "the cream of the media intelligentsia and the political class, from the fundamentalists, liberals, and the opportunist ecologists to the *passionara* of the eradicators" who described the event without historical justification as the work of "madmen of Islam"[12] "who were enveloped" . . . under the abominated name of Islamicism, the quintessence of all Oriental fanaticism, designed to give racist contempt the impeccable alibi of ethical and secular legitimacy."[13]

Le Monde, the French nation's most respected newspaper, turned to William Zartman, a political scientist from Johns Hopkins University, for explanations, but he wasn't much help. He confessed: "We academics have models of analysis, key categories; in the case of Algeria they do not work."[14]

Benjamin Stora explained the violence by the fact that Algeria celebrates violence with its repeated invocation of the war of independence.[15] He does not seem to consider the recent colonial history a part of explaining major postcolonial events. Stora's views on blocking colonial memories align with those of the French state. For instance, he stated in an interview in the midst of a heated debate about torture in the colonial period that "It is better to try to put an end to these wars of memory than to resuscitate them again and always."[16]

This is clearly a call against memory and whatever memory implies, especially justice, but coming from a historian, it is highly problematic. The craft of history resuscitates memories of the past. As a historian journalist, Stora himself produces memories of the past from within postcolonial French institutions. What Stora objects to is the past produced by the Algerian nation state, not the one produced by France. This stand is revelatory of the logic of postcolonial France toward its former colony. This contradiction in a larger French discourse about Algeria allows Stora to write:

> The perpetuation of the culture of war that rejects the political origins of contemporary nationalism ended up generating dangerous habits among a segment of the young generation. One cannot teach with impunity that the principle of armed struggle is central to the construction of the nation and be surprised at its application in reality.[17]

Violence has been central in the construction of the Algerian nation, but it has been central in the building of many nations, including France itself. The horrific violence and terror of the French revolution did not spare its own architects and makers and has been crucially important in the shaping and defining of modern France. "La Marseillaise," the national hymn of France, evokes "the fight" and "war" and cannot be called a hymn for peace:

> *Aux armes citoyens! Formez vos bataillons!*
> *Marchons, marchons,*
> *Qu'un sang impur abreuve nos sillons.*

> To arms, citizens! Form your battalions!
> Go ahead, Go ahead,
> May impure blood water our fields.

This celebrates violence perpetrated by the state and it is mandatory in French schools. Every year, letters are sent to the president of the French Republic requesting that the national anthem be changed. But the French state is not an exception. Violence is a daily celebration and practice of most nation states. As Arno Mayor once put it, "the founding myth of every society or state romanticizes and celebrates its primal bloodshed."[18] A long social-science tradition—Marx, Weber, Pareto, Gramsci, Althusser, Foucault, and Bourdieu—claims that every modern state celebrates violence and wields it daily (and primarily against its own citizens). Violence defines the nation-state and all states.

Through acts of violence, communities, groups, identities, and nations are born, defined, and redefined. Paul Ricoeur is right when he notes that the existence of human beings, who are by definition political, is guided by violence[19] and also when he notes that there is no community that was not born from an act that we can associate with violence.[20] But violence does not only found groups and identities or guide peoples' actions, it is rooted even in that concept called "liberty" which is central in liberal doctrine, as Richard Tuck argues.[21]

Stora explains the tragedy of Algeria by a phenomenon shared by all modern states—celebration and exercise of violence. What he overlooked is colonialism and the ways it has shaped the present in a way as to drastically change the makeup of Algerian society and implement a colonial culture that generated violent events. Stora is not alone in ignoring the tremendous effects of a country with a very long colonial history and a very recent date of independence.

Scholars from the former colonies who were born or living in France could not liberate themselves from French postcolonial discourse on Algeria. They were selectively asked to give their opinions about the country. Houari Addi argues that the violence results from the actions of the military and that the democratic process should have gone on—that the potential victory of the FIS would have reinforced a democratic culture.[22] For him, the FIS victory would have been a "fecund regression" (to where?), implying that going back would allow the nation to go forward (again one might ask, to where?). Linear timelines, marked by progress, regulate this vision of Algerian politics and the discourse it intends to analyze.

The main type of analysis displayed in the discourse of Addi is the idea that progress is possible only through the idea of democracy. Neither concept is subject to critical analysis. How does one define *progress*? Is progress still a useful concept, whether for analysis or to increase hope? Since democracy can be conceived and even practiced in a variety of ways (and not only in the liberal or neoliberal fashion), one might ask: What kind of democracy is applicable to Algeria, where an Islamic culture (itself the product of modernity) is dominant among the educated and uneducated, the young and old, and women and men?

The issue of violence—why citizens of the same nation kill each other mercilessly—is avoided in the work of political scientists who are solicited by the media. They do not explain that the violence is due to the military dictatorship. The institution of the military itself cries out for explanation: What is its history, its sociology, and its components (the high, low, and lower officers that compose it)? But the military is only one player in Algeria. Numerous other actors who are part of what has been going on since independence are overlooked. They are unrecognized as actors.[23]

Louis Martinez,[24] a French-born Algerian, draws from Charles Tilly (who himself drew from Hannah Arendt and Max Weber) in taking an instrumentalist approach to civil war by asking "What is it for?" For Martinez, war is an instrument by which people make wealth. But Martinez does not ask whether war is also the means by which people *lose* wealth—power, prestige, and life itself. He does not note that war has numerous facets. As Carol Nordstrom puts it, there are no local wars:

> Massive, interlinked and very international war-related industries make war possible in any location in the world. I have seen the same weapon vendors, mercenaries, military advisors, supplies, and military manuals—both illicit and formal—circle the globe.[25]

Wars, especially postcolonial wars, cannot be explained as if they are local events with national actors motivated solely by a desire for material wealth. Because France was repeatedly cited by the actors as integral to the conflict, the Algerian war of the 1990s should also be seen as a French postcolonial war.

Although the people of Algeria—whether sympathizers of the FIS or not—always speak about the involvement of France in the conflict, scholars such as Stora, Martinez, and Addi do not mention it. Those who mention France, such as Bruno Etienne, focus on a displacement of "hatred:"

> But at what moment does an actor—whether manipulated or not—go on to the act of self-destruction? And in what "objective" conditions does an entire society become "mad" to the point of massacring its own children, as was the case in Algeria in the 1990s? . . . Self-hatred was going to be transformed into hate for the Other. All the more so in that Algeria, like most Arab countries, had lost its Other: the native Jew and the foreign (and foreign-tongued) European. Brother was thus alone face-to-face with his different brother, Kabyle, Berber, Arab, Islamist. This then produced a civil war that was to cause more than a hundred thousand deaths.[26]

In fact, the massacres in Algeria were not ethnic. The leaders of the FIS themselves were from different "ethnicities" and regions in the country.[27] Arabs, Kabyles, and Berbers did not kill each other because they were Arabs, Kabyles, and Berbers, as Etienne suggests. The violence was distributed along ideological lines that involved not the state and its supporters, on one hand, and the Islamists and their supporters, on the other. Other political parties, intellectuals, artists, and groups that constituted civil society generally took their places on either side of this division. Second, Etienne takes France out the conflict ("Algeria . . . lost its Other"), whereas in the testimonies of the actors, France supported or even instigated the violence. The reference to colonialism in the form of "the foreign (and foreign-tongued) European" is clear in Etienne's statement. This indirect reference to the 1954 to 1962 Algerian war of liberation reminds readers of a time when members of the FLN engaged in ruthless combat against French colonial rule. It is as if in the 1950s Algerians were motivated solely by their hatred, not by the FLN's long war against a brutal colonization. What Etienne really says in the above statement is: *Having lost the French, whom they hated, the Algerians had no one to hate except themselves, and they did so, wholeheartedly and bloodily. They killed themselves because they had no French to kill.* In other words, if the French were still in Algeria, the Algerians would have killed them instead of killing each other. Etienne makes the French the victims of the violence in absentia. Underlying Etienne's statement is the old dichotomy of Orient versus Occident, Muslim versus Christian. The identities that he refers to—Berber, Kabyle, and Islamist—were created by colonialism and were not natural or even precolonial. Instead (and as chapter 1 demonstrates), they have been formed and politicized in a specific context—the context of colonization. Exploring the genealogy of postcolonial identities reveals that colonial power lingers in both the former colonies and the former metropoles.[28] Antagonistic identities within nation-states can lead to violence and not only in Algeria.[29] I return to this issue shortly.

In the English-speaking world, Hugh Roberts [30] has written essays on what he calls the civil war in Algeria and published them in *Algeria: The Battlefield* (2003). But information is itself a battlefield where human and cognitive casualties are too numerous to count. Roberts reproduces the discourse of the Frenchified intellectuals who were themselves actors in the tragedy. They decide the FIS as "populist" and state that its ideology is not compatible with democracy. This is a common discourse among many Frenchified intellectuals, whose elitism is based on their monopoly on French knowledge (called *modernity*). Because of this, the Algerians are called the "populace," and any ideology that would appeal to them is labeled "populist." Roberts does not seem to have had much contact with those who constitute the majority of the population and who provide the FIS with its legitimacy. He argues that the violence was the result of an Islamist violent wing, the Groupe Islamique Armé (the GIA) that clashed with the state as each aimed to control power. The crucially important issue of why ordinary citizens were sacrificed for the control of power is surprisingly overlooked. The important question of why citizens of the same nation turn in violence against each other is not even asked.

In all these studies of Algerian violence in the 1990s, political scientists and journalists are interested in the *instrumentalist* approach to violence. This approach—whose most articulate theorists are Weber and Arendt—attempts to understand violence as a means to achieve an end. Thus it seeks to comprehend the rationality of violence. It is sociological in character insofar as it examines how violent acts maintain social constructs. In this type of analysis, society contains conflicting ideologies and economic interests that create tensions and political contradictions. The scholar seeks the reason behind these to explain the eruption of violence.

The *cultural* approach is missing in the study of the violence in Algeria because scholars have been mainly political scientists using an instrumentalist approach. Also, in the midst of events, everybody is eager to know who the killers are and why they kill, and the *meaning* of the killings does not seem relevant to most.

Looking into the meanings of the killings requires a cultural, interpretive approach and a historical basis. The interpretative approach explored the meaning of violence. Analysts in this tradition (which is the dominant practice in the anthropology of violence today) focus on a constellation of meanings that are at play in violent confrontations. Meanings are produced, reproduced, consumed, and contested. Since violence involves various actors, such an approach allows researchers to study a violent event from different "subjective positions," as Joshua Cole put it, "and to examine how these subjectivities are themselves made possible and transformed by acts of violence."[31]

Focusing on the meaning of violence allows one to avoid the thorny question central to the instrumentalist approach: who did it and why? The anonymity behind the Algerian violence analyzed in this chapter makes answering this question difficult if not impossible. By side-stepping the question, however, and focusing on the *meaning* of the anonymous violence, I hope to demonstrate how we can make sense of what otherwise appears to be irrational. It is the reactions of the Algerian people and the ways that they have interpreted and accounted for the slaughter that interest me here.

This interpretative approach also allows us to move beyond a simplistic opposition of state versus Islamist groups and secular versus sacred, which continues to structure the commentary and analysis surrounding the events of the 1990s.[32] The interpretative approach includes all elements of Algerian society that are simultaneously the domain and the objects of violence.

To reframe the questions elicited by the acts of violence described earlier, we are no longer interested in merely answering the instrumentalist queries of "Who?" and "Why?" Neither are we concerned with transcribing different, competing meanings to the violence. Instead, we now can ask, "How did the historical formation of Algeria allow and condition the massacres on December 31, 1997, the first night of Ramadan, as well as those of the following month?" Given the anonymity of the killers, we can also ask: "What in the formation of the postindependence state enables such acts of violence to transgress the boundaries of prohibition? What are the elements of the culture of violence? How is the prohibited domain breached in this time and place?"

THE GEOLOGY OF VIOLENT EVENTS

Violence is a crisis and an experience, and an experience is a series of events. Experience creates identity, and identity allows experiences to be shared in an existentialist way.[33] Yet both historians and anthropologists seem to have abandoned the concept of the event as a useful category for social analysis.[34] Still, a few historians and anthropologists have attempted to bring events back to the domain of social analysis.[35] In what he termed the "return of event," Pierre Nora maintains that the historian cannot study an event at the time of its occurrence:

> The historian of the present has no part in the eruption of the volcano, whereas the historian of the past, availing himself of the passage of time, can artificially turn event-volcanoes into the markers with which he stakes out his terrain. Nevertheless, the historian of the present can regain his sovereignty by studying the volcano as a geologist would: his job is to identify the underlying geological strata; to map the internal expositions and secondary detonations, to locate the basic lines of stress and the mechanisms by which lave, after being expelled, is reabsorbed. A crisis, which is a complex of signals a crisis somewhere in the social system. There is a dialectical relation between the two phenomena, namely the dialectic of change, with which the historian of the present is just as ill equipped to deal as is the historian of the past.[36]

This process of a geologist is what I use here to explore the spectacular emergence of violent events, such as those that happened during the month of Ramadan. In every modern society, there are cultural layers and various forms of identities—cultural, political, economic, and sexual. These cultural strata underlie the landscape of an event and make its formulation possible—in the form of narration and names. Because events are narratives that attempt to give meaning to what happened, the system of meaning used—made from a set of cognitive categories—is not the same for all. And these categories are themselves forms of identity.

This section presents what Nora calls the "geological layers" of events—the cultural landscape in which action happens and in which narratives about it take shape, make sense, and circulate. Geological layers constitute what I call the "societal grammar" of a society, meaning the ensemble of various identities that are on display in a given society and that make action possible. I suggest that Algeria's societal grammar is an ensemble of postcolonial, cultural, and political identities at play. Here, I subscribe to the distinction of various forms of identities as suggested by Mahmood Mamdani:

> If we are to understand the specificity of political crises and the possibility of political action, we will need to distinguish political identity from both cultural and market-based identities. Political identities exist in their own right. They are a direct consequence of the history of state formation, and not of market or culture formation. If economic identities are a consequence of the history of development of markets, and cultural identities of the development of communities that share a common language and a meaning, political identities need to be understood as a specific consequence of state formation.[37]

Identities are never fixed or absolute. Within a group or even within one person, multiple identities may exist and overlap. The various forms of identities mentioned by Mamdani can be theoretically separated, but they usually do not develop in isolation, and once developed, they always fluctuate; they change by and in relation to various other identities. Still, Algerians' political, cultural, and economic identities all develop within colonialism, and postcoloniality is the field on which they are playing.

Colonial history is necessary to explain the violent events and transgressions of the postcolonial era. Anthropologists have long identified culture as an important element of conflict and violence.[38] But culture is not only a system of meaning by which actors comprehend the real. *It is a system of meanings that are infused with power by which actors create the real and act by it and on it.* It is a product of the imagination, yet these imaginary categories, products, domains, functions, and programs are historical by definition. Every category has a history of its own, as every category is defined by rules and constraints that regulate its relation to other categories. The history of this history and this relation is necessary to understand the political present. Hence, some anthropologists wish to make anthropology historical.

Even though the modern project of the historiographic state is oriented toward creating the European present, it cannot do so without affecting the past of colonized subjects. And thus, without reproducing a present for them—through narration of the past, which is narration in and for the present—the historiographic state produced a French Algeria with colonial subjects comfortably located within a Frenchified (and thus French) cultural landscape. It also created and sometimes reaffirmed colonial identities for the colonized populations. Thus, we saw that Berbers and Kabyles were located on the European side, however low they were in the racial European hierarchy. Arabs were confirmed in the position previously given them by Orientalist discourse of the metropole—nomadic conquerors in a colonial setting, in sharp opposition to Europe, and in conflict with the Berbers.

The historiographic state was inherited by the nation-state in Algeria. Surely, the transformation from colony to nation happened after changes, alterations, and redefinitions but within a colonial continuity. Postcolonial power—a new set of social and cultural relations mediated mainly, but not exclusively by discourse—emerged in Algeria. Postcolonial power is colonial power in transformation. Through its mutations, this power creates colonial effects in a setting that is, strictly speaking, no longer colonial. The colonial discourse that defined, named, and imposed a set of relations in the context of colonial modernity thus continues to affect the present in ways that are unpredicted, unintentional, but not unexplainable.

Most political identities that survived in postcolonial Algeria found their strongest formulations during the Algerian war for liberation (1954 to 1962). This event occurred at a time when political identities that transcended and even undermined cultural identities were born, formed, and reformed. The Algerian revolution was indeed the cradle of its national identity, and it shaped how the struggles and conflicts, sometimes deadly and often tenacious, over what constitutes Algeria's present and future were seen. This conflict was largely discursive and sought to define through language and by a specific set of categories the Algerian.

Here, the cultural identities of the actors were part of the making of political identities. Not all actors spoke the same language, and not all those who spoke the same language agreed on the meanings their words gave to things. The project in front of them was the same one that the historiographic state intended to make. For both, a modern nation and belonging to a territory—body and soul—were necessary conditions for personal identity. The historiographic state made this project a French one. Only those who shared the French experience were part of it. Those who shared this experience to a lesser degree might have been eligible but were still excluded, as were those who constituted its enemy—the Arabs.

The Algerian nation-state reversed French colonial ideology. It asserted what the colonial negated but without consistently negating what the colonial asserted. The Algerian nation was for all who lived within Algeria—French, Arabs, and Berbers. On this, there is agreement. But what does it mean to say Algeria is a nation?

The nation of Algeria had its cultural origins mainly in Salafism, a reformist ideology developed initially in India. Salafism found Arab expression in Egypt at the hand of a non-Arab scholar, theologian, and activist by the name of Afghani and his Egyptian disciple Muhammad Abduh. Salafism was essentially a response to the triumph of modernity, a response that stresses the fact that modernity is inherent to Islam and that it was only by a true understanding of the early, pure Islam of the Salaf (the ancestors) could Muslims find their old lost might and glory.[39] Soon after, Salafism found its way to the Maghreb, initially to Algeria and Tunisia and then to Morocco.[40] Even though it promoted educational reform, its political implications were not overlooked by the British (in Egypt) or the French (in Algeria). Through education and historical writings, Algerian Salafism created a distinguished culture within the colonial cultural landscape of Algeria. It transcended the dichotomy of Arab versus Berber and offered an alternate Algerian Muslim identity. The Salafi discourse, even in the writing of its most eloquent scholars (incluiding Ben Badis, Madani, and Mili) was clearly inseparable from the colonial discourse. It contained within itself the colonial logic of domination. As a subaltern discourse, it made French colonial discourse its focal point. Yet its ambiguity, the result of its contradictory reference, caused a great deal of epistemological confusion when it became a discourse of nationalism. Nothing illustrates this confusion better than the polemic between Ben Badis and Ferhat Abbas. The latter, a Frenchified intellectual, wrote about the Algerian nation: "I have asked history, I have asked the living and the dead; I have visited the cemeteries: no one talked to me about it." To which Ben Badis responded: "We too have looked in history in the present, and we have noticed that the Algerian nation has been formed and it exists."[41]

Wittgenstein maintains that to have an agreement, people first need conformity in what he calls "forms of life" or culture. Between the language of Abbas and Ben Badis is a significant gap that does not allow for agreement or even understanding. One can progress from Wittgenstein's statement by saying that to have an agreement, one needs to agree on forms of life and be able to understand forms of life that are different from one's own. The issue of language here is not whether Abbas wrote in French or Ben Badis in Arabic (both men understood both tongues) but that they did not understand each other's linguistic categories, implying an assumption that there were speaking about the same thing—which I argue is not the case.

The Salafi term for *nation* existed in Arabic. Poets, scholars, and travelers often referred to the nation as the *watan* (homeland). But this *watan* meant something different from the concept of nation as understood by Europeans and even European-educated Muslims in colonial societies. The concept of nation in their understanding was associated with that of tribalism. This is how Ferhat Abbas understood it, and this is how it was echoed in the acclaimed novel *Nedjma* by Kateb Yacine: "we are not a nation, not yet, you know that: we are only decimated tribes."[42] Everything is in the "yet"—a promise of fulfillment, not a remembrance but an awaiting for something absent; a will to become a nation, and everything that colonialism, not biology, prevented people from attaining. The Algerian war for liberation was nothing but an effort to achieve the will for it. The war was a demonstration of that will—a demonstration of becoming, not of having been.

Even though the discourse of nationalism was generated from the discourse of religious reformists, the two are different and cannot properly be understood without addressing this difference. In nationalism, a part is given to colonial discourse. The colonial discourse is also a discourse of difference: it formulates a negative image of Islam, asserts the inherent inability of the population to found a nation, and argues for the necessity of colonial presence for the creation of a modern polity, the concrete example of which is colonial society itself. The national discourse gives Islam a secondary place in its polity, agrees on the inability in the past to create a nation (and asserts its current and more so its future ability), rejects colonialism as an unjust system, but argues for the necessity of modernity, for the creation of a polity, the model of which is France itself.

By the end of the colonial period during the war for liberation, the armed struggle for independence progressed, and national ideologues imagined a nation born from the rubble of a colonial society that was doomed to be dismantled. Each political or cultural group imagined fundamentally different outcomes. Some, mostly French-educated youth, imagined the nation as secular with Arabic as its language and socialism as its ideology. Others, also mostly French-educated, imagined the nation as Berber first and foremost and secular with Tamazight as its language. Still others, mostly but not exclusively Arabized, imagined (or remembered) the nation as Arab and Islamic. Hence, there were three major antagonistic, competing projects—Arab nationalism, Berber nationalism, and Islamic nationalism.

Within the conceptual geology of Algerians, modes of identification are diverse, heterogeneous, and, in several instances, dangerously conflicting. The concept of the nation—at least in its European and American form—is not a dominant mode in Algeria. A nation, in the discourse of the state, means the Algerian nation, which has a uniting language (Arabic) and religion (Islam) and clear borders, beyond which there are threatening enemies (namely, Morocco, which Algeria fought twice—the first directly, the second by proxy—and has had limited diplomatic relations with). Even in this concept, the nation-state was not Arab for only after the uprising of 1988 was Arabic declared an official language. Its religion was not Islam; its law and its ideology were socialist. For the FIS, the Algerian nation is that of the *sha'b* (people) whose language is Arabic and whose religion is Islam, two factors that resisted colonialism and are resisting the "infidel" regime. Other factions think of themselves rather as part of the *umma,* whose struggle against "democracy, communism, liberalism" is only a means to the establishment of the caliphate. Berber nationalists, on the other hand, see the nation as Berber, a Tamazight conquered by the Arabs and dominated by them. But Berbers themselves are not a homogeneous group. The Shawiya are somewhat indifferent to Berber identity, and the Touareg have a strong Muslim identity and a greater sensitivity to the sacred language of the Qu'ran. The Kabyles have the strongest Berber identity and a regional identity.

Several anthropologists of violence identify the "crisis of the nation" as crucially important in understanding the violence of our time.[43] Arjun Appadurai, for instance, maintains that "part of the crisis is an increasingly violent relationship between the nation-state and its post-national Others."[44] To tackle the issue of violence, he suggests the following:

The first step is to recognize that there is a fundamental, and dangerous, idea behind the very idea of the modern nation-state, the idea of a "national ethnos." No modern nation, however benign its political system and however eloquent its public voices may be about the virtues of tolerance, multiculturalism and inclusion, is free from the idea that its national sovereignty is built on some sort of ethnic genius.[45]

For Appadurai, violence is mainly ethnic and is intended to cleanse the body of the nation from alien, impure elements. Appaduri seems to have in mind the European experience, where the formation of the nation-state and its enduring problems have been different than those in the Third World. An understanding of such differences, alluded to in the work of Benedict Anderson, would take into account the specificity of each historicity. To do so, one should distinguish between a nationalism that emerges based on the idea of "genius" expressed openly by enlightened minds of that nation and a nationalism that is based on the idea of "potentiality." One needs to distinguish between offensive nationalism (which is assertive, confident, exclusive, and cleansing) and defensive nationalism (which is uncertain, created out of a system of often colonial domination, ambitious, argumentative, dependent, challenging, marked by colonial domination, is homogenizing, and not cleansing). The first is European nationalism, the product of what Anderson calls *print capitalism*. The second is what was until recently called *Third-World nationalism* and is an import, the product of colonialism.[46] This said, one then needs to distinguish between violence as an act of cleansing the impure from the body of the nation and violence as an act of creating this body in the first place (homogenizing).

Benedict Anderson and Partha Chatterjee differ on how communities come to be imagined. For Anderson, print capitalism allowed a group of people in distant places to think of themselves as being alike. This model originated in Europe and the Americas and was exported to the Third World. Chatterjee disagrees with the last point and argues that the Third World imagined this beforehand.[47] A misunderstanding lies in the concept of imagination, which remains undefined by both Anderson and Chatterjee. Between the lines in both, imagination is creating—making something that is not real and is fictitious. But for Ricoeur, "imagination is first and foremost a restructuring of the semantic fields."[48] The Third World could be said to have imagined itself by restructuring semantic fields, but the change was also happening in colonial semantic fields. Chatterjee's work eloquently shows the connections between colonial discourse and national imagination. Given the connections and power relations between the two, national discourse, despite restructuring the colonial, had nothing but colonial categories by which to define itself.

The Algerian nation was claimed, celebrated, and articulated by different actors whose cultural and political identities were believed to be different from one another. For the elite, made of heterogeneous cultural elements unified by a political identity, Algerian nationalism defined the nation as Arab, secular, and socialist. Other groups that also claimed to have participated in the struggle against colonial rule saw (or rather imagined) the nation differently. For them, the nation was not a political project but a reality inscribed in Algerian history. Among these are the Salafi, the religious reformers, whose goal was to form the Muslim, Arab, Algerian nation in precisely the form that colonialism wanted to obliterate. Berber nationalists, on the other hand, identified the nation as a secular project with Tamazight as its national language.

All of this suggests that different political and cultural identities in postindependence Algeria were fundamentally at odds with one another, making it impossible to imagine the nation collectively. Such a task requires that there be an agreement on language and "forms of life"—that is, on culture. This is difficult to imagine in the case of Algeria.[49] Postcolonial Algeria was saturated with symbolic violence, and competing groups sustained the discourse of violence. Berber nationalists spoke about Arab conquests, Arab domination, Arab hegemony, and Arab repression of Berber culture. The Arabized masses spoke about French conquests, French domination, and continued French hegemony, especially in the form of the French party— the FLN that controlled and defended a secular state in the 1990s. The FIS, which inherited the Salafi discourse, used similar rhetoric as it called for the establishment of a Muslim nation. To return to Wittgenstein: "when two principles really do meet which cannot be reconciled with one another, then each man declares the other a fool and a heretic."[50]

Each set of actors speaks a historical discourse formed in a colonial context that, despite subsequent modifications still bears the imprint of the fundamental categories of colonial modernity. Such discourse provides a means of struggle and delimits the object for which it struggles. So the relevant historical horizon for analyzing Algeria's current violence does not begin with the canceled elections in January 1992. Since independence, the state of Algeria has been in violent relationship with its others. But violence is a discursive conflict before it translates into action and uses force. Again, the violence that raged in Algerian society in the 1990s, especially during the month of Ramadan, needs further interpretation.

TRANSGRESSION AND THE MEANINGS OF MODERN SACRIFICE

Violence is not necessarily transgression; and transgression does not need to be violent. The above discussion about the emergence of conflicting cultural and political identities in Algeria suggests the emergence of a culture of enmity (not adversity) when identities are seen as exclusive and thus *potentially* (and in some instances, *effectively*) violent—even if the violence is not expressed in blood and dead bodies. The main question regarding acts of transgression can also be asked in relation to the actors' interpretations. Here, I examine how two main actors interpreted the slaughters during the holy month of Ramadan

(1998 to 1999) and consider the societal grammar that has constituted the nation, its others, and the violence that envelops both.

Immediately after the massacre, the state-controlled media showed scenes of murdered men, women, and children, including horrific mutilations of bodies. In the eyes of Algerians, the massacre had all the required elements of transgression, most notably the element of sacrifice. The bodies were not only victims murdered for a cause. The transgressive violence became, to borrow from Henri Hubert and Marcel Mauss, a "procedure which consists in establishing a communication between the sacred and the profane, by the intermediary of a victim—a consecrated thing which is destroyed in the course of the ceremony."[51]

What happened during the month of Ramadan (and throughout the 1990s) in Algeria contradicts the idea that God put an end to the end of human sacrifice, as told in the Qu'ran (and in the Old and New Testaments). As Jill Robbins puts it, the story of Abraham's sacrifice "recounts the 'end' of sacrifice, the end of the practice of human sacrifice."[52] Islam is believed to be a reconnection with the Abrahamic religion and in that way not only will it reenact the sacrifice of an animal instead of a human, but it will recreate its own "end" of human sacrifice through the story of Mohamed himself. Abd al-Muttalib, his grandfather, was willing to sacrifice his son Abdullah, the Prophet's father. However, his life was spared when, under the advice of a seer *('arrâfa)*, the child was offered against the slaughter (or the sacrifice) of one hundred camels. Islam thus was born out of a sacrifice of origins, twice since Islam presents itself as an Abrahamic religion.[53]

The slaughter of an animal thus became the mark of Islamic sacrifice. This slaughter is often referred to as *dhabiha* or *dahiya*.[54] *Dhabiha* refers to the slaughter of an animal in ritual ceremonies, such as births, weddings, circumcisions, and funerals. *Dahiya* refers usually to the Abrahamic act, repeated by Muslims annually by slaughtering a lamb.[55]

The killings during the month of Ramadan were done with

knives, despite the existence of machine guns and the victims' requests to be shot instead of stabbed. The method points to killings that were intended to be acts of sacrifice. Yet if in Islamic tradition there was indeed an end to human sacrifice (as attested to by the adoption of the story of Abraham and the introduction of the narrative of the Prophet and his father, Abdullah), then how can its continuation in a modern era, in the context of nationhood and postcoloniality, be explained?

A number of my discussions with Algerians at the time of the events (during the month of Ramadan in Dec., 1997–Jan., 1998) and later pointed to a belief that the killers were often believed to be members of Groupe Islamique Armé (GIA) who considered their victims (innocent men, children, and women who did not offer any support to the army) as martyrs *(shuhada)*. The idea was that they died so that God could maintain a Muslim community and that, for this reason, they would go to heaven. This is the same belief held about animal sacrifices. The lambs killed on the day of sacrifice are also believed to have a life of heaven awaiting them. None of my interlocutors mentioned the story of the Khidr, a story of sacrifice in Islamic tradition that signals the existence, if not the necessity, of human sacrifice for the well-being of the *umma*. Although it has its origin in the Qu'ran,[56] the story of Khidr was expanded in the work of Qu'ran exegetes.[57] The story narrates the journey of Moses and his servant to the "meeting of the two seas." God sends them a Khidr to guide them in their journey, and the Khidr asks that his deeds not be questioned. Yet his deeds are horrific and involve the sinking of a boat of generous people who help Moses and the Khidr. In addition, the Khidr kills a child, seemingly for no reason. Horrified, Moses questions the Khidr and in doing so breaks their contract. The Khidr explains his deeds, informed by wisdom. For example, the killing of the child was a blessing to his parents, who otherwise would have been killed when the child grew into an unscrupulous killer. The point here is that from the perspective of those who pointed fingers at the FIS or the GIA, the discourse took its meaning and even its force of argument from within an Islamic tradition reinterpreted in a modern era marked by the interkilling of Muslims and citizens.

Sacrifice is not restricted to religion. The concept of sacrifice survived, unfiltered, in the secular to become a central element in the ideology of nationhood. As Ivan Strenski puts it: "the idea of sacrifice itself seems precisely one of those religious notions especially prone to migrate into politics. Notions like ritual and cultic giving—sacrifice—bear a natural affinity for civic giving—for heroism or martyrdom, in short for all those examples of patriotic offering of oneself in 'sacrifice' for the nation."[58] Since both the secular and religious are categories and thus some sacrifices are seen as religious and others are not, one might well look into the offerings given to (or even required by the nation of) its citizens. Since the nation is as abstract, mystic, and mysterious as the spirit of Hegel, one may well wonder whether the offerings required for the nation do not have similarities to those made to God. From a Durkheimian perspective, since religion is nothing but society, the nation is itself nothing but religion. But how do secular sacrifices and religious sacrifices differ?

During the 1981 riots in Casablanca, the Moroccan monarch, Hasan II, who was claimed to be "the symbol of the nation and the guarantor of its unity," addressed Moroccans in a televised speech with his usual expression "my dear people" *(sh'bi al'ziz):* "I am willing to sacrifice [*ndahi*] one-third of the people for the other two-thirds." The Casablanca riots of 1981 were triggered by food price increases and unfolded in a highly political climate while the king was on an official visit to Nairobi. They were seen as a serious threat to the existence of the monarchy and therefore the nation, according to the then-dominant national ideology. Hassan II's will to sacrifice was not to please God but rather to save the two-thirds who will constitute the nation, or his "dear people."

Although human sacrifice "ended" in religion, the nation continues to require it. First, human sacrifice in religion (the offering of blood to God) is not the same as the offering of oneself to the nation. In the first instance, the offering is made to please

God. In the second instance, the offering is made to protect a nation or even to create a nation. One offers human blood to God, and the other defends an entity against enemies. Human sacrifice continues to exist, not to the pleasure of God or the nation but rather to defend these entities from transgression. Yet at moments, such as the case at hand, what is sacrifice for some may be a transgression for others.

The mystery surrounding the Ramadan killings and their fluid meaning—not entirely a sacrifice and not really a transgression—may itself be the mark of modern and even postcolonial transgression. Once again, no one claimed responsibility, and all sides claimed innocence. The government, through its mass media, immediately pointed fingers at the oppositional Islamist party, FIS, describing it as "terrorist" and failing to distinguish between different factions. According to the state-sponsored media, the violence was the work of terrorists, and its primary purpose was to defeat the government. In making this argument, the government deployed its own instrumentalist logic, suggesting that Islam is only a means for power *(kursi)*. Following this line of reasoning, the massacres came to be perceived as a fundamental truth: the FIS and its supporters were enemies of Algerian society, failing to spare members of the army or civilian men, women, and children.

The state broadcast this discourse and bolstered it with horrific images. Despite its secular commitment, it drew on a certain interpretation of Islamic history and Islamic dogmas to assert FIS culpability. It used religious language to call the FIS a Khawarij, a reference to an Islamic sect that emerged in the eighth century and waged a ruthless war against the Muslim community, declaring them "infidels." Declaring fellow Muslims as infidels was (and is) central in the discourse of some Islamic political movements inscribed in the tradition of Sayyid Qutb and his theory of the *jahilya* of the twentieth century. His claim, often endorsed by extremist Islamists, is that Islamic societies sometimes degenerated into a state of *jahilya* and that Muslims have a duty to reestablish Islamic society and fight by *khitab* (discourse, persuasion) and by *harakat* (action, which many interpret as violence).[59]

In drawing on Islamic history and tradition, however, this discourse did not abandon the secular language of the state. It described the violence as "massacres" that were carried out by "terrorists," a term that first emerged during the colonial war of independence and was used by the French colonial state to describe members of the FLN. The term *terrorist* had already been tied to the party in power that was now condemning the violence of the Islamist oppositional party, FIS. That state identified the GIA, supposedly a group of armed veterans of the Afghanistan-Soviet war, known as the Afghans, as allegedly part of the FIS, who were designated as the perpetrators of the massacres. They were called by the state (and those who reproduce its discourse) *Kharjits*. According to one observer, "The GIA . . . classified all individuals as either enemies of Islam or supporters of jihad. Hence civilians were called on to choose sides under pain of death."[60] Their literature seemed abundant and was reproduced in state media, in tracts, and even in interviews conducted by the London-based Arabic newspaper *Al-Hayat*. And their discourse seemed to be coherent with the massacres of Ramadan. In his interview with *Al-Hayat*, Nabil Sahraoui, a leader of GIA states:

> GIA is a group with a Salafi creed and method it seeks to implement the law of God and to fight the apostate ruler in Algeria . . . Our goals consist in fighting the thoughts *(afkar)* and visions *(tasawwurat)* of Jahiliya, such as secularism, masonry, democracy, communism, and any thought or vision that differs from the path of the Salaf.[61]

At one point he adds,

> The *jihad* today is one of the greatest obligations [*fard 'ayn*], and a Muslim should know that the defense of Islam and Muslims by his life, his wealth, and his speech, is a duty. The assistance to the *Moujahidin* is an obligation.[62]

During a previous village massacre in the summer of 1997, a letter claiming to be from the GIA took responsibility for the violence and declared that the Algerian people were themselves "infidels."

In response to claims that the army failed to protect these villages, as it had a base a few miles away from the massacres, the state maintained that it was not possible to intervene in the middle of the night out of fear of roadside bombs or ambushes. But some Algerians claim that they saw the militants and recognized that they were Islamists—that they were from the same neighborhood and known to them as jobless young men who were sympathizers with the FIS.

Although the culpability of the GIA or the FIS seemed self-evident to the state and to some Algerians, it was denied by the FIS, whose members claimed their innocence and identified the state as responsible. According to the FIS, the killings were not carried out by Muslims, either by the armed wing of the FIS or by the GIA. The leaders and the sympathizers of the FIS accused the state of forming an armed group of men who wore Afghan clothing and disguised themselves as Islamists to eradicate real Muslims. According to the FIS, the massacres were an act of the government, continuing the French colonial policy against the population, using personnel who were officers in the French army before independence. Thus, according to the leader of the FIS, Abbasi Madani,

This regime [*nizam*] was founded to oppress the people and their freedom and to implement a pure dictatorial, military regime with no other objective but to punish the Algerian people for having led the resistance against colonialism and for having insisted on having their independence from France. What is happening to Algeria now is unheard of during colonialism. It is true that there were general massacres then. But then the murderer used to wear a French beret. Now this is happening in the name of Islam and hurts Islam in two ways: it kills the Muslim and it blames him for the killing.[63]

Other witnesses also pointed to the state and claimed to have evidence of its involvement. Most of those who claimed to be witnesses also claimed to be survivors of the massacres and moved as refugees in Europe. One woman, known only as C, spoke to the Association for the Defense of the Victims of the Massacres in Algeria, regarding similarly anonymous attacks in Ar-Raïss in August 28th, 1997:

> In the midst of the screams, they smashed the door and broke the windows. There were quite a number of them. My brother and father tried to defend us, but they were beaten to death by axes. My daughter tried to run away, but she was caught and slaughtered by two attackers. As for me, I tried to hang on to life, but I was beaten with an axe and an iron bar and knocked over. I was hit in the face and was bleeding everywhere, but when I was about to fall down, I clung to the beard of my killer. Although he had a long beard and Afghan clothes he was no Muslim for he was cursing God. The other attackers were also insulting God. As I told you, I clung to his beard, and it came off. He had a false beard.[64]

Although the state denied responsibility and accused the FIS of committing the slaughters, it found itself in a peculiar and dangerous situation. Through the different narratives surrounding the massacres, the victims revealed the state's inability to serve its primary function—to guard its territory and people against unlicensed transgression. The transgressive violence, in other words, created two victims—the civilians who were killed and the state. The state could no longer be credibly understood as maintaining a monopoly on the means of violence but instead could itself be subjected to violence, transforming it into a victim. This victimization was not a mere vulnerability or a decrease in power. Rather, it became an ideological means to launch new political state projects. The attacks on civilians, not far from military bases, enabled the Algerian state to launch new elections in 1998 from which the FIS was excluded, and to reconfirm its legitimacy at home and abroad. At home, security became more important than democracy and more important than the Islamic state. At home, the Algerian state found itself engaged in the "same" battle facing the "global community"— the "war on terror"—even before the tragic events of September 11, 2001. After this date, the GIA declared itself a global movement against the "crusaders" and their allies. They officially linked themselves to al-Qaeda in 2006, becoming al-Qaeda in the Islamic Maghreb, and adopted the suicide bombing tactics that are being used in Iraq and Afghanistan.

EPILOGUE OF VIOLENCE

Carol Nordstrom speaks of ethnography of the war zone,[65] without questioning the possibility of such an endeavor or clarifying what constitutes a war zone. The ethnography of war and violence in this sense, one can argue, is impossible. The "here" and "there" are as problematic as "special category." One can be in a war zone without seeing violence on the field or on the horizon. One can also be in a war-free zone where violence interrupts totally unexpectedly. In Algeria in the 1990s, ethnographic work was impossible because such research was not licensed and also because information itself was an important dimension of war. Some Western journalists were allowed into the country under specific conditions and were escorted after the fact to the zone that was affected by the violence. Yet they were prevented from speaking to people.[66] Algerian journalists were killed by anonymous parties. I did not witness the transgression and would not have liked to do so. I was not there in the middle of the first night of Ramadan or at any other time during the massacres. I got my the narratives about what happened and what was happening from dozens of people, several of them friends and colleagues, while I was either in Morocco, in France, or in the United States.[67] I received narratives from those who had been there and survived and visited several sites of the massacres in the summers of

2005, 2006, and again in the winter of 2007 in Algiers and Constantine.

In 2005, I spent the summer in Algeria, half of it in Algiers and the other half in Constantine and its mountainous areas, including Khenchela and Baghayy. By this time, Algerians spoke about what happened in the 1990s as the past. It was referred to usually as "the black years" *(les années noirs)*. My friends there, all of them Frenchified academics, have a specific view about what happened, and their discourse is the academic one. Yet it is different from the French one, like the one maintained by Louis Martinez or Benjamin Stora. According to them, the violence is chiefly the responsibility of the Islamists, who indoctrinated the youth *(les jeunes)*: "We used to see these young people with their backpacks going to the mountains and did not pay attention to what they were doing. They used to go by train and prepare for all of that."

Not far from the campus of the University of Algiers, on the street that faces its gate, my friend stopped and showed me a parking lot: "You see that park? I was walking one day, and I saw a car flying in the air. It was a car bomb. It was just right there." He pointed to a location on the other side of the parking, where the car, he said, exploded. He stopped walking, looked at the location of the bomb, and continued narrating: "I walked, as usual, to my apartment. It is just right there, and I will show you from the window. Yet I did not change anything in my habits. I did not want fear to rule my life. I kept doing exactly the same thing every day. From time to time, I used to hear that we were put on the death list; but I never paid attention to that. I did not seek to leave the country, like many of my friends. I stayed." He said all of this matter-of-factly, sounding neither proud nor sorry.

What struck me was the focus of his discussion—the youth. Those who fought were indeed young. Also, Algiers and Algeria is a young country, with 80 percent of the people under thirty years old. My friend then went on to speak about his own children, who were in their early twenties. I asked him what they thought about violence:

> They were indoctrinated too. We [my friend and his wife, who are highly educated] knew what they thought. We never discussed it. Yet we made it clear to them that they had their ideas and we had our own. For instance, even in the midst of the black years, we sat at the table for dinner, and we opened the bottle of wine every night.

The couple drinks, but the children do not out of Islamic conviction. In their apartment, everything is modern; it does not look different from any French apartment. The salon is furnished with modern sofas and a coffee table with French catalogues and art books. On the other side of the living room, there is a library with French books, mostly about Algeria and the Maghreb. The conversation is always in French, even when an Algerian friend comes to visit. I did not have a chance to meet his children.

I met Kamel, who was happy to introduce me to his father, Tahar. Tahar worked in Bentalha and in Sidi Mousa for over twenty years. Kamel was a young man in his midtwenties. He wore a T-shirt, blue jeans, and sneakers. The discussion started immediately, all in Arabic dialect, about what happened in Bentalha. He smiled and he said: "It is the army who did that." "How so?" I asked, and he repeated what I had heard—how not far from the place of the murders was the police station, and the army headquarters. He added in a matter-of-fact tone: "The Islamists don't have helicopters. There were helicopters flying over the place the whole night." Aicha, a university student whom I met and spoke to earlier in June, 2006 said the same thing. "But why does the army kill its own citizens?" I asked in both instances. Both Kamal and Aïcha repeated the same thing—that the sites of the massacres in Ben Mousa and Bentalha were known to be a base for Islamists and their supporters. I wondered whether generational differences affected

people's interpretations of what happened. Aïcha was not an
Islamist. Her head was not covered. She was young and quite
liberal in her views. She did not drink but felt comfortable going
to a restaurant that served alcohol. A student of philosophy, she
felt comfortable discussing Merleau-Ponty and Avicenna. Kamel
was not an Islamist either, but he had much less education. Unlike Aicha, he was a Kabyle. Neither would fit the physical description of an Islamist or a terrorist (beard, headscarf, loose
clothes) the ideological description (discourse on the Islamic
state, virulent discourse against the West, and so forth). Neither
was unemployed or poverty-stricken. However, in both cases,
there was a deep mistrust of the Algerian state. Neither had lived
through colonialism. Both were born after 1962, most likely in
the late 1970s.

Ten years after the events of September 1997 and of Ramadan
1998, on January 7, 2007, Tahar, Kamel's father, a taxi driver,
was driving me to Bentalha and Sidi Moussa. He seemed quite
reserved. Initially, he did not say much and did not even ask me
why I was going there. I asked him whether he ever visited Morocco. He said that he did. He spoke to me about his visits and
started complaining about the frontiers being closed. I said:
"Now you can go. They lifted the visa last year." He told me
that he prefers to drive, spend time there, and pack his car with
goods from Morocco. He referred to it as *Marrouk* and when he
spoke about Moroccans he referred to them as *mrarka*. Both
terms are pejorative when used by Moroccans, and I had to
struggle a bit to ignore this. I was aware that, when used by Algerians, the terms *Marrouk* and *mrarka* often lose their pejorative connotations. He spoke with fondness about the country
and about his *mrarka* friends. Indeed, he warmed up when
speaking about his friends. I then asked him whether he knew
Bentalha. He said that he used to work there for over twenty-
five years.

"What did you do?" I asked.

"I was a taxi driver for a construction company. I drove the
workers to and from the working place."

"You were not living there, were you?"

"No, it is a poor neighborhood."

"Is it a neighborhood?"

"Well, it is a village. Not big."

"When did you work there?"

"I just resigned a couple of years ago."

I knew that he must have worked there during the 1990s. So I asked him: "Were you there at the time of the massacre?"

"I was working there. But the massacres happened at night. I used to drive the workers after 5 pm and bring them to work early in the morning."

We reached a road thickly lined with orange trees on both sides, and he pointed out the road to me. He told me, "A friend of mine was driving and he was shot here, in this spot."

"Who shot him?"

"The terrorists [*al-irhabiyun*]," he said in a matter-of-fact tone. "The Islamists [*al-islamiyun*]. They shot him, and then they ran into the middle of the trees." He pointed to the left side of the trees. "I used to see them here. I used to drive and see them. I just kept on driving rather normally. I did not speed. Sometimes, they gestured to pass. But they never stopped me."

We crossed the military base. It was a *gendarmerie,* a type of police force for the countryside. Adjacent to it, there was a construction factory where Tahar used to work. The gendarmerie was only two miles from the town of Bentalha, which we soon reached. We drove down its main street, and it was clearly an Islamist town. All the women were veiled. A few school girls, not even nine years old, were leaving school running. One was totally covered with a black dress from head to toe. Most of the young men were dressed in jeans and shorts. From time to time, bearded middle-aged men with loose clothes could be seen. We passed the police station. I asked Tahar, "Can we walk?" He was too polite to say, "Are you out of your mind?" He just said: "It is dangerous. They could tell that we are not from here." Indeed, the town was small, all of the people we saw must have known each other. At the end of the main street, there was a very shallow river of dirty water *(ma al-harr)*. On the other side of the river, one saw almost nothing but orange trees. Tahar pointed to the river:

> This is where they used to come from. They'd cross the river at night and attack the village. They killed everybody. They also came with a list of people they wanted to kill. When they were done, they crossed the river again and disappeared into the trees.

He stopped the car, and we watched the entire main street. There was something interesting about it. It did not look like an old village. I tried to imagine how it was before. One could see the new village coming out of the old one. Most of the houses were rebuilt with modern material in the form of boxes with barred windows. A few houses were huts made of cheap and old material, mostly very thin iron called *qasdi*r. The village clearly had been a shanty town not very long ago and was so at the time of the massacres of September 1997. Its poverty persisted even with its new houses.

Tahar was an FLN believer. For him, the FLN brought independence. He remembered its heroic fight against the French and the injustice and the humiliation *(hugra)* of the French colonial system in Algeria. The problem is those beasts *(bhayim)*, he said:

> It is as if they were in a cage and then someone let them out. They hurried to the door and start dictating what to do. You see the man, he does not even know how to write his name, and he starts dictating *(yafti)*. They dictate what should be done. I knew one of them, he worked with us in the shanty. He goes on and on about what should be done. I knew he was one of them. At night, he is with them, during the day he is at the shanty. Then one day he stopped coming all together.

While driving back to the city of Algiers, everything looked peaceful. Tahar spoke about what had happened in the past with a strong conviction that it was all behind us. I was looking at the street to find out where we were. We were at Mourad Derouche. We then reached the plaza of the martyrs. One cannot miss the huge statue of the Emir Abdel Kader, with his sword, symbolizing the fight he carried out for the nation. A few minutes away by car was the plaza Ali Lapointe, a name that is known internationally from the movie *The Battle of Algiers*. I was surprised that the city was a memorial to colonial struggle. The names of men who died for the nation and whose deaths made the nation possible are engraved on it in a way that gives it its own identity. Everything in the city reminds one of colonial violence and the war for liberation.

The general sentiment among Algerians is that the days of the Ramadan tragedy are far behind the nation and that the state prevailed. Yet in the streets of Algiers and especially in its suburbs, one feels that the bloody days were not very long ago. In 2006 and 2007, armed groups killed 132 civilians and 160 security forces. The army killed 378 suspected terrorists. During my three stays, the state media announced almost daily the killing of a couple of "terrorists" here and there. In front of the Office of Human Rights, over fifty women (all mothers) and several older men gather rather quietly, demanding to know the fate of their sons, who disappeared during the "black years." I was told they gather every Wednesday. Although free to stand there, they were watched, and no journalist or anthropologist was allowed to approach them. Several soldiers and undercover policemen watched them. For these women and men, the tragedy continues today. The state has yet to give them an answer. The streets outside Algiers, especially between cities, still suggest a state of war. Heavily armed young soldiers from the countryside are seen at check points. Yet the state locations and symbols, such as police stations and government offices, continue to be targets of violence. As recently as December 12, 2007, the United Nations offices were targeted by violent attacks that continue to signal to officials, citizens, and the rest of world (now more connected than ever) that the violence in Algeria has not stopped.[68]

NOTES

1. Marshal Sahlins, "The Return of the Event, Again," *Culture in Practice* (New York: Zone Books, 2000), 293–351.
2. Dominic LaCapra, *History in Transit* (Ithaca: Cornell University Press, 2004).
3. For Merleau-Ponty, events are the result of the perception of an individual. Merleau-Ponty, *Phénoménologie de la perception*, 470. Krystztof Pomian argues that there must first be a change in the world and that this change must be perceived by several individuals. I believe Pomian misunderstood Merleau-Ponty. A happening in the world needs to be perceived and thus narrativized. The individual is a phenomenological subject in his statement, and one does not need several virtual individuals to define an event. Some of the founding events of human history were based on the perception of one person who might have indeed been a "victim" of "phantasms" and "hallucination," which Pomian believed are antithetical to the perception of an event. See Kryzystof Pomian, *L'ordre du temps* (Paris: Gallimard, 1986), 16–19. However, without really contradicting Merleau-Ponty, events (as narratives) change their signification in different contexts considering the different use they are subject to (as I show in chapter 4).
4. The entries of news I have is by no means exhaustive. For more entries about the massacres see Review de Press, Algérie, January 1998, No. 421–5). Mellah, Salima, *Les massacres en Algérie*, Comité Justice pour l'Algérie, Mai 2004. Online access: http://www.algerie-tpp.org/tpp/pdf/dossier_2_massacres.pdf
5. Nesroulah Yous, *Qui a tué à Bentalha?* (Paris: Decouverte, 2000).
6. Emile Durkheim, *The Elementary Forms of the Religious Life* (New York: Free Press, 1965).
7. Deborah Kapchan, *Gender on the Market* (Philadelphia: University of Pennsylvania Press, 1996).
8. Michael Taussig, "Transgression," in Marc Caylor, ed., *Critical Terms for Religious Studies* (Chicago: University of Chicago Press, 1998), 352.
9. Max Weber, "Politics as Vocation," *From Max Weber: Essays in Sociology* (Oxford: Oxford University Press, 1953), 78
10. George Bataille, *The Accused Share* (Zone: New Press, 1988).

11. As a resident in France, I witnessed firsthand all the reactions—from intellectuals, academics, Algerians, and other Maghrebis—to the emergence of the FIS.

12. Pierre Bourdieu, *Acts of Resistance* (New York: New Press, 1998).

13. Ibid.

14. Interview with William Zarthman, *Le Monde*, January 13, 1998.

15. Benjamin Stora, *"Algérie: absence et surabondance de mémoire"* in Mohamed Benrabah, ed. *Les violences en Algérie*. (Paris: Odile Jacob, 1998). By 2001, Stora was less certain about his own explanation and explained that the violence was also caused by the forgetting of "the founders of the nation." Stora must have meant that such forgetting deprived the nation of its meaning, hence a national crisis. See Benjamin Stora, *La guerre invisible, Algérie, années 90* (Paris: Presses de Sciences Po, 2001), 36–40. However, I would rather argue that the problem was not that the "founders of the nation" were forgotten; rather their presence was overwhelming in a nation with such recent colonial history whose lines are read even in the street names of the country. Therefore, there was a surplus of national meaning, most of it conflicting.

16. Interview with Benjamin Stora, *Nouvel Observateur*, no. 1884, December 14–20, 2000, 8.

17. Benjamin Stora, "Algérie: Absence et surabondance de mémoire." *In* Mohamed Benrabah, ed. *Les violences en Algérie*, 154.

18. Mayor, *The Furies*, 71.

19. Paul Ricoeur, *Histoire et vérité* (Paris: Hachette, 1955), 246.

20. Ricoeur, *La mémoire, l'histoire, l'oublie*.

21. That was the view of Richard Tuck, *The Rights of War and Peace: Political Thought and International Order from Grotius to Kant* (Oxford: Oxford University Press, 1999). Cited and discussed by by Talal Asad, *On Suicide Bombings* (New York: Columbia University Press, 2007), 59.

22. Houari Addi, *L'Algérie et la démocratie: pouvoir et crise du politique dans l'Algérie contemporaine* (Paris: Editions la Découverte 1994).

23. Ibid., 188

24. Louis Martinez, *The Algerian Civil War* (New York: Columbia University Press).

25. Carol Nordstrom, *A Different Kind of War Story* (Philadelphia: University of Pennsylvania Press, 1997).

26. Bruno Etienne, *Les combatants suicidaires* (Paris: Editions de l'Aube, 2005), 17–18, quote cited in Asad, *On Suicide Bombing,* 53.

27. See on this point Abderrahmane Moussaoui, *De la violence en Algérie* (Paris: Actes Sud, 2006), p. 84.

28. On this issue, see Abdelmajid Hannoum, "Notes on the (Post)Colonial in the Maghreb."

29. See Arjun Appaduri, *Fear of Small Numbers.* (Durham: Duke University Press, 2007).

30. Hugh Roberts, *Algeria, the Battlefield: Studies in a Broken Polity* (London: Verso, 2003).

31. Joshua Cole, "Intimate Acts of Unspeakable Relations," in Alec Hargreaves, ed., *Memory, Empire, and Postcolonialism* (Lanham: Lexington Books, 2005), 131.

32. Even the brilliant book by Moussaoui, the only anthropological study of violence in Algeria, did not liberate itself from this framework and therefore despite its anthropological dimension, his study is closer to the instrumentalist approach I describe in this chapter; see *De la violence en Algérie.*

33. LaCapra, *History in Transit.*

34. On anthropology and events, see Steve Caton, "Anger Be Now Thy Song: The Anthropology of Event," *Institute for Advanced Study Occasional Papers,* no. 5 (November 1999), 1–20. On history and events, see Pomian, *L'ordre du temps,* 7–36.

35. Most notably Pierre Nora, "The Return of the Events," *Histories: French Constructions of the Past* (New York: New Press, 1995); Marshal Sahlins, "The Return of the Event, Again," 293–351.

36. Nora, "The Return of the Events," *Histories: French Constructions of the Past,* 435.

37. Mahmood Mamadani, *When Victims Become Killers* (Princeton: Princeton University Press, 1996), 21–22.

38. Among many, Michael Taussig, *Colonialism, Shamanism, and the Wild Man* (Chicago: University of Chicago Press, 1987); Valentine Daniel, *Charred Lullabies* (Princeton: Princeton University Press, 1996).

39. For Salafism, see especially Malcolm H. Kerr, *Islamic Reform: The Political and Legal Theories of Muhammad 'Abduh and Rashid Rida* (Berkeley: University of California Press, 1966); Elie Kedourie, *Afghani and 'Abduh: An Essay on Religious Unbelief*

and Political Activism in Modern Islam (London: Frank Cass, 1966); Albert Hourani, *Arabic Thought in the Liberal Age, 1798–1939* (London: Oxford University Press, 1970).

40. On the question of Salafism in the Maghreb, see Jacques Berque, *Le Maghreb entre les deux guerres* (Paris: Seuil, 1967), English translation, *French North Africa* (London: Faber and Faber, 1967). On the founding figure of Salafism in Algeria, see Ali Merad, *Le réformisme musulman en Algérie* (La Haye: Mouton, 1967). See also James McDougall, *History and Culture of Nationalism in Algeria* (Cambridge: Cambridge University Press, 2006).

41. Cited in Le Tourneau, *L'évolution politique d'l'Afrique du Nord musulmane*, 314, 319.

42. Yacine, *Nedjma*, English transl. Bernard Aresu (Charlottesville: University of Virginia Press, 1991), 170–71.

43. Begona Aretxaga, *Shattering Silence* (Princeton: Princeton University Press, 1996); Allen Feldman, *Formations of Violence* (Chicago: University of Chicago Press, 1991), Asad, *On Suicide Bombing*.

44. Appadurai, "Patriotism and Its Futures," *Modernity at Large*, 168–169.

45. Appaduri, *Fear of Small Numbers*, 4.

46. Anderson, *Imagined Communities*.

47. Partha Chatterjee, *The Nation and Its Fragments* (Princeton: Princeton University Press, 1996).

48. Ricoeur, "Imagination in Discourse and in Action."

49. Ludwig Wittgenstein, *Philosophical Investigations* (Oxford: Blackwell, 1997), 88e.

50. Ludwig Wittgenstein, *On Certainty* (New York: Harper, 1972), 81e.

51. Henri Hubert and Marcel Mauss, *Sacrifice: Its Nature and Function* (Chicago: University of Chicago Press, 1964), 97.

52. Jill Robbins, "Sacrifice," in Marc Taylor, ed., *Critical Terms for Religious Studies* (Chicago: University of Chicago Press, 1998), 291.

53. For more details about this story, see Mohamed Ibn Ishaq, *The Life of Mohamed* (Oxford: Oxford University Press, 1957), 66–68. Tabari, *Târîkh* (Beirut: Maktabat Khayyât, nd.), 172–174. Also in Ibn Khaldûn, *'Ibar,* vol. 2, 378.

54. For sacrifice in Morocco, see Abdallah Hammoudi, *The Victims and Its Masks* (Chicago: University of Chicago Press, 1993).
55. For a description of this ritual in Morocco, see Elaine Combs-Schilling, *Sacred Performances: Islam, Sexuality, and Sacrifice* (New York: Columbia University Press, 1989); in Mecca, see Abdallah Hammoudi, *Une saison à la Mecque* (Paris: Seuil, 2005).
56. Qu'ran (18:60–82).
57. See, for instance, Ibn Ishaq, *The Life of Mohamed*.
58. Ivan Strenski, *Contesting Sacrifice* (Chicago: University of Chicago Press, 2002), 9.
59. Sayed Qutb, *Jahiliyat al qarn al 'ishrîn* (Beirut: Dar al-Shuruq, 1974). See also Gilles Kepel, *Prophet and Pharaoh* (London, Al Saqi Books, 1985)
60. Quoted in Louis Martinez, *The Algerian Civil War*, 000.
61. Interview with Nabil Sahrawi, *Al Hayat*, January 8, 2004.
62. Ibid.
63. Interview with Abbasi Madani, *Al Jazeera*, November 16, 2003.
64. "Voices of the Voiceless" in the *Association for the Defense of the Victims of the Massacres in Algeria*, Copenhagen, edited by M. Farouk, T. S. Senhadji and M. Ait Larbi, 1999, 218.
65. Nordstrom, *A Different Kind of War Story*; Freedman, *Formations of Violence*, 5n. 40.
66. Bernard-Henri Lévy, "Choses vues en Algérie" *Le Monde*, January 8–9, 1998. As a consequence of his inquiry in the "war zone," the report of Levy reproduces the official version of the army. See for a critique of Lévy's report in Francois Gèze and Pierre Vidal-Naquet, "L'Algérie de Bernard-Henri Lévy" In *Le Monde*, March 5, 1998.
67. In Princeton, a forum to discuss the "events" took place at the University in May 27 to 29, 1994. For a summary, see Abdallah Hammoudi and Stuart Schaar, eds., *Algeria's Impasse* (Princeton: Center for International Studies, Princeton University, 1995).
68. Despite the very low intensity of violence, it continues sporadically. The last most spectacular ones go back to July and June 2009 in eastern Algeria during which 18 soldiers and one civilian were killed. Source: *Al-Jazeera*, July 30, 2009.

Epilogue

The interview with the Moroccan academic that opens this book reveals much about postcolonial conditions in the Maghreb. The parallel that he draws between the role played by colonialism in his country and the industrial revolution in Europe suggests either a profound ignorance of colonialism or an extreme form of alienation or both. But in the end, we may wonder whether this man has any alternative other than gratitude, despite tremendous personal loss. Can he feel, think, or *be* otherwise?

Loss is undoubtedly real—and ubiquitous—in Maghreb societies, even among those who may not be aware of it. The Maghreb, like most regions of the world, has undergone violent transformations throughout the colonial period. People have lost something of their own being and had to modify their belief that things were as they originally believed them to be. This heritage of loss and disrupted destiny is carried, paradoxically, alongside an expressed (or unexpressed) recognition of what was gained and given in return—modernity. This paradoxical heritage is a defining characteristic of cultural postcoloniality in the Maghreb. Consider a statement made by Abdallah Laroui in what is still the most authoritative book on the history of the Maghreb:

> This is the great misdeed [*méfait*] of colonization. It stops historical evolution and obliges the colonized to remake it backwardly.

215

Hence in principle, every colonization is a condemnation to death.[1]

At the same time, Laroui advocates modernity for the present and the future of the Maghreb against what he calls "cultural retardation" and "medievalization."[2] In his work, modernity is equated with Europe but (surprisingly and conveniently) never associated with colonialism.[3] One may wonder how the two can be dissociated, but this opinion is not unique to Laroui, the Moroccan nationalist historian. Third-World nationalism in general dissociates modernity from colonialism, despite the fact that modernity originated in colonialism and was born with the conquest of the Americas, as Enrique Dussel argues.[4]

Laroui is an eloquent and a rigorous defender of modernity, despite its responsibility for the tragic death of historical evolution. Modernity may well be worth the price, considering Laroui's strong discourse in its favor. As a national historian, he participates in the triumph of modernity (France), even when he engages in a rigorous critique of colonialism, the purpose of which is to write a national history of the Maghreb.[5] This was one way by which Third-World nationalism contributed to the triumph of modernity. The relationship between the two is more than a genealogical one, meaning that one was born out of the other. Rather, both are part and parcel of the same web of significance. Stated differently, modernity "here" (in Europe) extended itself, through various forms of violence, to "there" (non Europe). It manifests itself by a variety of discourses as well as by a variety of critiques of them, that is, of meta-discourses, of self-critique. Hence, the fact that one cannot "provincialize," that is, displace modernity by a modern discourse, no matter how radical it may be in its critique. Neither is rejection a possibility from within modernity.[6]

My interview with the Moroccan academic took me back to an incident I witnessed in primary school in 1974. Two of my classmates challenged our French teacher, Madame Garcia, on the topic of colonialism. From where I sat at the front of the classroom, I could see her blush. Timidly and awkwardly, she responded that colonialism was not a bad thing, that it did not exploit and that it was something good that was brought to help people have civilization. The idea that people were not civilized before the arrival of the French sounded bizarre to me. The two questioners laughed loudly at her answer, making her blush even more. I did not fully comprehend the situation, but I knew that my teacher's discourse of colonialism agreed with another discourse I heard in the streets, which seemed to be nostalgic for colonialism. It claimed that in colonial times, schools, public hospitals, and work conditions seemed to be better.[7] The French were viewed positively. Sometimes they were even referred to as *Shurfa* (perhaps sincerely, perhaps sarcastically).[8] Although my two classmates were critical of colonialism, they were more Frenchified than the rest of the class, which was composed mostly of children from low-income families from the countryside. They spoke French with a French accent, dressed modernly, and were at ease with themselves—qualities that I considered very French. They looked refined and knew this, and their attitudes toward their classmates reflected it. There was so little contact between them and the others, especially those from the regions around the small Atlas mountains (Hajab, Azrou, Ifrane, Ain Louh) that the classroom seemed to be made up of French children and *indigène* children. Frenchness undoubtedly indicated class. The two students were complaining about the very thing that gave them distinction—in the classroom, and in society as a whole.

Domination leaves no viable alternative, and soon the dominated can no longer see even the possibility of change on the horizon. The only means of change left at their disposal are the very means used to subjugate them. The colonized find themselves in a modern present that they neither invented nor have the ability to change, particularly as they are taught to conceptualize using modern categories in the same language of the discourse that has decided these categories. Hence, the postcolonial epistemological dilemma, difficult to overcome by deconstructive critique, often leads to the reproduction of what Chakrabarty calls "a narrative of despair"[9]—a narrative that says nothing at the end but that *"We are doomed. Not even History can save us."*

In the national discourse of the Maghreb, ambiguity toward colonialism is unmistakable, in large part due to nationalism. The positive discourse of modernity was omnipresent in my high school curriculum: we were citizens of a country on the road to modernity. At the same time, we read two conflicting texts that reinforced ambiguity toward colonialism. One was assigned in an Arabic literature course—a text by the Salafi Moroccan nationalist ideologue Allal al-Fasi, where he writes about colonialism and exploitation. The second text was assigned in a French course, Fanon's *The Wretched of the Earth*. Both of these texts were about colonial dispossession of the colonized. While Fanon was relatively unknown to us and more difficult to understand, we understood Fasi's text beyond expectation. Rumor had it that Fasi urged the poor to fight and make sacrifices for independence, yet at the same time urged the bourgeoisie of the city of Fes to send their children to school and prepare them for key positions in society after independence. Thus, we read his text believing that the man was a hypocrite when he denounced colonialism.[10]

Whether this rumor was true, I cannot say. But it was a narrative that has what James Scott calls a "hidden script"[11]—that is, it is a narrative of subjugated people accounting for and dealing with their postcolonial condition. In this case, the rumor explained the postcolonial condition in which the poor masses ended up with nothing, while the bourgeoisie (identified with the old bourgeoisie of Fes) gained from a struggle in which they were believed to be outsiders. "Fasis" are portrayed in Moroccan popular culture as cowards who are incapable of a physical fight, let alone a collective resistance. As a teenager, I found this rumor in a novel by Tahar Benjelloun, *Moha le fou, Moha le sage*, but Benjelloun was simply echoing how an important nationalist was viewed by disadvantaged Moroccans. In all of this, modernity was separate from colonialism, so much so that we thought of colonialism as a military presence of the French and of modernity as all of the wonderful things that they left after they departed—hospitals, schools, railroads, and a language and a way of life to be appreciated and sought after, by travel and exile if necessary.

Again, this ambiguity toward colonialism is not unique to Morocco. During the Algerian war of the 1990s, I interviewed Algerian intellectuals and listened to what they had to say both formally and informally about the tragedy. The consensus among those I spoke with was that the problem plaguing Algerian society was Islamism—specifically, the FIS. Even justifying the use of weapons was taboo and would immediately earn one the dreadful label of "Islamist," and put him in the camp of the enemy. There was less agreement that the problem of Algeria was indeed the state. (All of this has been expressed in numerous publications.) At only one time during those interviews did I hear a Frenchified intellectual blame France. He said: *"C'est la France qui nous a foutu de la pagaille."* [It is France that has created this mess for us]. I was surprised and intrigued, as France was not often mentioned as the party responsible for postcolonial violence in Algeria. Only Islamists criticized postcolonial France and considered it the sole party responsible for what they considered to be a coup d'état. The same view was echoed by ordinary people that I interviewed, and not all of them sympathizers with the FIS. But in their view, France is present in Algeria through a segment of society they call *"hisb fransa"* (party of France). But again to hear an intellectual blaming France for *"la pagaille"* seemed a rarity to me. When I asked him to explain, he said "Until 1947, all we wanted was to become part of France, and France was rather categorical about our exclusion [from the French nation]. The Violette project[12] finally accepted that Algerians could become French but under certain conditions, meticulously selected."

This complaint about colonial France was not about its colonial practices, but about the premature cessation of its civilizing mission. If modernity had not been aborted, then Algerians would not have endured a civil war. This is a discourse of ambiguity that blames modernity for its shortcomings and yet applauds it as a great boon.

The Algerian state may systematically denounce colonialism, but at the same time its people consume French modernity uncritically and avidly. Modernity is not questioned as a colonial product whose effects on society are gruesome and deadly. The state's critiques have ended up being read, like the discourse of Fasi in Morocco, as a way to legitimize the rule of a party and not as a means of improving living conditions for the people. As I was told in one of my interviews during the violence of the 1990s, these officials spoke French fluently, displayed its signs, consumed its products, and took their families on shopping expeditions to Paris during the civil war.

This state of affairs is not representative of all Algerian society. A less ambivalent discourse on French colonialism is often associated with the discourse of Islamists who are perceived as anti-Western, antimodern and thus antirational. The critique of colonialism and postcolonial culture was one of the strategies deployed by leaders of the FIS to undermine their opponents (all of whom fell under the category of *hisb fransa*) and critique the state (the FLN). During its campaign, the FIS declared over and again that it would hold France accountable for colonial crimes against the Algerian people and replace French with English as the country's second language (English was considered to be a noncolonial language). The FIS's rhetorical strategy competed with the discourse of nationalism and eclipsed it. It appeared less ambiguous and thus more genuine. The FIS successfully intervened in the discursive domain where nationalism showed its limitations and perhaps made France better understand and appreciate its connection to the Algerian nationalism of the FLN. Although Algerian diplomats appearing in French media were fluent in French, FIS members seemed to speak it awkwardly or not at all, whether because they were unwilling to use it or did not know it.

It is interesting to see how the French news media interpreted the success of the FIS strategy. For a political analyst such as Paul Balta, then considered a leading expert on the Arab world, this phenomenon could only be explained by the fact that, for these young people, modernity is "at their door, but not within their reach" (Balta, writing in *Le Monde*, played with words here: *"une modernité à leur porte mais pas à leur portée"*).[13] In other words, they protested not against modernity itself, but against their inability to attain it. The assumption expressed in Balta's statement is that modernity is desired, pursued, and thus valued and appreciated even by those seemingly against it. Their protest is only an expression of frustration. Given the nature of the problem, one can logically conclude that the solution is clear: give modernity to young people in Algeria and their frustration and protests will cease. For Balta the problem of Algeria is the lack of modernity (not its presence, as this book argues), which reveals that French postcolonial institutions cannot free themselves from a colonial discourse.

Again, whether in colonial, national, or postcolonial discourse, modernity seems to be rarely questioned. Yet the Mahgreb societies preceded modernity and will undoubtedly outlive it. Historians and anthropologists cannot change this fact. I do not claim that modernity's absence will result in these societies' sudden death. My goal is not programmatic or prophetic. It is simply to point out that modernity established itself by destroying things and that modernity is dominant even in the discourse of some of its trenchant critics, including me. Since historians and anthropologists can only historicize its establishment and show the complexity of its politics, they are themselves contingent upon it. One of the points I have tried to demonstrate in this book is that modernity was a project that was associated with the rise of Western Europe, that (through colonial conquests and different forms of governmentality) displaced other cultural civilizing projects, other imaginaries, and that created a new imaginary—a new self and a new being, a new center and a new periphery. The point is not whether this project was worth the price or determines our survival but whether we can understand the price paid by the "natives" in a transaction in which they held little power. The killings and mutilations of the 1990s and today were created by the culture of modernity in Algeria. Colonialism violently rearranged people, land, and cultures in a way that created a new destiny for Algeria, and it has given birth to new identities, new ideologies, and new ways of being. What happened in the 1990s cannot be understood without the history of modernity in Algeria, which is a colonial history.

The term *modernity,* as used in this book, refers to French colonial knowledge and its various forms. The preceding chapters focus on moments in which modern knowledge created its own realities in the colonies and demolished other realities in the process. Modernity is inherently pluralistic, even at times of colonial uncertainty that are marked by intense violence. Its methods are multiple: weapons, torture, human degradation, symbolic domination, economic pressure, and regimes of knowledge (about nationalism, religion, democracy, human rights, transparency, multiculturalism, and transnationalism).

In the previous chapters, the word *modernity* is often used with the adjective *colonial* to situate the type of modernity experienced in the colonial transformation of Algeria, via conquest and science. Sometimes, the term *modernity* is left unmodified because modernity, as a discourse and a historical condition, is always changing (although violence remains a constant in its many manifestations). In fact, the changing dynamics of modernity are marked by fluctuating intensities of violence. For instance, Prussia's 1870 defeat of the French changed conditions and discourse in France itself. Meanwhile, in Algeria, local people's understandings, actions, interactions, and reactions caused the colonizers to adjust as well. The Algerian uprising of the 1870s temporarily turned the colonial regime (along with its core values of science and European superiority) topsy-turvy and forced it to change. The uprising demonstrated that the local population was not passively devoid of rational thought and common sense. Their pragmatism and ability to anticipate colonial actions made them important players in colonial politics, demonstrating a fatal blind spot in the modern field of vision. Yet this important lesson was hard for French colonials to learn. They preferred to believe that their mistake was merely at the level of ethnographic accuracy and not at the level of modern colonial epistemology as a whole.

The acts and actions of "natives" shook modern confidence in a specific mode of knowledge (ethnography) and led to investment in a different mode of knowledge (history). This is an important shift (noted several times in chapter 4) between a modern form of knowledge (ethnography) that stresses observation and experience to assure more effective rule and another form of knowledge (history) that privileges archives and archeology— transforming these into modern narratives, and thus bringing the past under the control of the present.

The shift from the ethnographic state to the historiographic state was dictated by a conflict within modernity itself, but it is also the result, at least in part, of the oppressed local population resisting and even attempting to overthrow the project of modernity to cease being its victims. Modernity, with its inherent violent processes, can be forced to change only when faced with reciprocal acts of violence, no less modern and violent. When Fanon states that "colonialism is violence by its very nature and can only be fought by greater violence,"[14] he is referring to a historical and sociological condition he witnessed. Yet, the idea is a familiar one. Marxist scholars and Marx himself have maintained the same thesis about the modernity of capitalism, stating that it could be defeated only by violence, that is by revolution. Even in postwar French society, violence—in the view of Sartre and Foucault in his footsteps—is the only effective way to overthrow a modern society that rules and is based on violence and repression. Neither Marx nor Sartre nor Foucault could see that bourgeois society *is* modern society and therefore that challenging bourgeois society by its own means of physical and symbolic governance may be pointless. To overthrow such a society by modern means would only bring about a renewed modern society that would be no less violent and no less oppressive.

Associating modernity with violence has required that I explain violence itself. I have attempted to do this in the previous chapters and to continue in this epilogue. Violence has one effect—destruction, including the destruction of lives, emotions, spaces, bodies, languages, practices, beliefs, thoughts, dreams, and possibilities, both in the present and future. Violence creates something new—a new social imaginary with other languages, emotions, practices, beliefs, thoughts, dreams, and possibilities. The effect of violence is transformative even as it is destructive. Violence also has degrees of intensity that go from very low, even invisible, to highly explosive. Violence has many forms, including political violence, textual violence, physical violence, and symbolic violence and can be sporadic or structural, sacrificial or arbitrary, global or domestic, tribal or modern.

Although the violence waged by the members of the Algerian FLN against the French colonial system was perceived as either criminal or terrorist, the latter being a more intense and organized version of the former (in the view of the colonial state), such violence was itself the product of what it fought—modernity. When it overthrew the colonial system, it replaced it with a similar system that was also modern and national. Postcolonial Algeria inherited what it fought, and thus the social dynamics of its society remained similar (if not identical) to those that were replaced.[15] Fanon notes that the national bourgeoisie replaced the colonial bourgeoisie, and he argues that the culture of the national bourgeoisie is a product of colonial culture. Because of Fanon's modern subjectivity, he was surprisingly blind to the Islamic discourse of the "native," which was actually omnipresent in the discourse driving the Algerian war of liberation. Islam is totally absent in Fanon's writings, and he only vaguely references tradition or folklore. Part of this omission may be explained by one of the main theses of this book—that in colonial Algeria, the intense dynamics between local and colonial caused the distinctions between the two to become blurred. Fanon must have seen a national culture in the modern culture of Algeria. Yet the discourse that Fanon saw as only national is seen by colonial sociologists, such as Jacques Berque, as a religious reformist discourse.[16]

Violence, I have argued, is first evident as a conflict in discourse. Before the Algerian war of liberation, a Muslim (Salafi) modernist discourse was forged in the context of colonization and integrated substantially modern categories (albeit with modification) such as the nation, progress, knowledge of history, earthly salvation, and so on. This discourse was created in reaction to and thus also in relation to the colonial discourse. It is modern and yet, for modern Muslims, unmistakably Islamic. It was appropriated (with further modifications) by a younger generation of Algerians who were schooled in French modernity and yet created a discourse that opposed and yet was part of colonial discourse. This oppositional discourse resulted in violent attacks against people and property. The legacy is an ongoing engagement with and antagonism toward France that is alive to this day.

Postcoloniality in Algeria is marked by what I call a *societal grammar* formed in the colonial period. Various identities—political, cultural, and economic—are the products of a colonial history and a colonial political dynamic that changed the cultural landscape of Algeria. Understanding this societal grammar is necessary for understanding the violence that exploded in 1992 and continues to take lives and damage the nation in various ways. The self-declared Islamic discourse is not a distinct element of the conflict. As I have argued in this book, it is just as modern as secular discourse even though sociologists seem eager to draw a religious and secular dichotomy. I have tried to show that the FIS threatened not to take Algerians backward in time or to establish an Islamic state but rather to eliminate a century of French modernity in Algeria. The FIS claimed that it only wanted to replace one form of modernity with another (even as it replaced French with English, the language of global modernity).

Algeria has continued its march toward the future, carrying within itself modernity and Islam, terms that are not only inseparable but mutually defining, interestingly enough not only in Algeria, but also in France itself.[17] This is why, for many observers, the violence of the 1990s was seen as a repeat of the colonial war of the 1950s.[18] At the conclusion of this work, I can say only that the violence Algeria experienced in the 1990s was not a repeat but a continuation of divisions, tensions, and conflicts created in the colonial epoch. The culture of colonial modernity continues to generate events in the present, other transformations notwithstanding.

NOTES

1. Laroui, *L'histoire du Maghreb*, 351. Nationalism has not considered colonialism a crime but has considered some deeds to be crimes. A *méfait* is a *fait* that is badly done and thus can be either undone and/or redone differently (*défait* and/or *refait*). Crimes that result in historical death—which he does not associate with French colonization as such but with every colonization—require justice (that is, trial and punishment). The use of a correct language to describe colonial deeds makes one avoid positing the criminality of the enterprise.

2. See especially Laroui, Abdallah. *The Crisis of the Arab Intellectual*. See also Abdallah Laroui, *Islam et moderité* (Paris: La Découverte, 1987). Laroui has not abandoned this discourse, even in recent interviews. See Abdallah Laroui, "Grande Interview with Abdallah Laroui," in *Economia*, 4, (October 2008–January, 2009) 121–134.

3. Laroui's history of Moroccan nationalism does not make a parallel between modernity and colonialism. Following Jacques Berque, who was formulating a hypothesis on the line of Braudelian argument about the Mediterranean, Laroui dates the advent of modernity in the Maghreb back to the fifteenth century, not to the eighteenth or nineteenth century. For the argument of Berque regarding modernity in the Maghreb, marked by the foundation of modern state throughout the sixteenth and seventeenth centuries, see "Une entrée dans le temps moderne," *Ulémas, fondateurs,*

insurgés du Maghreb: XVIIe siècle (Paris: Sindbad, 1982), 13–43. Laroui thus argues for the continuation of an interrupted history. See Laroui, "Grande Interview." Also, *L'histoire du Maghreb*. This line of argument, like Salafi reasoning before it, contributed to the creation of the condition of the acceptance of modernity in a "home" where there was a strong resistance against it offered by Islam. In essence, it says: "we should be modern because modernity was part of our heritage."

4. See Enrique Dussel, *The Invention of the Americas: Eclipse of "the Other" and the Myth of Modernity* (New York: Continuum, 1995). Dussel shows how modernity originated in the conquest of the Americas by Holland, Spain, Portugal, France, and Britain, thus allowing Europe to go beyond the region of the Mediterranean and become a "world-system." This event, he argues, was marked by a denial of "the other." This denial not only marked its birth, but also its very condition. Modernity recognizes only itself. Maybe this is what Asad refers to when he states that "modernity extinguishes various possibilities". See interview with David Scott titled: "The Trouble of Thinking" in *Powers of the Secular*, ed. David Scott and Charles Hirschkind (Stanford: Stanford University Press, 2006), 274.

5. For more on this point, see Hannoum, "Notes on the (Post)Colonial in the Maghreb" *Critique of Anthropology*: 336–341.

6. Dipesh Chakrabarty, *Proventializing Europe* (Princeton: Princeton University Press, 2003). Chakrabarty also wrote that the rejection of "modernity" is "in many situations, politically suicidal." Instead, he proposes to "provincialize" it. However, Europe cannot be displaced by a discourse that owes its very existence to modern figures such as Marx and Heidegger. Consequently such an ambitious discourse is part and parcel of that which it seeks to displace. Hence, an epistemic impossibility. Nonetheless, Chakrabarty managed to produce a brilliant modern critique, but not a displacement.

7. This discourse is often understood as "nostalgia" for colonialism. Daho Djerbel, an Algerian historian of colonialism believes that "nostalgia of the colonial epoch is unfortunately real." See interview with Yassine Temlali at http://www.ldh-toulon.net/spip.php?article1129. However, this discourse, often times is formulated as a positive memory of colonialism, is nothing but a sarcastic cri-

tique of the state that does for people less than what the French supposedly did.

8. *Shurfa* is the name given in Morocco to those who are believed to be descendants of the Prophet and is a title of nobility associated with a high degree of charisma. It also bestows a great deal of legitimacy on the current Moroccan monarchy, believed to be Sharifian. For more on the concept, see Clifford Geertz, *Islam Observed* (Chicago: University of Chicago Press, 1971), 45–47

9. Chakrabarty, *Proventializing Europe*.

10. To me, the second part was confirmed later when I read it echoed in Tahar Benjelloun's novel, *Moha le fou, Moha le sage* (Paris: Seuil, 1978).

11. James Scott, *Domination and the Arts of Resistance* (New Haven: Yale University Press, 1990).

12. According to the 1936 Blum-Violette project, some Muslim Algerians could become French citizens without renouncing their Muslim status. The project targeted the *evolués* (the Frenchified Algerian elite and former soldiers), who were asking for equal status with metropole French. The project was rejected by both those who desired independence and the ulta-Europeans and was revoked by the Senate in 1938. See Charles-André Julien, *L'Afrique du Nord en marche* (Paris: Omnibus, 2002), 113.

13. I read this in *Le Monde* at the beginning of the Algerian tragedy in early 1990s and am unable to find the exact reference for it.

14. Fanon, *The Wretched of the Earth*.

15. Marnia Lazreg makes a similar point regarding the use of violence against the Algerian FLN and the use of violence by the FLN against France and against the Algerian FIS (and its supporters). Marnia Lazreg, *Torture and the Twilight of Empire* (Princeton: Princeton University Press, 2008), 256.

16. Berque, *Le Maghreb entre les deux guerres*.

17. Historian Joan Scott wrote about the politics of the headscarf: "depending on particular national histories, the idealization of the nation has taken various forms. In France, it has taken the form of an insistence on the values and beliefs of the republic, said to be the realization of the principles of the Enlightenment in their highest, most enduring form. This image is mythical: its power and appeal rest, to a large degree, on its negative portrayal of Islam." Joan Scott, *The Politics of the Veil* (Princeton: Princeton University

Press, 2007), 7. Since the nineteenth century, it has been virtually impossible to speak of Islam without speaking of modernity. This is apparent even in radical Islamist discourses. But one cannot speak of modernity without speaking of its others (it denies and it needs at the same time).

18. Among others, Pierre Bourdieu, "Dévoiler et divulguer le refoulé," in Joseph Jurt, *Algérie—France—Islam* (Paris: L'Harmathan 1997), 24; Asia Djebar, *Le nouveau quotidian,* December 4, 1997. Lazreg, *Torture and the Twilight of Empire,* 256–257.

Selected Bibliography

Abdel-Malek, Anouar. "Orientalism in Crisis." *Diogenes* 44 (Winter 1963), 103–140.

Abraham, Philip. "Notes on the Difficulties of Studying the State," in *Journal of Historical Sociology* (1986): 58–89.

Abu El-Haj, Nadia. *Facts on the Ground*. Chicago: University of Chicago Press, 2001.

Addi, Houari. *L'Algérie et la démocracie: pouvoir et crise du politique dans l'Algérie contemporaine*. Paris: Editions la Découverte, 1994.

Ageron, Charles Robert. *L'Algérie algérienne de Napoléon III à de Gaule*. Paris: Sindbad, 1980.

Ageron, Charles-Robert. *Les Algériens musulmans et la France, 1871–1919*. Paris: Presses Universitaires de France, 1968.

Al-Aiachi-Moula-Ahmed, *Voyages dans le sud de l'Algérie et des états barbaresques de l'ouest et de l'est*. Trans. Adrian Berbrugger. Paris: Imprimerie impériale, 1846.

Alderman, Derek H. "Place, Naming and the Interpretation of Cultural Landscapes." In Brian and Peter Howard *Ashgate Research Companion to Heritage and Identity*. Burlington: Ashgate Publishing, 2008: 195–214.

Anderson, Benedict. *Imagined Communities*. London, Verso, 1992.

Anonymous [Ismael Urbain], *Indigènes et immigrants*. Paris: Challamel, 1862.

Anonymous. *La Kabylie: recherches et observations sur cette riche contrée de l'Algérie par un colon.* Paris: Maistrasse et Wiart, 1864.

Appaduri, Arjun. *Fear of Small Numbers.* Durham: Duke University Press, 2007.

Appaduri, Arjun. *Modernity at Large.* Minneapolis: University of Minnesota Press, 1996.

Archives Chateaux de Versailles, *les archives d'outre mer,* Paris. Carton H, Carton H 191, Carton H 193, Carton H 375.

Arendt, Hannah. *On Violence.* New York: Harvest Books, 1969.

Arendt, Hannah. "Race-Thinking before Racism," *The Origins of Totalitarianism.* New York: Harcourt, Brace & Wold, Inc., 1966.

Aretxaga, Begona. *Shattering Silence.* Princeton: Princeton University Press, 1996.

Arnold, Bettina. "The Past as Propaganda: Totalitarian Archeology in Nazi Germany." *Antiquity* 64 (1990): 464–478.

Aron, Raymond. *Dimensions de la conscience historique.* Paris: Plon, 1961.

Aron, Raymond. *Les etapes de la pensée sociologique.* Paris: Gallimard, 1967.

Asad, Talal. *The Formation of the Secular.* Stanford: Stanford University Press, 2001.

Asad, Talal. *Genealogies of Religion.* Baltimore: Johns Hopkins University Press, 1996.

Asad, Talal. *On Suicide Bombings.* New York: Columbia University Press, 2007.

Asad, Talal. "Religion, Nation State, Secularism," in *Nation and Religion* (Princeton: Princeton University Press, 1999), 187–203.

Aucapitaine, Henri. *Le pays et la societé kabyle.* Paris: Bertrand, 1857.

Azmeh, Aziz. *Ibn Khaldûn in Modern Scholarship.* London: Third World Center for Research, 1981.

Balibar, Etienne. "Dissonances within *Laïcité.*" *Constellations* 11, no. 3 (2004): 353–367.

Balout, Lionel, et al. *Vingt-cinq ans d'histoire algérienne: recherches et publications.* Algiers: Latypo-Litho et Carbonel, 1956.

Barthes, Roland. *A Barthes Reader.* New York: Farrar, Straus and Giroux, 1982.

Barthes, Roland. "Le discours de l'histoire." *Social Science Information* 6 (1967): 56–75.

Barthes, Roland. *Mythologies*. New York: Hill & Wang, 1972.

Barthes, Roland. "L'écriture de l'événement." *Communications* 12 (1968): 108–112.

Bataille, George. *The Accused Share*. Zone: New Press, 1988.

Bel, Alfred. *La religion musulmane en Berbérie*. Paris: Geuthner, 1938.

Benjamin, Walter. *Illuminations*. New York: Schocken, 1969.

Benjelloun, Tahar. *Moha le fou, Moha le sage*. Paris: Seuil, 1978.

Berbrugger, Adrien. *Algérie historique, pittoresque et monumentale*. Paris: Delahaye, 1843.

Berque, Jacques. "Ibn Khaldûn et les bédouins" *Maghreb: histoire et sociétés*. Algiers: Duculot, 1974.

Berque, Jacques. *L'intérieur du Maghreb*. Paris: Gallimard, 1978.

Berque, Jacques. *Ulémas, fondateurs, insurgés du Maghreb: XVIIe siècle*. Paris: Sindbad, 1982.

Berque, Jacques. *Le Maghreb entre les deux guerres*. Paris: Seuil, 1967.

Berque, Jacques. "Vingt ans de sociologie maghrebine." *Annales: Economie, Société, Civilisation* 11 (1956): 286–324.

Biesse-Eichelbrenner, Michèle. *Constantine: la conquête et le temps des pionniers*. Honfleur: Marie, 1985.

Blachère, Régis. "La place d'Ibn Khaldun dans l'humanisme arabo-islamique." *Revue des Deux Mondes* (October 1972): 70–79.

Blumenberg, Hans. *The Legitimacy of the Modern Age*. Cambridge: MIT Press. 1983.

Bodenhorn, Barbara, and Gabriele Von Bruck. *The Anthropology of Names and Naming*. Cambridge: Cambridge University Press, 2006.

Bou Aziz, Yaha. *Thawrat 1871: Dawr al Muqrani wa al Haddad*. Algiers: Al-Sharika al Wataniya, 1978.

Bourdieu, Pierre. *Acts of Resistance*. New York: New Press, 1998.

Bourdieu, Pierre. "Dévoiler et divulguer le refoulé." in Joseph Jurt *Algérie, France, Islam*. Paris: L'Harmattan, 1997.

Braudel, Fernand. "A propos de 'L'histoire de l'Afrique du Nord de Ch. Andre Julien.'" *Revue Africaine* (1933): 37–53.

Brunschvig, Robert. *La Berbérie orientale sous les Hafsides.* Paris: Adrien-Maisonneuve, 1982.

Bugeaud, Thomas. *Par l'épée et par la charrue.* Paris: Presse Universitaire de France, 1948.

Bugeaud, Thomas. *De l'établissement de légions des colons militaires dans les possessions français du nord de l'afrique.* Paris: Firmin Didot, 1838.

Bugeaud, Thomas, and Daumas Eugene. *Exposé de l'état de la société arabe, du governement et de la législation qui la régit.* Algiers: Imprimerie du gouvernement, 1844.

Burke, Edmund. "Two Critics of French Rule in Algeria: Ismael Urbain and Frantz Fanon." *Franco-Arab Encounters.* Beirut: American University of Beirut, 1996. 329–344.

Carette, Ernest. *Etudes sur la Kabylie proprement dite.* Paris: Imprimerie nationale, 1848.

Carette, Ernest. *Recherches sur l'origine et les migrations des principaux tribus de l'Afrique septentrionale et partculièrement de l'Algérie.* Paris: Imprimerie Nationale, 1853.

Cassirer, Ernest. *An Essay on Man.* New Haven: Yale University Press, 1994.

Castoriadis, Cornelius *Domaine de l'homme.* Paris: Seuil, 1986.

Castoriadis, Cornelius. "The Imaginary: Creation in the Social-Historical Domain." Paisley Livingston, ed., *Order and Disorder.* Menlo Park, Calif. : Benjamin/Cummings Pub. Co., Advanced Book Program, 1984.

Castoriadis, Cornelius. *L'institution et l'imaginaire.* Paris: Seuil, 1975.

Cate, Edouard. *Petite histoire de l'Algérie.* Algiers: Jourdan, 1889.

Caton, Steve. "Anger Be Now Thy Song: The Anthropology of Event." *Institute for Advanced Study Occasional Papers,* No. 5, November 1999. 1–20.

Celik, Zynep. *Urban Forms and Colonial Confrontations.* Berkeley: University of California Press, 1997.

Certeau, Michel de. *Ecriture de l'histoire.* Paris: Gallimard, 1975.

Certeau, Michel de. "L'histoire et le réel." *Dialectiques* 14 (1976): 42–62.

Chakrabarty, Dipesh. *Proventializing Europe*. Princeton: Princeton University 2003.

Chatterjee, Partha. *The Nation and Its Fragments*. Princeton: Princeton University Press, 1996.

Cheddadi, Abdesslam. *Ibn Khaldûn revisité*. Casablanca: Toubqal, 1999.

Clancy-Smith, Julia. *Rebel and Saint*. Berkeley: University of California Press, 1994.

Cohn, Bernard. *An Anthropologist amongst Historians*. Oxford: Oxford University Press, 1987.

Cohn, Bernard. *Colonialism and Its Forms of Knowledge*. Princeton: Princeton University Press, 1996.

Cole, Joshua. "Intimate Acts of Unspeakable Relations." In Alec Hargreaves, ed., *Memory, Empire, and Postcolonialism*. Lanham: Lexington Books, 2005. 125–141.

Collingwood, Robin George. *The Idea of History*. Oxford: Oxford University Press, 1963.

Combs-Schilling, Elaine. *Sacred Performances: Islam, Sexuality, and Sacrifice*. New York: Columbia University Press, 1989.

Conrad, Joseph. *Heart of Darkness*. New York: Bantam, 1981.

Daniel, Norman. *Islam and the West: The Making of an Image*. Edinburgh: Edinburgh University Press, 1960.

Daniel, Valentine. *Charred Lullabies*. Princeton: Princeton University Press, 1996.

Danto, Arthur. *Narration and Knowledge*. New York: Columbia University Press, 1986.

Daumas, Eugène. *Moeurs et coutumes d'Algérie*. Paris: Hachette, 1953. Originally published 1855.

Daumas, Eugène. *La vie arabe et la société musulmane*. Paris: Lévy, 1869.

Daumas, Eugène, and Paul-Dieudonné Fabar. *La Grande Kabylie*. Paris: Hachette, 1847.

Davis, Nathalie Zemon. *Society and Culture on Early Modern France*. Stanford: Stanford University Press, 1975.

De Sacy, Silvestre. "Déclaration aux Algériens." *Revue Africaine* 6 (1962): 150–156.

De Slane, William. *L'histoire des Berbères d'Ibn Khaldûn.* Algiers: Imprimerie du Gouvernement, 1852–1856.

De Slane, William. *Prolegomènes historique d'Ibn Khaldun.* Algiers: Imprimerie du Governement, 1863.

Devaux, Charles. *Les Kebailes du Djerdjera,* Marseille: Camoin, 1859.

Dielter, Michael. "Our Ancestors the Gauls: Archeology, Ethnic Nationalism, and the Manipulation of Celtic Identity in Modern Europe." *American Anthropologist* 96, no. 3 (September 1994): 584–601.

Dirks, Nicholas. *Castes of Mind.* Princeton: Princeton University Press, 2001.

Djebar, Asia. *Le nouveau quotidian,* December 4, 1997.

Djerbel, Daho. *Interview.* http://www.ldh-toulon.net/spip.php?article1129.

Ducheron, Francine. *Bordj-bou-Arreridj pendant l'insurrection de 1871 en Algérie.* Paris: Plon, 1873.

Ducos, Edouard. *L'Algérie: quelques mots de réponse à la brochure, La vérité sur l'Algérie par le général Ducrot.* Paris: E. Dentu, 1871.

Ducrot, Auguste. *La vérité sur l'Algérie.* Paris: E. Dentu, 1871.

Durkheim, Emile. *The Division of Labor in Society.* Trans. G. Simpson. London: Free Press, 1933.

Durkheim, Emile. *The Elementary Forms of the Religious Life.* New York: Free Press, 1965.

Dussel, Enrique. *The Invention of the Americas: Eclipse of "the Other" and the Myth of Modernity.* New York: Continuum, 1995.

Emerit, Marcel. "La lutte entre les généraux et les prêtres au début de l'Algérie française." *Revue Africaine* (1949): 65–125.

Emerit, Marcel. "Le problème de la conversion des musulmans de l'Algérie." *Revue Historique* 223 (1960): 63–84.

Emerit, Marcel. *Les Saint Simonians en Algérie.* Paris: Société d'édition, 1941.

Eisenstadt, S. N. "Multiple Modernities," *Daedalus* 129 (200): 1.

Enfatin, Prosper. *Colonisation de l'Algérie.* Paris: Bertrand, 1843.

Etienne, Bruno. *Les combatants suicidaires.* Paris: Editions de l'Aube, 2005.

Fabian, Johannes. *Time and the Other.* New York: Columbia University Press, 1983.

Faidherbe, Louis Léon César. *Instructions sur l'anthropologie de l'Algérie.* Paris: Hennuyer, 1874.

Fanon, Frantz. *The Wretched of the Earth.* New York: Grove Press, 1963.

M. Farouk, T. S. Senhadji and M. Ait Larbi, edit. Voices of the Voiceless" in the *Association for the Defense of the Victims of the Massacres in Algeria,* Copenhagen, 1999. online access: http://www.hoggar.org/books/Massacres/11Voiceless.pdf

Feldman, Allen. *Formations of Violence.* Chicago: University of Chicago Press, 1991.

Feraud, Charles. *Les interprètes de l'armée d'Afrique.* Alger: Jourdan, 1876.

Fischel, Walter. "Ibn Khaldûn's Use of Historical Sources" *Studia Islamica,* No. 14 (1961), 109–119.

Forest, Louis. *La naturalisation des Juifs algériens et l'insurrection de 1871.* Paris: Société française d'imprimerie, 1897.

Foucault, Michel. *L'archeologie du savior.* Paris: Gallimard, 1969.

Foucault, Michel. *The Archeology of Knowledge.* New York: Pantheon, 1972.

Foucault, Michel. "Governmentality." In Graham Burchell, Colin Gordon, and Peter Miller, eds., *The Foucault Effect.* Chicago: University of Chicago Press, 1991.

Foucault, Michel. *Il faut défendre la société.* Paris: Hautes Etudes, 1997.

Foucault, Michel. "Qu'est-cequ'un anteur?" *Dits et Ecrits.* Paris: Gallimard, 1994.

Frémeaux, Jacques. *Les Bureaux arabes dans l'Algérie de la conquête.* Paris: Donël, 1993.

Fournel, Henri. *Les Berbères: études sur la conquête de l'Afrique par les Arabes.* Paris: Imprimerie nationale, 1875.

Fournel, *Etudes sur la conquête de l'Afrique par les Arabes.* Paris: Imprimerie Nationale. 1857.

Fure-Biguet, G. *Histoire de l'Afrique septentrionale sous la domination musulmane.* Paris: Charles-Lavauzelle, 1905.

Furet, François. *Interpreting the French Revolution.* Cambridge: Cambridge University Press, 1981.

Gallo, Max. On laïcité positive. www.liberation.fr/evenement/010189216-ancienne-conception-de-la-laicite-est-depassee (accessed September 19, 2009).

Gallo, Max. On Muslims and their faith. www.lefigaro.fr/debats/20060208.GIG0209.htm?073334 (accessed September 19, 2009).

Gautier, Emile-Félix. *L'Algérie et la métropole.* Paris: Payot, 1920.

Gautier, Emile-Félix. "Le cadre géographique de l'histoire en Algérie." *Histoire et historiens de l'Algérie.* Paris: Felix Alcan, 1930, 17–35.

Gautier, Emile-Félix. "Native Life in North Africa." *Geographical Review* 13 (1923): 27–39.

Gautier, Emile-Félix. *Les siècles obscurs.* Paris: Payot, 1927.

Geertz, Clifford. *Islam Observed.* Chicago: University of Chicago Press, 1971.

Geertz, Clifford. *The Interpretation of Cultures.* New York: Basic Books, 1975.

Geertz, Clifford. *Local Knowledge.* New York: Basic Books, 1983.

Geertz, Clifford. "La religion, sujet d'avenir." *Le Monde,* May 6, 2006. 000.

Geertz, Clifford. *Works and Lives: The Anthropologist as Author.* Stanford: Stanford University Press, 1984.

Gellner, Ernest. *Muslim Society.* Cambridge: Cambridge University Press, 1981.

Gèze, François and Vidal-Naquet, Pierre, "L'Algérie de Bernard-Henri Lévy." *Le Monde,* March 5, 1998.

Giddens, Anthony. *The Consequences of Modernity.* Stanford: Stanford University Press, 1990.

Giradet, Raoul. *L'idée coloniale en France.* Paris: La Table Ronde, 1972.

Gobineau, Arthur. *Essai sur l'inégalité des races humaines.* Paris: Firmin Didot, 1853–1855.

Gobineau, Arthur. *The Inequality of Human Races.* Trans. Adrian Collins. New York: H. Fertig, 1967.

Greimas, Algirdas-Julien, and Courtès, Joseph. *Dictionnaire raison né du language.* Paris: Hachette, 1979.

Greimas, Algirdas-Julien. *Du sens II: Essais sémiotiques.* Paris: Seuil, 1983.

Greimas, Algirdas-Julien. *Structural Semantics.* Lincoln: University of Nebraska Press, 1983.

Greimas, Algirdas-Julien. "On Chance Occurances in What We Call the Human Sciences," *On Meaning,* trans. Paul J. Perron and Frank H. Collins, foreword by Frederic Jameson. London: Pinter, 1987.

Gsell, Stéphane. *Histoire ancienne de l'Afrique du Nord.* Paris, Hachette, 1914–1930.

Gsell Stéphane. *Les monuments antiques de l'Algérie.* Paris: Thorin, 1901.

Gsell, Stéphane, et al. *Histoire et historiens de l'Algérie.* Paris: Alcan, 1931.

Guha, Ranajit. *Elementary Aspects of Peasant Insurgency in Colonial India.* Durham: Duke University Press, 1999.

Guha, Ranajit. "The Prose of Counter-Insurgency." *Subaltern Studies.* Oxford: Oxford University Press, 1988.

Hammer, Joseph de. "Sur l'introduction à la connaissance de l'histoire, célèbre ouvrage d'Ibn Khaldûn." *Journal Asiatique.* (1822): 267–78.

Hammoudi, Abdallah. *Une saison à la Mecque.* Paris: Seuil, 2005.

Hammoudi, Abdallah. *The Victim and Its Masks.* Chicago: University of Chicago Press, 1993.

Hammoudi, Abdallah, and Stuart Schaar, eds. *Algeria's Impasse.* Princeton: Center for International Studies, Princeton University, 1995.

Hannoum, Abdelmajid. "L'auteur comme autorité en ethnographie coloniale" in Francois Pouillon et Daniel Rivet, ed., *La sociologie musulmane de Robert Montagne.* Paris: Maisonneuve & Larose, 2000, 251–266

Hannoum, Abdelmajid. *Colonial Histories, Post-Colonial Memories.* Portsmouth: Greenwood, 2001.

Hannoum, Abdelmajid. "Colonialism and Knowledge in Algeria: The Archives of the Arab Bureau." *History and Anthropology* 4 (2001): 343–379.

Hannoum, Abdelmajid. "The Historiographic State: How Algeria Once Became French" in *History an Anthropology* 19 (2008): 91–114.

Hannoum, Abdelmajid. "Notes on the (Post)Colonial in the Maghreb" *Critique of Anthropology*, 29, no.3 (2009): 324–344.

Hannoum, Abdelmajid. "Paul Ricoeur on Memory." *Theory, Culture, and Society* (2005): 123–137.

Hannoum, Abdelmajid. "Translation and the Colonial Imaginary: Ibn Khaldûn Orientalist." *History and Theory* 42 (2003): 61–81.

Hannoum, Abdelmajid. "Translation and the Imaginary." *Anthropology News* (November 2002).

Hanouteau, Adolphe, and Aristide Letourneau. *La Kabylie et les coutumes kabyles*. Paris: Imprimerie Nationale, 1872.

Hartog, François. *Régimes d'historicité*. Paris: Seuil, 2003.

Hjelmslev, Louis. *Prolégomènes è une théorie du language*. Paris: Minuit, 1968.

Hourani, Albert. *Arabic Thought in the Liberal Age, 1798–1939*. London: Oxford University Press, 1970.

Hubert, Henri, and Marcel Mauss. *Sacrifice: Its Nature and Function*. Chicago: University of Chicago Press, 1964.

Hugonnet, Ferdinand. *Français et Arabes en Algérie*. Paris: Sartorus & Challamel, 1860.

Hugonnet, Ferdinand. *Souvenirs d'un chef du Bureau arabe*. Paris: Michel Levy, 1858.

Hussein, Taha. *Etude analytique de la philosophie sociale d'Ibn Khaldûn*. Paris: Vrin, 1919.

Ibn Ishaq, Mohamed. *The Life of Mohamed*. Oxford: Oxford University Press, 1997.

Ibn Khaldûn, Abderrahmane. *Histoire des Berbères*. Trans. William de Slane. Algiers: Imprimerie du gouvernement, 1852–1856.

Ibn Khaldûn, Abderrahmane. *Kitâb al-ʿibar was dîwân al mubatadaʿ wa al khabar fî ayyâmi al ʿarab wa al barbar wa man ʿâsarahum min dhawî al sultân al akbar*. Beirut: 1959. 7 vols.

Ibn Khaldûn, Abderrahmane. *Muqaddima*. Beirut: Dar al Kutub alʿIlmiya, n.d.

Ibn Khaldûn. *Muqaddima*. Trans. by Frantz Rosental. Princeton: Princeton University Press, 1967.

Ishaq, Khalil. *Précis de jurisprudence musulmane et principes de législation musulmane civile et religieuse selon le rite malikite*. Trans. Nicholas Perron. Paris, Imprimerie nationale, 1848–52.

Issawi, Charles. *An Arab Philosophy of History: Selections*. Princeton: Darwin Press, 1987.

Jakobson, Roman. *Language and Literature*. Cambridge: Harvard University Press, 1987.

Kapchan, Deborah. *Gender on the Market*. Philadelphia: University of Pennsylvania Press, 1996.

Kapferer, Jean-Noel. *Rumeurs: le plus view media du monde*. Paris: Seuil, 1987. English translation, *Rumors: Uses, Interpretations, and Images*. New Brunswick: Transaction Publishers, 1990.

Kedourie, Elie. *Afghani and 'Abduh: An Essay on Religious Unbelief and Political Activism in Modern Islam*. London: Frank Cass, 1966.

Kepel, Gilles. *Prophet and Pharaoh*. London, Al Saqi Books, 1985.

Kerr, Malcom. *Islamic Reform: The Political and Legal Theories of Muhammad 'Abduh and Rashid Rida*. Berkeley: University of California Press, 1966.

Khalidi, Tarif. *Arabic Thought in the Classical Period*. Cambridge: Cambridge University Press, 1994.

Koselleck, Reinhart. *Future Pasts*. New York: Columbia University Press, 2004.

LaCapra, Dominic. *History in Transit*. Ithaca: Cornell University Press, 2004.

Lapasset, Ferdinand. *Apercu sur l'organisation des indigènes*. Paris: Dubos, 1850.

Lapène, Edward. *Tableau historique, moral et politique sur les Kabyles*. Metz: Academie Royale, 1846.

Laroui, Abdallah. *The Crisis of the Arab Intellectual*. California: University of California Press,1976.

Laroui, Abdallah. "Grande Interview with Abdallah Laroui." *Economia* 4 (October 2008–January, 2009): 121–134.

Laroui, Abdallah. *L'histoire du Maghreb*. Paris: Maspero, 1973.

Laroui, Abdallah. *Islam et modernité*. Paris: La Découverte, 1987.

Lavigne, Albert. *Le régime du sabre.* Paris: Lacroix, 1871.

Lazreg, Marnia. *Torture and the Twilight of Empire.* Princeton: Princeton University Press, 2008.

Le Tourneau, Roger. *L'évolution politique de l'Afrique du Nord musulmane.* Paris: Colin, 1962.

Lévi-Strauss, Claude. *Structural Anthropology.* New York: Basic Books, 1976.

Lévi-Strauss, Claude. *Structural Anthropology II.* Trans. M. Lyton. Chicago: University of Chicago Press, 1983.

Lévy, Bernard-Henri. "Choses vues en Algérie" *Le Monde,* January 8–9, 1998

Littré, Emile. *Dictionaire de la language française.* Paris: Hachette, 1863–1872.

Madani, Abbas. *Interview.* Aljazeera, November 11, 2003.

McDougall, James. *History and the Culture of Nationalism in Algeria.* Cambridge: Cambridge University Press, 2006.

Malarkey, James. "The Dramatic Structure of Scientific Discovery in Colonial Algeria: A Critique of the Journal of the *Société Archéologique de Constantine* (1853–1876)" in *Connaîssances du Maghreb,* Paris: CNRS in Jean Claude Vatin, ed., 137–160.

Mamdani, Mahmood. *Citizen and Subject.* Princeton: Princeton University Press, 1996.

Mamadani, Mahmood. *When Victims Become Killers.* Princeton: Princeton University Press, 2001.

Man, Paul de. "'Conclusions' on Walter Benjamin's *The Task of the Translator.*" *Yale French Studies* 97(2000): 10–35.

Marçais, George. *La Berbérie musulmane et l'Orient au moyen age.* Paris: Aubier, Montaigne, 1946.

Marçais, William. "Comment l'Afrique du Nord a été arabisée." *Annales de l'Institut d'Etudes Orientales, Algiers* 4 (1938): 1–21.

Marona, Mabel, Enrique Dussel, and Carlos Jauregui. *Coloniality at Large.* Durham: Duke University Press, 2008.

Martinez, Luis. *The Algerian Civil War.* New York: Columbia University Press, 2000.

Marx, Karl. *The Eighteenth Brumaire of Louis Bonaparte.* New York: International Publishers, 1935.

Masqueray, Emile. *La formation des cités chez les populations sédentaires de l'Algérie.* Aix-en-Provence: Edisud, 1983.

Mayor, Arno. *The Furies: Violence and Terror in the French and Russian Revolutions.* Princeton: Princeton University Press, 2000.

Mellah, Salima, *Les massacres en Algérie,* Comité Justice pour l'Algérie, Mai 2004. Online access: http://www.algerie-tpp.org/tpp/pdf/dossier_2_massacres.pdf

Merad. *Le réformisme musulman en Algérie de 1925 à 1940.* La Haye: Mouton, 1967.

Mercier, Ernest. "La bataille de Poitiers et les vraies causes de recul de l'invasion arabe." *Revue historique* 7 (1878): 1–13.

Mercier, Ernest. "Ethnographie de l'Afrique septentrionale: notes sur l'origine du peuple berbère." *Revue Africaine* 15 (1871): 420–433.

Mercier, Ernest. *L'histoire de l'établissement des Arabes dans l'Afrique septentrionale.* 3 vols. Constantine: Marle, 1875.

Mercier, Ernest. "La race berbère: véritable population de l'Afrique septentrionale." *Société Archéologique de Constantine* 39 (1905): 23–59.

Mercier, Ernest. *Questions algériennes.* Paris: Challamel, 1883.

Merleau-Ponty, Maurice. *Adventures of the Dialectics.* Trans. Joseph Bien. Evanston: Northwestern University Press, 1973.

Merleau-Ponty, Maurice. *Phénomenologie de la perception.* Paris: Gallimard, 1945.

Meschonnic, Henri. *Modernité Modernité.* LaGrasse: Verdier, 1988.

Mink, Louis. *Historical Understanding.* Ithaca: Cornell University Press, 1987.

Monglave, Eugène. *La Kabylie.* n.p., 1857?.

Monteil, Vincent. *"Les Bureaux arabes au Maghreb (1833–1961)."* *Esprit,* November, 1961: 575–606.

Moussaoui, Abderrahmane. *De la violence en Algérie.* Paris: Acts Sud, 2006.

Napoleon III. *Lettre sur la politique de la France en Algérie addressée par l'Empereur au Marechal de Mac Mahon.* Paris: Imprimerie Nationale, 1865.

Nietzsche, Friedrich. *Basic Writings of Nietzsche.* New York: Modern Library, 2000.

Nora, Pierre. *Histories: French Constructions of the Past.* New York: New Press, 1995.

Nordstrom, Carol. *A Different Kind of War Story.* Philadelphia: University of Pennsylvania Press, 1997.

Obyesekere, Gananath. *European Mythmaking in the Pacific: The Apotheosis of Captain Cook.* Princeton: Princeton University Press, 1992, 1996.

Peyronnet, Raymond. *Livre d'or des officiers et des affaires indigènes.* Algiers: Imprimerie Algérienne, 1930.

Pomian, Krystztof. "Les archives." In Pierre Nora, ed., *Lieux de mémoire.* Paris: Gallimard, vol. 3, 1992: 162–233.

Pomian, Krystztof, *L'ordre du temps.* Paris: Gallimard, 1986.

Prochaska, David. *Making Algeria French.* Cambridge: Cambridge University Press, 1992.

Qayrawani, Mohammed ibn abi-El-Raïni. *Histoire de l'Afrique,* trans. E. Pellissier and Ch. Remusat. Paris: Imprimerie Impériale, 1845.

Quatremère, Etienne. "Ibn Khaldûn's Muqaddima." in *Notices et extraits des mss de la Bibliothèque impériale,* vols. 16–18 (Paris: 1858).

Rabinow, Paul. *French Modern.* Cambridge: MIT Press, 1989.

Rambaud, Alfred. "L'insurrection algerienne de 1871." *Nouvelle Revue* (October 1–October 15, 1891): 000–000.

Rapport fait au nom de la commission d'enquête sur les actes du gouvernement de la defense nationale. Versailles: Imprimeurs de l'Assemblée Nationale, 1872.

Régnier, Philip. *Ismayl Urbain: voyage d'Orient.* Paris: L'Harmattan, 1993.

Reig, Daniel. *Homo orientaliste.* Paris: Maisonneuve, 1988.

Reinaud, Joseph. "Ibn Khaldûn." *Nouvelle biographie générale.* vol. 25. 1861.

Renan, Ernest. "De la part des peuples sémitiques dans l'histoire de la civilization." *Mélanges d'histoire et de voyages.* Paris: Calmann Levy, 1864. 1–25.

Renan, Ernest. "Qu'est-ce que c'est qu'une nation?" *Oeuvres Complétes.* Vol. 1. Paris: C. Levy, 1947.

Renan, Ernest. "La société berbère." *Mélanges d'histoire et de voyages.* Paris: Calmann Levy, 1878.

Review de Press, *Algérie,* January 1998, No. 421–5.

Reynaud, Pellissier de. *Annales algériennes.* Paris: J. Dumain, 1854.

Reynold, Dwight, ed. *Interpreting the Self.* Berkeley: University of California Press, 2001.

Richard, Charles. *De la civilisation du peuple arabe.* Algiers: Dubos, 1850.

Richard, Charles. *Etudes sur l'insurrection du Dhara (1845–1846).* Algiers: Besancenez, 1864.

Richard, Charles. *Du gouvernement arabe et de l'institution qui doit l'exercer.* Algiers: Bastide, 1848.

Ricoeur, Paul and Canto-Sperber, Monique. "Laïcité d'exclusion" in *Le Monde,* December 11, 2003:

Ricoeur, Paul. *Evénement et sens" L'évenement en perspective,* edited by Jean Lepetit. Paris: EHESS, 1991, 41–56.

Ricoeur, Paul. *Histoire et vérité.* Paris: Hachette, 1955.

Ricoeur, Paul. "Imagination in Discourse and in Action." In Gillian Robinson and John Rundell, eds., *Rethinking Imagination.* New York: Routledge, 1994. 000–000.

Ricoeur, Paul. *La mémoire, l'histoire, l'oubli.* Paris: Seuil, 2000.

Ricoeur, Paul. "Les paradigmes de la traduction." *Esprit* (1999): 8–19.

Ricoeur, Paul. *Temps et récit.* Vol. 1. Paris: Seuil, 1985.

Rinn, Louis. "Deux chansons kabyles sur l'insurrection de 1871." *Revue Africaine.* (1887): 55–71.

Rinn, Louis. "Deux documents indigènes sur l'histoire de l'insurrection." *Revue Africaine.* (1891): 21–37.

Rinn, Louis. *Histoire de l'insurrection de 1871 en Algérie.* Algiers: Jourdan, 1891.

Roberts, Hugh. *Algeria, the Battlefield: Studies in a Broken Polity.* London: Verso, 2003.

Robin, Nil. *L'insurrection de la Grande Kabylie en 1871.* Lavanzelle, 1901.

Robin, Nil. "Les imessebelen" *Revue Africaine* 108 (November 1874): 401–412.

Robbins, Jill. "Sacrifice." In Marc Taylor, ed., *Critical Terms for Religious Studies*. Chicago: University of Chicago Press, 1998. 285–297.

Sacy, Silvestre de. *Chrestomathie arabe* (1808).

Sacy, Silvestre de. "Ibn Khaldûn." In *Biographie universelle*. Vol. 21. 1818.

Sacy, Silvestre de. *Relation de l'Egypte par Abd-Allatif*. Paris: Treuttel et Würtz, 1810.

Sahlins, Marshal. *Culture in Practice*. New York: Zone Books, 2000.

Sahraoui, Nabil. "Interview." *Al Hayat*, January 8, 2003.

Said, Edward. *Orientalism*. New York: Vintage, 1979.

Sarkozy, Nicolas. Speech about *laïcité*. Catholique.org (accessed September 9, 2009)

Saussure, Ferdinand. *Cours de linguistique générale*. Paris: Payot, 1985.

Schulz, F. E. "Sur le grand ouvrage historique et critique d'Ibn Khaldûn." *Journal Asiatique* 7 (1825): 213–300.

Scott, James. *Domination and the Arts of Resistance*. New Haven: Yale University Press, 1990.

Scott, Joan. *The Politics of the Veil*. Princeton: Princeton University Press, 2007.

Shibutani, Tamotsu. *Improvised News: A Sociological Study of Rumor*. Indianapolis: Bobbs-Merrill, 1965.

Shatzmiller, Maya. *L'historiographie mérinide: Ibn Khaldûn et ses contemporains*. Leiden: E. J. Brill, 1982.

Simar, Théophile. *Etude critique sur la formation de la doctrine des races au 18è siècle et son expansion au 19è siècle*. Brussels: Lamertin, 1922.

Stoler, Ann. "In Cold Blood: Hierarchies of Credibility and the Politics of Colonial Narratives." *Representations* (Winter 1992): 151–189.

Stora, Benjamin. "Absence et surabondance de mémoire." In Mohamed Benrabah, ed. *Les Violences en Algérie*. Paris: Odile Jacob, 1998.

Stora, Benjamin. *L'Algérie en 1995: la guerre, l'histoire, la politique*. Paris: Michalon, 1995.

Stora, Benjamin. *La guerre invisible, Algérie. Années 90*. Paris: Presses de Sciences Po, 2001.

Strenski, Ivan. *Contesting Sacrifice.* Chicago: University of Chicago Press, 2002.

Tabari, *Târîkh.* Beirut: Maktabat Khayyât, nd.

Tacitus, *Agricola.* Cambridge: Harvard University Press, 1970.

Taine, Hyppolite. *La Fontaine et ses fables.* Paris: Hachette, 1861.

Taine, Hyppolite. *Histoire de la littérature anglaise.* Paris: Hachette, 1863.

Taine, Hyppolite. *De l'intélligence.* Paris: Hachette, 1861.

Talliart, Charles. "La faculté d'Alger." In Stéphane Gsell, ed., *Histoire et Historiens de l'Algérie.* Paris: Librarie Felix Alcan, 1931. 363–80.

Taussig, Michael. *Colonialism, Shamanism, and the Wild Man.* Chicago: University of Chicago Press, 1987.

Taussig, Michael. "Culture of Terror-Space of Death: Roger Casement's Putumayo Report and the Explanation of Torture." *Comparative Studies in Society and History* 26, no. 3 (1984): 467–497.

Taussig, Michael. "Transgression." In Marc Taylor, ed., *Critical Terms for Religious Studies.* Chicago: University of Chicago Press, 1997: 349–363.

Tassy, Garcin de. "Suppélement à la notice de M. de Hammer." *Journal Asiatique* 4 (1824): 158–161.

Taylor, Charles. *A Secular Age.* Cambridge: Harvard University Press, 2007.

Tocqueville, Alexis de. *De la colonie en Algérie.* Paris: Complexe, 1988.

Tocqueville, Alexis de. *Oeuvres complétes.* Paris: Gallimard, 1991.

Touraine, Alain. *La critique de la modernité.* Paris: Fayard: 1992.

Trouillot, Michel-Rolph. Silencing the Past: Power and the Production of History. Boston: Beacon Press, 1996.

Tuck, Richard. *The Rights of War and Peace: Political Thought and International Order from Grotius to Kant.* Oxford: Oxford University Press, 1999.

Trumelet, Corneille. *Histoire de l'insurrection des Ouled Sidi Cheikh de 1864 à 1880.* Algiers: Jourdan, 1880.

Urbain, Ismael (published under George Voisin). *L'Algérie pour les Algériens.* Paris: Michel Levy Frères, 1861.

Urbain, Ismael. "Du gouvernement des tribus de l'Algérie." *Revue de l'Orient et de l'Algérie* 2 (1847): 241–259.

Urbain, Ismael, (published under Anonymous) *Indigènes et immigrants.* Paris: Challamel, 1861.

Urbain, Ismael. "Les Kabyles du Djurdjura," *Revue de Paris* 36 (1857): 91–110.

Urbain, Ismael. "La tolérance de l'Islamisme," *Revue de Paris* (XXXI) (April 1856): 63–81.

Vatin, Jean Claude. *L'Algérie des anthropologues.* Paris: Maspero, 1973.

Vatin, Jean Claude, et al., eds. *Connaissances du Maghreb.* Paris: Editions du Centre National de la Recherche Scientifique, 1984.

Veer, Peter van der and Lehman, Hartmut (ed.). *Nation and Religion.* Princeton: Princeton University Press, 1999.

Venti, Lawrence. *The Scandal of Translation: Towards an Ethic of Difference.* New York: Routledge, 1998.

Verne, Henri. *La France en Algérie.* Paris: Challamel, 1869.

Voisin, George. (Pseudoname for Ismael Urbain). *L'Algérie pour les Algériens.* Paris: Lévy Frères, 1861.

Vossion, Louis. *Si-el-hadj Mokrani et la révolte de 1871.* Paris: 1905.

Walsin, Esterharz, M. *De la domination turque dans l'ancienne regence d'Alger.* Paris: Gosselin, 1840.

Waterbled, E. "L'insurrection kabyle." *Revue des Deux Mondes* 108 (1873): 625.

Weber, Eugen. *Peasants into Frenchmen.* Stanford: Stanford University Press, 1976.

Weber, Max. *From Max Weber: Essays in Sociology.* Oxford: Oxford University Press, 1953.

White, John. "Taine on Race and Genius." *Social Research* 10 (February 1943): 76–99.

Whorf, Benjamin. *Language, Thought, and Reality.* Cambridge: MIT Press, 1956.

Winichakul, Thongchai. *Siam Mapped: A History of the Geo-Body of a Nation.* Honolulu: University of Hawaii Press, 1994.

Wittgenstein, Ludwig. *On Certainty.* New York: Harper, 1972.

Wittgenstein, Ludwig. *Philosophical Investigations.* London: Blackwell, 1997.

Wolf, Eric. *Peasant Wars of the Twentieth Century.* New York: Harper Colophon, 1973.

Worms, M. "Recherches sur la constitution de la propriété territoriale dans les pays musulmans et subsidiarement en Algérie." *Journal Asiatique* (1844).

Yacine, Kateb. *Nejdma.* Paris: Seuil, 1956.

Yacine, *Nedjma,* English transl. Bernard Aresu. Charlottesville: University of Virginia Press, 1991.

Yacono, Xavier. *Les Bureaux arabes.* Paris: Larose, 1953.

Yous, Nesroulah. *Qui a tué à Bentalha?* Paris: Découverte, 2000.

Yver, George. *Correspondance du Capitaine Daumas (1837–1839).* Algiers: Soubiron, 1912. Reprinted Algiers: Editions el Maarifa, 2008.

Zarthman, William. "Interview." *Le Monde,* January 13, 1998.

Index

HARVARD MIDDLE EASTERN MONOGRAPHS

1. *Syria: Development and Monetary Policy,* by Edmund Y. Asfour. 1959.

2. *The History of Modern Iran: An Interpretation,* by Joseph M. Upton. 1960.

3. *Contributions to Arabic Linguistics,* Charles A. Ferguson, Editor. 1960.

4. *Pan-Arabism and Labor,* by Willard A. Beling. 1960.

5. *The Industrialization of Iraq,* by Kathleen M. Langley. 1961.

6. *Buarij: Portrait of a Lebanese Muslim Village,* by Anne H. Fuller. 1961.

7. *Ottoman Egypt in the Eighteenth Century,* Stanford J. Shaw, Editor and Translator. 1962.

8. *Child Rearing in Lebanon,* by Edwin Terry Prothro. 1961.

9. *North Africa's French Legacy: 1954-1962,* by David C. Gordon. 1962.

10. *Communal Dialects in Baghdad,* by Haim Blanc. 1964.

11. *Ottoman Egypt in the Age of the French Revolution,* Translated with Introduction and Notes by Stanford J. Shaw. 1964.

12. *The Economy of Morocco: 1912-1962,* by Charles F. Stewart. 1964.

13. *The Economy of the Israeli Kibbutz,* by Eliyahu Kanovsky. 1966.

14. *The Syrian Social Nationalist Party: An Ideological Analysis,* by Labib Zuwiyya Yamak. 1966.

15. *The Practical Visions of Ya'qub Sanu',* by Irene L. Gendizier. 1966.

16. *The Surest Path: The Political Treatise of a Nineteenth-Century Muslim Statesman,* by Leon Carl Brown. 1967.

17. *High-Level Manpower in Economic Development: The Turkish Case,* by Richard D. Robinson. 1967.

18. *Rebirth of a Nation: The Origins and Rise of Moroccan Nationalism, 1912-1944,* by John P. Halsted. 1967.

19. *Women of Algeria: An Essay on Change,* by David C. Gordon. 1968.

20. *The Youth of Haouch El Harimi, A Lebanese Village,* by Judith R. Williams. 1968.

21. *The Problem of Diglossia in Arabic: A Comparative Study of Classical and Iraqi Arabic,* by Salih J. Al-Toma. 1969.